CITY AND SUBURB

JOHNS HOPKINS STUDIES IN URBAN AFFAIRS

Center for Metropolitan Planning and Research
The Johns Hopkins University

David Harvey, *Social Justice and the City*

Ann L. Strong, *Private Property and the Public Interest*: *The Brandywine Experience*

Alan D. Anderson, *The Origin and Resolution of an Urban Crisis*: *Baltimore, 1890–1930*

James M. Rubenstein, *The French New Towns*

Malcolm Getz, *The Economics of the Urban Fire Department*

Ann L. Strong, *Land Banking*: *European Experience, American Prospect*

Jon C. Teaford, *City and Suburb*: *The Political Fragmentation of Metropolitan America, 1850–1970*

CITY AND SUBURB

The Political Fragmentation of Metropolitan America, 1850-1970

Jon C. Teaford

The Johns Hopkins University Press
Baltimore and London

This book has been brought to publication with the generous assistance of the Andrew W. Mellon Foundation.

Manufactured in the United States of America

The Johns Hopkins University Press, Baltimore, Maryland 21218
The Johns Hopkins Press Ltd., London

Library of Congress Catalog Number 78-20519
ISBN 0-8018-2202-5

Library of Congress Cataloging in Publication data will be found on the last printed page of this book.

CONTENTS

TABLES

ACKNOWLEDGMENTS

In the preparation of this book many people have been of invaluable assistance. Professor Samuel Daykin of Ohio State University aided me in obtaining use of library facilities. Professor Kenneth Jackson of Columbia University offered useful suggestions on the manuscript, and Professor Stanley Kutler of the University of Wisconsin was of special help in the preparation and publication of the work. I acknowledge the patience and support of Mr. Henry Tom, the editor for this project, and thank Mrs. Joyce Good and her staff who typed and retyped the manuscript.

1

INTRODUCTION

Driving into Chicago from the west, one enters the metropolitan area at the city of West Chicago, passes through the village of Winfield, proceeds to the city of Wheaton and the village of Glen Ellyn, then rolls on through the bewildering array of Lombard, Villa Park, Elmhurst, Hillside, Westchester, Broadview, Maywood, Forest Park, Berwyn, and Cicero before reaching at last the city of Chicago. Municipality follows municipality as invisible city limits crisscross the suburban sprawl of housing tracts, neon-lighted commercial strips, and mammoth shopping malls. One passes the city hall of one municipality, the fire station of another, and the police headquarters of still another, each dedicated to serving its own small fragment of the urban area. Stray strips of one community intrude into the heart of its neighbor, and municipal limits zigzag in a boundary design rivaled only by the principalities of the Holy Roman Empire. This is the modern metropolis, a fragmented mass familiar to urban Americans from Boston to San Francisco. Throughout the nation a jumble of "Heights," "Parks," and "Woods" surround the modern central city, dividing the metropolis both legally and socially into a myriad of communities. In Chicago, in New York, in Los Angeles, or in Miami, the pattern is the same. Hundreds of separate governments rule a single urban area.

The result of this fragmentation is inefficiency, confusion of authority, and disparity in shouldering the burdens of the metropolis. Five municipal water authorities pump water to a region that could be served by one. Ten police departments engage in jurisdictional tangles that unified rule would eliminate. Twenty city councils enact ordinances for their particular segments, thus stymieing efforts at regional planning. Velvet-lawned suburbs escape full responsibility for the welfare and crime problems of the central cities; and while industry-rich suburbs enjoy a low tax rate, low-income residential communities suffer the burdens that arise from a poor tax base. Twentieth-century municipal limits are not simply lines on a map; they pose formidable barriers to equity and to cooperation within the metropolitan region.

Urban planners, political scientists, and other thoughtful critics have long decried governmental fragmentation, and such metaphors as "crazy quilt" and "mosaic" have become virtual clichés when applied to metropolitan America. In the early 1850s, citizens from the seriously divided Philadelphia metropolitan area warned that "these divisions and unseen lines and complications of powers" could "paralyze or arrest every effort to advance the common welfare and to suppress general evils."[1] Forty years later a Massachusetts commission investigating the government of metropolitan Boston reported on "the economies of consolidation" and observed that "by concentration of management and responsibility . . . it is frequently possible to increase the efficiency of a public service and to relatively lessen the cost."[2] Moreover, in 1930 a special committee of the National Municipal League found that suburban fragmentation resulted "in sectional treatment of problems which are essentially metropolitan, in radical inequalities in the tax resources of the several political divisions, and in jurisdictional conflicts."[3]

Following World War II, suburbia and the jigsaw map of metropolitan America came under even closer scrutiny as critics blamed central-city woes on suburban indifference and obstinacy. No one was more articulate in his attacks than Robert Wood, a political scientist and the secretary of housing and urban development during the late 1960s. Writing in 1958, Wood observed that "by ordinary standards of effective, responsible public services, the mosaic of suburban principalities creates governmental havoc." Wood preached that nineteenth-century notions of grass-roots democracy hampered policy planning in the modern metropolis, and he blasted suburbia as an illiberal, intolerant bastion of conformity.[4] During the following decade still others wrote of "the eroded central city and the crazy quilt triviality of suburbia" that threatened "to destroy the potential of our maintaining and reconstructing meaningful political communities at the local level."[5] Even a traditional defender of the suburban way of life such as *Better Homes and Gardens* published an article that claimed "we are still attempting to meet the crushing problems of suburban chaos with a horse-and-buggy system of government."[6]

Yet amid the cries for consolidation and centralization, many defended the virtues of local control and dispersion of authority. Suburban officials have long feared the loss of local power that would result if the central city swallowed its smaller neighbors through annexation. In 1878 a disgruntled resident in a recently annexed section of Boston warned that "a careful supervision of its own interests is essential to the well-being of every community, and this can never be so easily and effectively done in a large as in a small body politic."[7] By the 1920s suburban Saint Louis officials were referring to consolidated metropolitan rule as a "monstrosity," and ten years later a suburban Milwaukee editor summed up the attitude of many when he described centralized authority as "a big, robot system of government."[8] More recently the ghettos and neighborhoods of America's central cities have produced an array of leaders demanding a dispersion of authority, and many have responded to these cries for neighborhood rule. In 1969 novelist Norman Mailer ran for mayor of New York City and centered his campaign on the slogan "power to the neighborhoods."[9] One year later Mailer's victorious opponent, John Lindsay, announced a "Plan for Neighborhood Government" that sought to "reduce the alienation and distance that citizens feel toward a remote city government."[10] And in 1974 the president of the Center for Governmental Studies in Washington, D.C., defended metropolitan fragmentation because he valued "civic participation and a sense of community as highly as efficiency and economy."[11]

By the 1970s, then, the chorus of reformers included dissonant cries for both centralization and decentralization, for unified metropolitan rule and dispersed neighborhood power. One side spoke of the efficiency, equity, and policy planning benefits that supposedly would result from consolidation; the other shouted for greater popular participation and for local self-determination. One sought to broaden the power of city hall, and the other sought to limit it.

This study will seek to trace the history of these sometimes conflicting strands in American law and thought. It will describe the tradition of local self-rule and the legal structure that reflected this tradition. But it will also examine the annexation and consolidation campaigns of the past century and the quest for unified metropolitan government. The American desire for expansion, growth, and for improved public services has frequently been pitted against the equally prevalent traditions of local autonomy and separatism, and this book will recount the history of that clash.

Traditionally many have conceived of this conflict as a contest between a wealthy, narrow-minded suburbia dedicated to antique Jeffersonian ideals of grass-roots government and a poor, suffering urban core strangling in the noose of suburban obstinacy. According to popular myth, suburbia has consistently and successfully blocked all efforts at unification and metropolitan reform, has perpetuated social injustice in the nation, and is responsible for many of the nation's urban ills. The metropolitan conflict has been depicted as a simple two-sided duel with all of suburbia allied in defense of its privileged position against the attacks of its irreconcilable enemy, the central city. Many, such as Wood, have had no difficulty in identifying the good guys and the bad in this clear-cut black and white struggle.[12] Too often Americans have regarded dispersion and centralization, the suburb and the city, as irrevocably opposed and totally inconsistent.

Americans, however, have not always conceived of dispersed power and centralized control as mutually exclusive concepts incapable of peaceful coexistence. Instead, during the 1920s and 1930s, concerned suburbanites initiated a campaign to reconcile the two traditions through a federal form of metropolitan rule that would create a central unifying authority but preserve local units. These suburban residents were not blind fools indifferent to the welfare and progress of the central city but instead ranked among the proudest boosters of Pittsburgh, Cleveland, and Saint Louis. Yet they clung to their suburban loyalties as well, caught between a fondness for the small-town suburb and that modern dynamo of American business culture, the central city. Suburbia's great critic, Robert Wood, expressed a typically suburban attitude when he said of his own suburban hometown of Lincoln, Massachusetts: "Lincoln is undoubtedly an anachronism and it is probably obstructive to the larger purpose of the Boston region ... but it is a very pleasant and hospitable anachronism."[13]

By the 1920s and 1930s many upper-middle-class gentry likewise found the suburbs very pleasant and hospitable obstructions to the welfare of the metropolis. Consequently they sought to refashion the urban structure of government in order to achieve the best of two worlds. This work describes their efforts and the formidable obstacles that blocked their path, thus delaying the realization of metropolitan reform.

2

THE FRAGMENTATION OF THE METROPOLIS, 1850–1910

The late nineteenth century was a period of extraordinary urban growth as millions of Americans migrated into metropolitan areas. In this great age of urbanization, the factory began supplanting the farm and the labor scene began shifting from the field and pasture to the workshop and office. Urban Americans were building homes, raising office towers, paving mile after mile of new streets, and laying mile after mile of new sewers. They were also creating legions of new municipalities, for as the urban population proliferated so did the governmental units of the metropolis. By the first decade of the twentieth century scores of municipalities would clutter the map of each of the nation's major metropolitan counties, and each year cartographers would busily add new dots and circles along the outskirts of cities like New York and Chicago. By 1910 the census bureau had begun differentiating between metropolitan population and central-city population; the division between city and suburb was already recognized as a reality. The fragmentation of metropolitan America had begun, and the first strand of the suburban noose was tightening around the large central cities.

This division and subdivision of the metropolis was made possible through a legal structure, developed in the nineteenth century, that maximized the opportunity for local self-rule. In 1868 the eminent legal authority Thomas Cooley observed that "the American system is one of complete decentralization, the primary and vital ideal of which is, that local affairs shall be managed by local authorities."[1] And during the following four decades Americans seemed dedicated to realizing the ideal as Cooley had stated it. Local self-determination was the rallying cry of Americans, and this meant that each fragment of the metropolis would enjoy the right to govern itself and to decide its destiny. Local self-government was a sacred element of the American civil religion, and the nation's lawmakers were devout in their adherence to the faith. Legislators were not to fashion a centralized bureaucracy in charge of local government such as existed in many European nations. Instead, they were to manufacture a legal apparatus that placed power within the grasp of the local populace and permitted the creation of manifold governmental units, especially in the expanding metropolitan regions.

Nowhere is this devotion to local self-rule more evident than in the laws governing municipal incorporation. Whereas prior to 1800 incorporation and urban self-government had been privileges, by the close of the nineteenth century they had become rights. In Great Britain and in colonial America the municipal charter had been a cherished grant by the crown, often bestowed in exchange for a cash payment by the city fathers. New York City's aldermen paid £1,000 to the royal governor for that municipality's charter of 1731, and the privileges and property awarded by the grant seemed to justify the price.[2] During the nineteenth century, however, most state legislatures abdicated responsibility for the grant of municipal privileges through passage of general laws that authorized local voters to decide questions of incorporation. Under the general incorporation laws, municipal government was available to any community of voters that chose to exercise it. No central authority intervened to coordinate or restrict the creation of municipal units within the metropolitan area. Local self-government was no longer bestowed by the state; it was assumed by the citizenry. Any cluster of a few dozen houses and stores with urban aspirations had the right to incorporate itself. As Cooley had observed, local affairs were to rest in the hands of local authorities, and permissive incorporation laws aided in the realization of this ideal.

Western legislatures, burdened with demands to incorporate manifold speculative town sites, were the first to create general procedures for incorporation. Every speculator and pioneer store clerk hoped that his town site would be the future hub of western commerce, government, and culture, a city destined to overshadow Athens and Rome. But one of the first steps in this progression to imperial glory was incorporation, and consequently swarms of developers badgered their state legislators for municipal charters. Seeking to satisfy these requests, lawmakers created a mechanism that would allow every village of a few hundred residents to incorporate without bothering the legislature.

Such laws began appearing in the statute books as early as the first decades of the nineteenth century. In 1808 the legislature of the Louisiana Territory empowered the district courts of common pleas to incorporate towns if two-thirds of the residents of the town petitioned for incorporation.[3] Nine years later the state lawmakers of Indiana also surrendered responsibility for incorporating municipalities because "the granting of charters to each would be productive of much loss of time to this General Assembly." Consequently, the Indiana legislature authorized local residents to establish municipal governments if two-thirds of the qualified voters in the prospective town favored incorporation.[4] During that same year the Ohio legislature enacted a measure that permitted county commissioners to incorporate any town of "forty householders or upwards" if two-thirds of these householders petitioned for municipal status.[5]

Other states were to follow the example of Ohio and Indiana, with Missouri enacting a general municipal incorporation law in 1825, Illinois in 1831, Pennsylvania in 1834, Arkansas and New York in 1837, Iowa in 1847, Wisconsin in 1849, Tennessee and California in 1850, and Michigan in 1857.[6] These measures generally included a minimum population requirement for incorporation, a procedure whereby the residents of the community would themselves decide the question of incorporation, and provisions for supervision of the process by county officials. Thus Iowa required prospective towns to contain five hundred inhabitants, whereas New York, Pennsylvania, Wisconsin, and Michigan required a minimum of three hundred persons in incorporated villages or boroughs. California set the minimum at two hundred, Illinois at one hundred fifty, and Tennessee at one hundred. Indiana never imposed a minimum limit during the nineteenth century, and Ohio lowered its minimum requirement to thirty householders, with the exception that lakeside resorts could incorporate with only fifty inhabitants.[7]

In each state, incorporation required the approval of either a majority or two-thirds of the village voters, and this approval was to be expressed either in an election on the issue or through signatures on an incorporation petition. County courts, commissioners, or boards of supervisors determined the validity of petitions and elections, authorized the final incorporation of the community, and in some states judged the merits of incorporating a village or town and redrew proposed boundaries. But county officials rarely exercised these discretionary powers. For the most part the question of self-government for nascent urban centers was not to be decided at the discretion of either county officials or the central legislative authorities. It would depend instead on the will of the local voter.

Despite a seeming desire to free the legislature of unnecessary tasks, many state assemblies continued to pass special incorporation acts throughout most of the nineteenth century. Even in states where legislators continued to bestow local self-government through special laws, municipal incorporation became a right available to any aspiring community. Between 1803 and 1848 the Mississippi legislature incorporated 105 cities and towns, and during the single decade of the 1830's it handed out 71 municipal charters.[8] During the first five years of Alabama's statehood, the legislature rubbed-stamped 28 incorporation measures, granting powers of self-government to such abortive urban centers as Hazle-Green, Sparta, and Triana.[9] Likewise, Michigan's legislature continued to enact special incorporation laws throughout the century, although the legislators made no attempt to limit the right of any cross-roads hamlet to elect a mayor and village council. In 1879 the Michigan legislature incorporated the villages of Gallien with 413 inhabitants, White Cloud with a population of 440, Clare with a population of 502, Farwell with 521 inhabitants, and the metropolis of Sebewaing containing 553 residents.[10] Among lawmakers in Lansing and in other state capitals, there was little desire to limit the proliferation of small political units or to restrict the creation of local governments. Instead, local power was readily distributed and easily obtained.

With such a permissive attitude prevailing, the number of municipal corporations in the United States soared throughout the nineteenth century. As early as 1868, 419 municipal corporations dotted the map of Ohio and 12 suburban municipalities clustered in Hamilton County within a ten-mile radius of downtown Cincinnati. By 1910 the number of municipalities in Ohio totaled 784, with 31 in Hamilton County alone. From 1890 to 1910 the number of incorporated cities and villages in Cleveland's Cuyahoga County soared from 11 to 23.[11] Thus, by the beginning of the twentieth century, the split between city and suburbs already divided Ohio's largest metropolitan areas, as municipalities proliferated along the urban fringe.

Fragmentation also typified the pattern of local government in Illinois. By 1910 there were 1,066 municipalities in the state of Illinois, a greater number than in any other state. Cook County residents organized 10 new municipalities each decade from 1860 to 1890. The rate then accelerated with the creation of 26 additional villages between 1890 and 1900 and 14 others during the following decade. By 1910 at least 73 incorporated towns, villages, and cities had existed in Cook County, and though some had consolidated with Chicago, 66 still survived, each governing a separate fragment of the metropolis. At the same time, there were also 26 townships exercising governmental authority, scores of school districts, and over 20 park commissions.[12] To the north, in Lake County, Chicago residents were laying out country estates and purchasing summer retreats; the result was a clutter of municipalities in this county as well. In 1910 Lake County could claim 20 incorporated cities and villages, and Highland Park, Highwood, Lake Forest, Lake Bluff, North Chicago, and Waukegan already lined Lake Michigan's shores.

In both counties the right to local self-government extended to small communities as well as large. Since 1872 state law had required a minimum population of three hundred prior to incorporation, yet in 1910 three of Cook County's villages contained less than that number as did two of Lake County's corporations. The recently incorporated village of Hainesville had a population of only sixty-six, indicating that incorporation was a right available to even the smallest community. Sixteen of the Cook County municipalities contained less than five hundred inhabitants, and fifteen others had populations of between five hundred and one thousand.[13] Gradually, during the late nineteenth and early twentieth centuries, the residents of Cook County had spawned a mass of municipal midgets.

Elsewhere this same trend was evident. In 1880 Michigan could claim 229 incorporated cities and villages, but during the following thirty years this number was to double, reaching a total of 459 in 1910. Twenty of these corporations were in Wayne County, where Detroit is located; and already the villages of Grosse Pointe, Grosse Pointe Farms, Grosse Pointe Park, Hamtramck, and Highland Park ruled the urban frontier. By 1910 Minnesota contained 645 municipalities, 18 of them in Hennepin County, where Minneapolis is located. Only 3 cities and villages had existed in Hennepin County in 1880, but thirty years later Richfield, Edina, Saint Louis Park, Golden Valley, and Robbinsdale ringed the southern and western boundaries of the city.[14] In 1910 Pennsylvania could boast of 880 cities and boroughs, with 65 clustering in Pittsburgh's Allegheny County. Little New Jersey contained 242 municipalities in 1910, and 50 incorporated cities and villages cluttered the map of suburban Bergen County. Meanwhile, 499 municipalities governed the small towns and metropolitan areas of New York, and Westchester County alone contained 26 city and village governments, with Yonkers, Mount Vernon, and Bronxville clustering along the New York City border. In 1910 Massachusetts could claim 354 incorporated towns and cities, 32 of them crowded within a ten-mile radius of downtown Boston. Only 185 municipal corporations existed in the less populous state of California, but 25 of these were within the fast-growing county of Los Angeles, and their number was increasing rapidly.[15] Throughout the nation lawmakers had adhered to the principle of local self-determination; they had permitted the organization of a plethora of independent suburban domains through the passage of permissive incorporation laws.

Yet permissive incorporation laws were only the means by which fragmentation occurred and not the underlying cause of this fracturing of the political map. The incorporation statutes explain how the metropolis divided and subdivided, but they do not explain why. To find the reasons for this fragmentation, one must examine the motives for incorporation, the underlying reasons for the creation of twenty-five municipal governments in Los Angeles County, sixty-five in Allegheny County, and seventy-three in Cook County. By creating permissive rules for incorporation, legislators had fabricated the tools needed for partitioning urban America. But it was the social and economic factors in American life that provided the motives for this Balkanization.

The political fragmentation of the metropolis was, in fact, partially a reflection of the social and economic particularism emerging in industrializing America. By the late nineteenth and early twentieth centuries, the American metropolis included a hodgepodge of people of widely divergent economic, social, and cultural interests. Metropolitan areas were fragmenting into zones of industry, zones of truck farming, middle-class neighborhoods, lower-class neighborhoods, black ghettos, Italian districts, German sections, and Polish enclaves. And each segment of this segregated metropolis sought different policies from its local government. Owners of glue factories, slaughterhouses, and fertilizer plants detested municipal ordinances regulating industrial filth, while middle-class residents along elm-lined streets applauded such measures. The imbibing Irish, Czechs, and Italians differed radically from the bluenose Methodists and Presbyterians of American birth in their views on local liquor laws. Homeowners in new suburban tracts and neighboring farmers who still tilled their fields and supplied the urban markets differed markedly in their attitudes toward streets, lighting, and water. Divergent groups demanded divergent ordinances and programs, and the simplest way for each to achieve its ends was to separate and form independent municipalities. Each could escape the other by forming a separate suburban domain. This political process of fragmentation into segregated units thus reflected the cultural and economic fissures in the nation. Political fragmentation came not only as a result of the legal structure; it was also the product of a fragmentation within urban society. Political particularism did not create the social and economic barriers dividing the metropolis. Instead, it was, in large part, a consequence of these barriers, a consequence of the divisions within American society during the late nineteenth and early twentieth centuries.

Social and economic segregation had not always characterized the metropolis. Before the mid-nineteenth century, the American city was an integrated mass without sharply differentiated social or economic sectors. In 1820 the workshops of artisans stood nearby the homes of upper-middle-class merchants, and many houses served as both place of business and residence. City councils might relegate slaughterhouses to a special zone of industrial filth, but zoning ordinances, restrictive deeds, and subdividers' dreams did not partition the city into separate realms for housing, manufacturing, and commerce. Moreover, social segregation was a rarity, since rich and poor lived in proximity to one another. Ethnic ghettos were not common, for the American city was still ethnically homogeneous, and the population was overwhelmingly white, Protestant, and of British or at least of northern European ancestry. Shanty districts did ring the outer rim of the city, and a few exclusive streets or squares did add social luster to the American metropolis, but the houses of the poor clustered in narrow alleys behind the houses of the rich, and everyone lived within walking distance of both slums and mansions. No one could escape the realities of economic inequity, of wealth and poverty.[16]

In the middle and late nineteenth century, however, industrialization and immigration rent the integrated fabric of the urban scene. A momentum for social and economic segregation developed as workshops grew into factories and as the Roman Catholic Irish, Poles, and Italians supplanted the native poor. While members of the middle class had tolerated the nearby artisan's workshop, they now fled from the factory. Lawyers, doctors, and middle-class businessmen loathed the idea of living in the shadow of a steel mill, and the mid-century advent of streetcar transportation provided a means by which they could travel to houses distant from centers of employment. Middle-class urban dwellers too grew increasingly isolated from America's poor as they used the streetcar to commute far from the abhorrent Irish and their saloons, the Germans and their beer gardens, and the alien Slavs. The nation and the city were becoming a complex mélange of varied institutions and differing persons, and the prevailing trend was toward separatism, not unity.[17]

The clashing forces of diversity were as evident along the urban fringe as in the heart of the metropolis, for suburban America was not a uniform expanse of middle-class dwellings with neat lawns and teetotaling WASPs. This was the real estate developer's image, the picture created by entrepreneurs anxious to lure buyers to the edge of the urban world. But all the diversity of the nation was present in suburban America, and the desire to separate was strong.

In suburban Chicago, fingers of manufacturing stretched outward along the tracks of the Atchison, Topeka & Santa Fe, the Chicago and Northwestern, and the Illinois Central railroads. In 1865 meat packing entrepreneurs laid out the Union Stockyards in suburban Lake, beyond the Chicago city limits. In the 1880s George Pullman built his giant railroad car works in suburban Hyde Park; and oil refineries, steel mills, brick yards, and other noxious concerns followed the leads of Pullman and the meat packers. As a result, although the north shore conformed to the developer's dreams of upper-middle-class suburbia, the south and west sides included expanses of industry. Likewise, in the Pittsburgh metropolitan area, the hills were topped by the houses of the prosperous while the valleys and ravines were choked with the smoke and fumes of the mills. And in the Cincinnati region, Procter & Gamble built the world's largest soap manufacturing plant in a suburban valley adjacent to the village of Saint Bernard.

The hills and ravines of suburban Pittsburgh and Cincinnati also housed people of widely divergent backgrounds. Around the lowland mills crowded the immigrants, the Slavs, the Germans, the Italians, and the Irish with their tolerance for saloons and their devotion to the Roman Catholic church. On the hills lived the Presbyterians with their abhorrence for alcohol and their dedication to Protestantism. In 1910, 11 percent of the population of the Pittsburgh suburb Edgewood was foreign born, whereas in the industrial suburb of Rankin 51 percent were immigrants. The Cleveland suburb of Newburg was 35 percent foreign born, but a few miles to the north only 15 percent of East Cleveland's population was born abroad. And in the Chicago metropolitan area the suburb of Cicero was 42 percent foreign born, whereas in adjacent Oak Park the foreign born constituted only 17 percent of the population. Social segregation was a facet of both urban and suburban life as newcomers from Europe flocked to the urban periphery as well as to the urban core.

Thus a mood of separatism characterized the metropolis of the late nineteenth and early twentieth centuries. By 1910 suburban America was a segregated collection of divergent interests, industrial and residential, Protestant and Catholic, truck farmer and commuter, saloon habitué and abstainer. Each group had its own particular goals and desires, its distinctive views on taxation, pollution, morality, planning, and ethnicity. Some segments sought a taxation policy that would benefit industry or a lenient attitude toward industrial pollution. Others sought ordinances that would safeguard local purity from the threats of saloons and wicked women, whereas still other segments worked to sustain human iniquities. Some suburban residents and subdividers hoped to protect the beauty of their neighborhoods as well as their property values by excluding undesirable forms of development; others hoped to preserve ethnic and social purity. Each of these segments sought to escape from the others and to achieve its goals by taking advantage of the state's willingness to abdicate its control over the creation of municipalities. Thus, a permissive legal structure abetted the emergent separatism of the late nineteenth and early twentieth centuries; the result was political fragmentation.

The advantages of permissive incorporation in a segregated society were clearly evident in the creation of municipal tax havens. In 1800 the taxable value of properties within the city varied across a relatively narrow range with the blacksmith's forge, tailor's shop, and rope factory valued at less than the merchant's mansion. There were no tax-rich industrial districts, and tax-exempt institutions were generally on a small scale and constituted a relatively minor burden. By 1900, however, the range of taxable properties in the metropolis was enormous, stretching from a few hundred dollars for the worker's shack to millions for the giant steel mill or massive oil refinery. The tax portrait of the city had formerly been one with subtle shadings, but by the beginning of the twentieth century it was a picture with harsh contrasts. Metropolitan regions throughout the nation contained zones of widely varying tax resources, including areas of giant industry, undeveloped land producing little revenue, and tax-exempt colleges and public institutions. Lenient incorporation procedures allowed certain fragments to profit from this situation. For example, residents could incorporate suburbs that included only highly valued properties, thereby escaping the financial responsibility of providing services for tax-exempt lands or for land of low valuation. By taking advantage of permissive incorporation laws, suburbanites could thus create new municipalities whose boundaries excluded expensive burdens.

It was this desire to evade taxes that motivated the founders of the Chicago suburb of South Evanston. In 1873 South Evanston refused to join with the village of Evanston; fearing higher taxation in Evanston, it chose instead to incorporate as a separate municipality. The problem stemmed from the fact that the property of Northwestern University was tax-exempt, though it comprised one-tenth of the total valuation of Evanston and even though the university enjoyed all of the municipal services. The result was higher taxes for other Evanston property holders, and the people of South Evanston refused to subsidize Northwestern in this manner. The interests of the college community of Evanston and the residential community of South Evanston differed, and South Evanston elected to pursue a separate and independent course. Not until 1892, after South Evanston had repeatedly failed to obtain a source of uncontaminated water, did the residents of that community agree to consolidate with their neighbor to the north. Safe water had assumed a higher priority than low taxes, and one fragment of the Chicago metropolis ceased to exist.[18]

Typical of the conflict between rural and semirural taxpayers was the struggle that led to the incorporation of Brooklyn Heights, Ohio, in 1903. Brooklyn Heights was largely a community of truck farming and greenhouse agriculture dedicated to serving the urban market in adjacent Cleveland. Because of its intensive cultivation, the property in Brooklyn Heights received a higher tax valuation than did property in other regions of Brooklyn Township, and Brooklyn Heights residents believed that they were paying too much to the township and receiving too little in return. Local residents consulted an attorney who told them that the only way to escape was to incorporate. Thus they formed an independent municipality and evaded responsibility for subsidizing services in the tax-poor areas of the township.[19]

Manufacturing concerns also sought to escape heavy taxation by creating municipal fiefdoms in outlying districts. The Standard Oil Company, always a leader in industry, pioneered this technique in the 1890s when it backed the incorporation of Whiting in the seriously fragmented Calumet region of northwestern Indiana. Standard had originally intended to locate its midwestern refinery within the city of Chicago, but Chicago residents complained about possible air pollution and Standard feared the high city taxes. Consequently, in 1891 the company chose to escape the regulatory and taxing power of Chicago by locating its works just outside the city limits in the unincorporated community of Whiting. By 1894 the adjacent debt-ridden city of Hammond was casting covetous eyes on the rich tax resources of Whiting and began proceedings to annex the community. Fearing the heavy tax burden that would result, Standard Oil encouraged separate incorporation of the company-controlled town. Under Indiana law a municipality could annex unincorporated territory without approval of the residents in the area to be annexed, but a city in Hammond's population class could not absorb an incorporated neighbor without voter sanction. Consequently, incorporation was the surest defense against an invasion by Hammond's tax collectors.[20]

There followed a lengthy period of litigation and political intrigue. Separatists declared darkly that any Whiting man who supported the Hammond city administration was "an enemy to his town," and the Hammond newspaper reported that Whiting residents were "trying to move heaven and earth to undo the annexation proceedings."[21] Eventually Whiting achieved independent municipal status, but from the beginning the town was clearly Rockefeller property. Two of the first three mayors were Standard officials who dedicated themselves to maintaining a low tax rate conducive to the interests of the oil company. Yet Whiting residents accepted their servitude, and at the time of incorporation the local newspaper conceded that Standard Oil "does what it does well and economically," and consequently "it follows ... that the town will be well and economically conducted."[22]

A few years later the industrial village of Munhall, immediately south of Pittsburgh, recognized the tax advantages of incorporation and followed the example of Rockefeller's Whiting. Munhall was the site of Andrew Carnegie's Homestead Steel Plant, a lucrative giant from which surrounding Mifflin Township derived the bulk of its tax revenues. Consequently, residents in rural Mifflin Township paid low taxes, although township authorities seemed to spend a disproportionate amount of the revenues in these rural regions. Carnegie company officials and Munhall residents alike resented paying so much while receiving so little, and thus in 1901 they petitioned the county court for incorporation. Munhall's voters approved the incorporation proposal, and the village seceded from the township in order to enjoy the benefits of its wealth and avoid the expenses of rural roads and schools.[23]

The Carnegie interests would soon reap the rewards of incorporation. In 1907 an investigator of social conditions in the Pittsburgh region reported that the "artificial division" of the south bank of the Monongahela into various local government units "relieves the Steel Corporation from much of its responsibility as a property holder." The steel works shouldered a light tax burden, for Munhall's tax rate was one-half that of the adjoining but less industrialized borough of Homestead. Moreover, the factory managers did not need to worry about irritating or venal local officials, for according to one observer "the influence of the Carnegie Steel Company practically dominates borough action and has made the local government efficient and without suspicion of graft."[24]

The examples of South Evanston, Brooklyn Heights, Whiting, and Munhall demonstrate the temptation to incorporate in the segregated metropolis of the late nineteenth and early twentieth centuries. Universities and homeowners, greenhouse operators and truck farmers, manufacturers and agrarians all gathered along the urban fringe, and these distinctive groups had distinctive notions about financing suburban government. In a consolidated metropolis each would have to compromise with the others and share the financial burdens of local rule. But America's permissive incorporation procedures allowed some to profit by separating from their neighbors.

Manufacturers may have been escaping taxation, but taxes were not the only bane of industry. Municipal regulation or suppression of foul-smelling, filthy industries also irked many manufacturers and caused some to take advantage of permissive procedures to create suburban havens. Giant industries produced giant problems, and pollution was one of the most prominent industrial problems. The artisan's workshop of 1800 had not belched billows of smoke into the lungs of middle-class homeowners, and in an economy of such workshops the segregation of residence and manufacturing facility was not necessary. In contrast, the factory of 1900 was irritating to residential neighbors, and segregation of houses and mills often seemed most convenient and desirable. Consequently, many manufacturers withdrew from the heart of the city and sought to create suburban industrial enclaves protected by pliant, made-to-order municipal governments that would impose no bothersome regulations.

For example, in 1892 Patrick Cudahy, president of the Cudahy Packing Company, moved his slaughterhouse out of Milwaukee due to a proposed city ordinance defining meat packing plants as undesirable nuisances and forbidding such businesses to locate within the city. Cudahy founded the village of Cudahy, south of the Milwaukee municipal limits, relocated his plant there, and secured incorporation of the factory suburb in 1895. During its first decade, the village of Cudahy consisted only of the Cudahy plant and houses for Cudahy plant workers. With such a community in his pocket, Patrick Cudahy could now butcher his hogs and cattle in an atmosphere free from the persecution of local officials.[25]

In the Saint Louis metropolitan area meat packers also realized the advantages of municipal separatism. Beginning in 1872 stockyards and packing plants had clustered immediately north of East Saint Louis, Illinois. By 1906 manufacturing interests in the area no longer wished to deal with the bothersome township authorities, and they arranged the creation of a municipal corporation named National City. The packing companies built about forty frame houses next to the factories and moved in a sufficient number of employees to meet the population requirement for incorporation. As a result, the packers escaped interference from local authorities who might complain of the odors or filth of the slaughterhouses and stockyards. The National City mayors were usually officers of the ruling companies, and officials of the surrounding cities of East Saint Louis, Brooklyn, Venice, and Fairmont City exercised no jurisdiction over this enclave of industrial privilege.[26]

Moreover, National City's municipal tax assessor was an employee of the meat packers and loyally served his industrial masters. Though the Swift, Armour, and Morris properties were worth millions, the National City assessor valued these plants at only $117,000.[27] In this Saint Louis suburb, as in the Pittsburgh and Chicago suburbs of Munhall and Whiting, permissive incorporation and political fragmentation definitely meant extra cash in the pockets of industrialists.

Other such industrial refuges developed in suburban areas throughout the nation as manufacturers sought to minimize municipal restraints and local taxation. The borough of Rankin, in the eastern suburbs of Pittsburgh, boasted of being the richest municipality in the nation, having a magnificent concentration of industry that paid an admirably low tax rate. West Milwaukee was an incorporated tax island of many industries and few houses, and manufacturers laid out Granite City in suburban Saint Louis as an ideal industrial haven. South Saint Paul was the site of stockyards and packing houses in the Twin Cities region, and smelting interests founded Denver's industrial suburbs of Argo and Globeville. Fragmentation served the interests of American manufacturers, and as a consequence industrial suburbs proliferated.

Suburban incorporation, however, protected not only the purses of harried industrialists but also the morals of embattled Christians. In the divided metropolis of the late nineteenth and early twentieth centuries, a segment of the population held resolute views on drink, and they wanted their local government to reinforce their moral goals. Repeatedly moral crusaders took advantage of the permissive incorporation laws to protect their suburban communities from the "corrupt influences" of the metropolis. Whiskey and saloons were special targets of these pious souls, and many suburban municipalities owe their origins to the righteous fears of nineteenth and early twentieth-century teetotalers.

This motive was prominent in the incorporation of suburban Pasadena, California, in 1886. A colony of upstanding Hoosiers had founded the Pasadena community during the 1870s. By the mid-1880s, however, a saloon had opened its doors in the righteous community, and shocked residents realized that the only means of excluding such dens was through incorporation and passage of municipal ordinances prohibiting the sale of alcohol. Unfortunately South Pasadena residents protested that "incorporation was not essential to the good of the community" or necessary to "keep out the dram shop." Thus the community split, with Pasadena voting in favor of incorporation and South Pasadena remaining unincorporated.[28]

With Pasadena off-limits to alcohol, the saloon element threatened to move their business to South Pasadena. Alarmed South Pasadena residents now reconsidered the question of municipal government and the possibility of annexation to Pasadena. Two and one-half miles separated the two communities, and hilly terrain formed a topographical barrier to union. Consequently in 1888 South Pasadena chose to incorporate as a separate municipality rather than join its northern neighbor.[29]

Meanwhile, the Los Angeles County community of Monrovia was also choosing incorporation as a safeguard against immorality. By the fall of 1887 a saloon had located in the midst of the upright settlement, and municipal rule was the only means of ousting this liquor trade. Monrovia's citizens voted 110 to 1 in favor of incorporation, and among the first acts of the new city government was the closing of the saloon. The southern-born deputy city marshal marched into the lair of demon rum and drawled to the bartender, "We-all have incorporated and we-all don't want you here. This place is closed now."[30] The desire to exclude alcohol had thus resulted in three new municipalities in Los Angeles County, and this same motive would lead to further fragmentation of the region. In 1887 and 1888 Pomona and Compton also petitioned for incorporation, primarily in order to exclude alcohol, and in each case the forces of temperance achieved self-government and a ban on liquor.[31]

The whiskey question likewise encouraged the creation of suburban municipalities in the Chicago metropolitan area. One of the chief motives for the incorporation of Oak Park in 1902 was the desire to escape the rule of the wet-dominated town of Cicero and its largest settlement, Austin. The leader of those forces favoring separate incorporation claimed that "the greater growth of Austin would bring in a class of inhabitants that would favor the saloon."[32] Slavic persons with little aversion for alcohol were rapidly settling the Austin area, and the native American Protestant population of Oak Park feared the immoral influences that might accompany these foreigners. According to one Oak Park resident, "census reports show that Austin was filling up with a class of people who ... would be likely to oppose Oak Park's well-known temperance policy," and already the Ridgeland neighborhood was forming "an unholy alliance with the saloon and race-track element of Hawthorne" on Cicero's south side.[33] The focus of power in town politics seemed to be shifting from the forces of good to those of evil, and to avoid dominance by the saloon element Oak Park sought separation. The result was the division of Cicero between 1899 and 1902, with Austin joining the city of Chicago, Cicero remaining an incorporated town, and dry Oak Park and Berwyn achieving independent municipal status and the power to "prohibit (as well as regulate) the sale of liquor."[34]

Occasionally incorporation was a device for creating suburban islands of sin rather than enclaves of sanctity. For every suburban saint there was at least one sinner, and the sinners sought protection just as did the saints. In a society sharply divided over questions of morality, a persecuted sportsman, gambler, or saloon keeper could find solace and sanctuary by obtaining powers of self-government, thereby excluding the pernicious forces of morality. Moral divisions had not fragmented the cities of Georgian America, and neither temperance movements nor moral reformers had seriously threatened the carnal pleasures of urbanites. In Victorian America the reformers were rampant, the moral fissures in the metropolis were wide and deep, and this moral fragmentation further encouraged political fragmentation.

Race track developers found permissive incorporation laws especially convenient. For example, in 1903 E. J. (Lucky) Baldwin sponsored the incorporation of Arcadia, California, so that he could build a race track in that community free from the interference of Los Angeles County's vigorous moralists. Baldwin was a notorious roué who repeatedly figured in paternity and divorce suits, and one judge proclaimed that "Baldwin's reputation as a libertine, if not national, was certainly more than local."[35] Southern California's foes of sin, led by the Anti-Saloon League, could imagine with horror what Baldwin was planning for Arcadia, and they now warned that the community was "to be made a gambling hell and booze pleasure park."[36] The colorful Baldwin retorted, "Damn it, we'll show 'em a race track and plenty of it, the long-haired kickers."[37] According to his enemies, Baldwin met the statutory population requirement by importing "Huntington's illiterate peon gang" and by settling them temporarily on his ranch. Moreover, he provided all voters with free watermelons on election day, and they unanimously approved incorporation, dutifully electing a city council consisting of Baldwin and his employees.[38] Immediately following the election, the seventy-five-year-old Baldwin relaxed on "his cool, vine-clad porch, surrounded by three charming brunettes" and speculated with reporters about the possibility of Arcadia becoming the "Monte Carlo of the West."[39]

In 1904 the opening of Ascot Park raceway on the edge of Los Angeles halted Baldwin's plans momentarily. But the fate of Ascot Park would prove the wisdom of Baldwin's separatist policy, for in 1907 the priggish city of Los Angeles annexed Ascot Park, closed the course, and expelled track betting from its corporate limits. Now Baldwin carried out his scheme, founded Santa Anita raceway on his ranch in Arcadia, and realized his dream of a gambling resort in Southern California. At the opening of the track, Baldwin told reporters, "I desire no other monument. This is the greatest thing I have ever done, and I am satisfied."[40]

In the Cleveland metropolitan area racing enthusiasts also incorporated their own independent haven of gambling and amusement. Glenville Park, in suburban Glenville, was one of the leading race tracks in the country in the late nineteenth century and was known throughout the world by prominent horse breeders. In 1902, however, the forces of morality captured control of Glenville's government, and the new mayor announced that race track betting would no longer be permitted. The following year, the city of Cleveland annexed the track, and racing enthusiasts again prepared to hold their races complete with the usual betting. But Cleveland Mayor Tom Johnson was no more willing to permit gambling within the city limits than the Glenville officials had been. A squad of Cleveland police descended on the track and ensured that the will of the mayor was enforced. The track owners attempted to conduct races without betting, but this proved a failure, and in 1904 and 1905 the illustrious track was closed except for the running of a single day of exhibition racing.[41]

Cleveland race fans, however, were not willing to allow the sport of kings to wither under the oppressive hand of bluenose city administrators. Therefore, they decided to escape the interference of local authorities by locating a new track in a made-to-order municipality, a municipality that would shelter rather than suppress horse racing. In 1908 the distinguished local horseman Bert O. Shank moved some temporary colonists to his farm, located ten miles southeast of downtown Cleveland. If these colonists remained on the farm for thirty days, then they would qualify as legal residents of the farm and Shank's property would have a sufficient resident population to qualify for incorporation. After thirty days of lounging and drinking beer, the colonists, together with Shank and his stable hands and trainers, voted on the incorporation issue. Not surprisingly, incorporation won by a unanimous vote. After the electorate chose Shank as mayor of his farm, he paid off his temporary guests and they departed, having created another suburban domain, the village of North Randall.[42]

Work soon began on the construction of the Randall Raceway, and a second track, Thistledown Park, was later constructed on the farmland. By 1930 North Randall contained the two finest race tracks in the state and only 107 inhabitants. Through much of its history horses would outnumber people, but the municipal structure had served to protect the sporting interests of one segment of a metropolitan population with widely varying views about the pursuit of pleasure.

Elsewhere permissive incorporation laws also allowed the creation of suburban municipalities that tolerated or encouraged activities outlawed in the central city or in the more respectable suburbs. The numerous municipalities on the east bank of the Mississippi across from Saint Louis early developed into havens of immorality. Madison, Illinois, incorporated in 1891, could claim seventy saloons by the early twentieth century and was a leading rendezvous for criminals.[43] Hamtramck, Michigan, incorporated in 1901, soon gained fame as a center for saloons, brothels, gambling dens, and roadhouses in the Detroit metropolitan area.[44] In 1905 Vernon, California, achieved corporate status and with it, immunity from Los Angeles' blue laws and from county interference. If you were looking for an all-night bar, wanted to watch a prize fight, or felt like shooting dice in early twentieth-century Los Angeles, the independent municipality of Vernon was the place to go.[45]

Thus the fragmented metropolis resembled a moral checkerboard with alternating squares of sin and sanctity. In the Pittsburgh region sober-minded steel company officials ensured that no saloons moved into the borough of Munhall. But according to a local resident, the adjoining borough of Homestead in 1908 could claim "at least 65 saloons, 10 wholesale liquor stores, a number of beer agents, innumerable 'speakeasies,' " and a chief of police who ran a gambling club.[46] The diversity of American moral attitudes was as evident in the suburbs as in the central city. Suburban incorporation provided a means by which each fragment of the divided metropolitan population could institutionalize its beliefs on the subjects of amusement and morality.

Permissive incorporation, however, also served the interests of those with higher aesthetic sensibilities than Lucky Baldwin or B. O. Shank. Throughout the late nineteenth and early twentieth centuries municipal incorporation was a significant means of protecting the beauty and property values of a well-planned suburban subdivision and of excluding the ugliness so common to the metropolis. Though professional urban planning was in its infant stages, there were some imaginative real estate developers who endeavored to create scenic suburban tracts. Their interests differed from those of the suburban manufacturer, saloon keeper, and race track operator. And to protect these interests and safeguard their model communities, they resorted to the device of municipal incorporation. These men did not want their handiwork tarnished by central city invaders with more pedestrian tastes. Instead, developers sought to preserve their communities and they used the tool of incorporation to achieve this end.

For example, in 1872 J. O. Woodruff platted Woodruff Place, a suburb of Indianapolis. The deeds prohibited the building of any structures within a certain distance from the street; and grassy malls with flowing fountains, flower beds, and iron statuary ran down the centers of the roadways. Real estate advertisements publicized "its spacious lots with original forest trees, its high and commanding situation, its refreshing esplanades," and one suburban booster claimed that it was patterned after the Vatican Gardens.[47] It was the showplace of Indianapolis, the home of Booth Tarkington's *Magnificent Ambersons*, and residents of Woodruff Place did not wish the central city to destroy the genteel beauty of their community. Consequently, from 1876, when Woodruff Place was incorporated, to 1961, residents fought every effort by the city of Indianapolis to annex their seventy-seven-acre village.[48] In 1895 one separatist argued that an autonomous Woodruff Place was "able to cut the grass on the esplanades and vacant lots." But, he asked, "Will the city do this, and run our fountains? We think not!"[49] When Woodruff Place was originally incorporated, Indianapolis' city attorney suggested more mercenary motives for the suburb's separatist stance and viewed it "as an attempt to escape the payment of city taxes."[50] Promoters of the suburb also claimed that "a man who lives there will not have to pay city tax . . . and the difference of taxation . . . will amount to a sum worth considering."[51] But no matter how high the suburban tax rate soared, Woodruff Place residents persistently defended their elegant autonomy from the philistines of Indiana's capital city, even though that city completely surrounded the park-like suburb as early as the 1890s.

Aesthetic considerations also influenced the pattern of separatism in suburban Saint Louis. In 1902 a real estate developer, E. G. Lewis, decided to create a town named University City just beyond the limits of

Saint Louis; he planned to "lay it out under one great engineering plan as the most beautiful residence section conceivable." According to Lewis, "when it had acquired enough population, I would incorporate it as a separate city" and "having the municipal power, I could always protect it." This farsighted developer believed that "if anybody should erect a soap factory, for instance, adjoining our residence section, on which we were spending enormous sums for improvements, we could condemn that property, or . . . make it a city park."[52] Thus, through use of municipal powers, Lewis planned to protect the beauty of his perfect suburb and to ensure steadily increasing property values.

In the Chicago metropolitan area, the municipal governments of Lake Forest, Riverside, and Kenilworth also worked to preserve the distinctive suburban plans of their villages.[53] Zoning ordinances and planning commissions were not yet among the paraphernalia of municipal rule, but village leaders in these and similar municipalities could exclude industrial nuisances, create and maintain parks, refuse to annex undesirable areas, and take other measures to protect the prestige and appearance of their communities. In Woodruff Place, University City, and Kenilworth suburban developers and village fathers all realized that municipal government was a useful tool in preserving the sylvan beauty of suburbia.

Suburbanites also viewed municipal government as a useful tool for defining the separate social identity of their community. Class and ethnic barriers divided one fragment of suburbia from another, and many suburban dwellers wanted municipal boundaries to conform to these class and ethnic lines. Ethnicity was a factor in the moral rift in suburbia, but ethnic animosity was not solely a consequence of differing views on alcohol. The divisions in metropolitan society ran deeper than that, and they caused many to use permissive incorporation laws as weapons in a war against those of differing race, nationality, or social station.

For example, Oak Park's citizenry favored legal separation from Cicero not only because of the liquor issue but also because of a general sense of social separation from the remainder of the town. As early as 1891 a Cicero resident observed that there had been "such jealousy between Austin and Oak Park that citizens of the latter declared there was no 'tone' in Austin, while Austinites retorted that Oak Parkers were all aristocrats and wore ruffled nightshirts."[54] Four years later an Oak Park lawyer claimed that Austin parents "did not send their children to school."[55] And in 1901 an Oak Park leader commented that "there is no commercial or social intercourse" between residents of the north and south sides of Cicero.[56] An Oak Park newspaper noted that "we have little in common with the villages of the south side" of Cicero, and "they are in fact no more to us ... than if they were twenty miles away instead of four or five."[57] According to this Oak Park editor, "each village should control ... municipal matters according to its own ideas of what is best," and separate incorporation "will enable us to give our undivided attention to our own affairs."[58] In the following few months, Oak Park's upper-middle-class, Protestant, American-born residents would incorporate independently, severing governmental ties with the increasing number of foreign-born, working-class Roman Catholics in Cicero. Village boundaries would conform to social boundaries in the Chicago metropolis, with suburbanites creating a system of municipal apartheid.

Elsewhere this pattern of social separation also was evident. Cincinnati's suburb of Saint Bernard, incorporated in 1878, was almost wholly German and Catholic, while nearby College Hill was American and Protestant. Saint Louis's eastern suburb of Brooklyn, incorporated in 1874, was overwhelmingly black, and according to a magazine account written in 1908 it was "governed solely by negroes ... who believe that a higher degree of civilization is attainable for them through isolation from the whites." Only one white man was ever known to hold office in Brooklyn, and the village's mayor tolerated the few Caucasian residents but believed that "it would be better to have complete isolation from whites" than to create a mixed society.[59] In 1887 some white gentry in Atlanta, Georgia, drafted plans for a separate black municipality adjoining the city's southern boundary. According to the *Atlanta Constitution*, "it will be literally a negro town," and "its Mayor will be a colored citizen, the members of its Municipal Council will be colored, the police will be colored; in fact, the corporation functionaries will be of dark complexion."[60] Backers of the scheme were unsuccessful in creating this suburban enclave of black power, but their hopes were representative of the separatist feelings of many Americans.

Thus in Atlanta, Saint Louis, Chicago, and Los Angeles the advantages of separatism seemed readily apparent. Throughout the nation, urban areas were dividing and subdividing on the basis of economic function and social characteristics, and municipal incorporation was serving the separatist instincts of many. Incorporation was a pliant tool that could serve the economic, moral, or immoral ends of an individual, business corporation, or community as well as the aesthetic ends of a developer. Incorporators might seek to suppress factories or to protect them. They might want to nail closed the barroom doors or to fling them wide open. The urban population was resolving itself into separate geographic spheres—factory zones, ethnic neighborhoods, upper-middle-class retreats, race track havens—and each zone sought local self-government as a means of protecting its own particular interests by staving off interference from its adversaries. Separate incorporation formalized the barriers between the fragments of society, allowing each to pursue its separate goals. The advantages of separate incorporation were manifold, the means of achieving independent municipal status were available, and the result was a rising rate of municipal births.

Yet particularism did not underlie the founding of all suburban municipalities. Other motives existed for incorporation, and perhaps the single most important motive was not separatism but the desire for improved public services. The late nineteenth century was a period in which material comfort was valued highly. New technology and growing wealth resulted in a rising standard of living for Americans, especially middle-class suburban Americans. Material expectations rose rapidly, as was evident not only in the increased demand for consumer goods but also in the expansion of municipal services. By 1900 urban and suburban Americans were demanding many more public services than they had in 1850, and for the most part only a municipal government had the authority to meet these demands.

Municipalities introduced a vast array of new public services and facilities to satisfy the rising expectations of nineteenth-century Americans. At the beginning of the twentieth century, the flush toilet was standard equipment for the middle-class house as was the bathtub, and municipal waterworks and sewage systems made these conveniences possible. Gas lighting and electric illumination were both innovations of the nineteenth century, and municipalities made them available through franchise grants to private companies or through municipally owned plants. The streetcar was introduced in cities throughout the nation, and municipalities likewise contracted for this transportation service. This era also witnessed the development of the public library, the public park, and the professional police and fire fighting force, all of which were demanded by those accustomed to urban living and supplied by the municipality. Moreover, by the last decade of the century, cities began applying asphalt to their streets, eliminating the cobblestone and wooden pavements of the past, and erecting row after row of brilliant electric arc lights. Those who migrated outward to the urban periphery in the late nineteenth century expected all of these facilities and services, and municipalities provided them either through direct action or through a franchise with a public utility company.

Thus suburban residents demanded a safe supply of water, an adequate fire and police force, street lighting and paving, drainage and sewers, all the public amenities they had known in the city and expected to enjoy wherever they lived. Existing township and county governments, however, generally did not possess the authority to provide such services. No state during the nineteenth century authorized counties to build waterworks, lay sewer systems, construct gas or electric plants, or provide the range of urban amenities. Prior to 1898 only two states authorized counties to establish public libraries, and the first county park was not created until 1895.[61] Likewise, townships outside of New England were authorized to provide only limited services appropriate to rural living. The county and township existed primarily for the maintenance of rural roads, the care of the poor, and the administration of justice. If one wanted those services that urban Americans had come to accept as necessary, then one had to live within a municipal corporation. And for suburbanites this meant either annexation to the central city or incorporation of a new suburban municipality.

In many cases annexation was not possible because it was impractical for the central city to assume the burden of services to outlying areas. Numerous suburban communities developed on the urban fringe too far from the mass of the central city for annexation to be a viable alternative. In the New York City and Chicago areas, for example, the metropolitan populations did not move outward from the centers in neat concentric circles but spread outward along commuter rail lines. A thin finger of population stretched northward along Lake Michigan to Lake Forest and along Long Island Sound to Rye; others extended westward from Chicago into the Illinois prairie and eastward from New York City into Long Island. But between these fingers the land remained rural and undeveloped so that the pattern of settlement was attenuated rather than compact, rendering unified government and a unified system of public services difficult.

Elsewhere natural and political boundaries discouraged attempts by the central city to annex suburban zones and thus to provide these outlying areas with municipal services. Ravines, rivers, and mountain ridges separated the suburban population centers of the Pittsburgh area and hampered the provision of municipal services throughout the region. The broad expanse of San Francisco Bay separated San Francisco from its eastern suburbs while mountainous terrain divided the central city from much of San Mateo County to the south. In Los Angeles County the metropolitan area developed in noncontiguous bits and pieces, divided by topographical barriers. And in the New York City, Cincinnati, and Saint Louis areas state boundaries divided the metropolis, requiring that Hoboken and Bayonne in New Jersey, Covington and Newport in Kentucky, and East Saint Louis in Illinois fend for themselves. In 1900 nine of the twenty most populous cities in the United States were on state or international boundaries. Municipal corporations were created under state laws, however; there was no such thing as an interstate municipality. Consequently, state boundaries posed insuperable barriers to consolidation; they necessitated the founding of suburban municipalities.

Suburban residents also resorted to incorporation when the central city lagged in its annexation efforts. Philadelphia annexed no additional territory after 1854, and the boundaries of Saint Louis remained fixed after 1876. By 1910 suburbanites in both areas were spilling over the corporate limits and founding new governments. Pittsburgh failed to annex substantial territory between 1870 and 1900, and scores of surrounding municipalities developed in the interim. Prior to 1869 Cincinnati failed to pursue an aggressive policy of boundary adjustment, and a cluster of communities in the surrounding hills sought and obtained incorporation. Chicago did not annex any new territory from 1869 to 1887, and as a result villages and cities sprang up in clusters around its boundaries. Minneapolis and Saint Paul failed to adopt a forceful policy of territorial expansion after 1890, and there too suburban municipalities appeared. Urban America was expanding at a rate worthy of the most ardent booster's wildest dreams, yet all too often the central city failed to respond quickly enough to this centrifugal surge. Fears of central-city stagnation were lulled by continued rapid population growth in the urban core; and annexation often meant an additional and costly tax burden for the central city. Thus, many cities hesitated before making additional conquests, and when the central city hesitated, new municipal corporations arose to fill the governmental vacuum.

This simple desire for improved services is evident in the incorporation efforts of many outlying areas. In 1868 the residents of the Hyde Park district of metropolitan Boston sought creation of still another town government because of the need for municipal services in that fast-growing commuter community. Four thousand people had congregated in the Hyde Park settlement, which was located on the periphery of three existing towns. But none of these towns provided the area with the services demanded by a suburban populace. Local schools were inadequate, the village streets had "for their pavement stumps and roots of trees," and these rude thoroughfares were also unlighted. No local fire department existed nor was there a local police force. Incorporation seemed the best means to remedy these woeful inadequacies, and consequently Hyde Parkers demanded and received the right to municipal rule.[62]

The same circumstances prevailed in Wilkinsburg, Pennsylvania, in the 1880s. By 1886 Wilkinsburg was fast becoming a fashionable suburb of Pittsburgh, and the population had tripled to 2,500 within the previous fifteen years. Yet Wilkinsburg lacked street paving and lighting, sewers, fire protection, and other municipal amenities. Some property owners laid boards or cinders along the streets to serve as sidewalks, but many allowed pedestrians to slog through the mud. Others sought to obtain street lighting through voluntary contributions from merchants and residents, and some homeowners combined to build small sewers emptying into the local streams. But such efforts did not satisfy those who demanded urban services, and they petitioned for incorporation. Fearing increased taxes, some older residents opposed the change. One argued that the incorporation campaign "was started by a lot of those city 'fellers' who want to introduce new-fangled city improvements at the taxpayers' expense—such things as sewers, paved streets, public water supply, and bath tubs—'fellers' who are too lazy to bring a tub up from the cellar on a Saturday night." The bathtub devotees proved victorious, however, as Wilkinsburg soon achieved municipal status.[63]

The problems of South Omaha differed from those of Wilkinsburg, but suburban Nebraskans followed the example of their eastern counterparts and turned to incorporation as an answer to their community's ills. South Omaha, the site of the giant Union Stock Yards, was one of the largest livestock centers in the nation. It was a rough, workingman's town without polish and without the advantages of government. Many residents hoped to remedy these shortcomings, and in 1886 suburbanites petitioned for incorporation, complaining in the petition of "how we are exposed without any protection against tramps and murderers—having no jail, no church, one school house (and that falling to decay), one saloon for every twenty inhabitants, one gambling house, two houses of ill-fame, ... [and] no constable proper here." According to one observer, there was strong opposition to incorporation "among the moneyed men who talked expenses and cared more for the present nickel than for the future good of the city." The syndicate, which laid out the town and built the stockyards, refused to support the creation of a government that might introduce costly improvements. But a majority of the taxable inhabitants signed the incorporation petition, and thus they obtained municipal status. The local South Omaha newspaper lauded the organization of this new government, for "it means for South Omaha, protection to public business and private enterprise, the regulation of license and the control of unlawfully disposed persons, the care of streets and precaution against fire, in short, the legalized supervision of the business interests of the community."[64] Incorporation in South Omaha meant order, safety, and a welcome departure from the mayhem of the past.

The simple desire for public order and improved services is also evident in the incorporation efforts of Denver's suburbs. In 1890 those who favored the incorporation of Elyria, Colorado, circulated a long list of community problems that demanded the attention of a municipal government. They claimed that Elyria should incorporate because of the lack of drinking water, the need to drain the streets, the "widespread nuisance from the stench of dead animals," the need for a larger school, and the lack of electric street lights. Moreover, Elyria required a city marshal because of the lawlessness of "men who congregate at the saloons and fight, carouse and shoot their pistols." Observers further noted that a dog tax was "one of the innovations that . . . secured lots of votes from the municipality." In 1890 there were about six dogs to every family in Elyria, and one leading citizen confided to a Denver reporter that "we desire to decrease the number of dogs to one for a family." Dogs, desperados, sewage, and sanitation were all problems that confronted the unincorporated suburb, and municipal government was thought to be the panacea for these suburban ills. [65]

Across the country innumerable other outlying communities availed themselves of the advantages of incorporation. In 1871 the inhabitants of West Cleveland voted to incorporate because they needed "greater power over roads, public grounds and police than is presently enjoyed." [66] Seventeen years later, the Cincinnati suburb of Norwood chose to incorporate in order to fulfill "hopes for greater improvements." [67] And to the north the Columbus suburb of Grandview Heights incorporated in 1906 after the central city refused to extend gas and electric service to residents in the area. In 1892 the residents of Whitefish Bay, a summer retreat outside Milwaukee, decided to organize as a municipality in order to establish a school of their own. The existing school was in the extreme southwest corner of Milwaukee Township, and Whitefish Bay residents did not like "the idea of sending their children 2½ miles through snow and storm." [68] In 1898 Azusa, California, in Los Angeles County, incorporated in order to improve the community streets and secure a more adequate system of water distribution. [69] In 1907 residents of northern Middleburg Township to the south of Cleveland complained of inadequate schools and law enforcement and demanded incorporation. Eventually, in 1914, these residents achieved their goal and created the village of Brook Park, one of three municipalities carved out of Middleburg Township. [70] Meanwhile, in 1908 the community of Roseland, New Jersey, located eight miles from the heart of Newark, separated from Livingston Township and incorporated as a borough because the township failed to provide adequate school facilities for the expanding suburban population. [71]

During the late nineteenth and early twentieth centuries, then, scores of suburbs incorporated in order to obtain those public services that the central city was as yet unwilling or unable to offer. The material expectations of Americans were rising as were their demands for municipal government and for its services. The residents of Hyde Park wanted a fire department; people in Wilkinsburg longed for bathtubs; those in South Omaha wanted a police force; the residents of Elyria needed drainage. In 1800 Americans would have accepted a volunteer fire department and muddy streets; they would have foregone indoor plumbing and professional law enforcement. But in 1900 more modern services were regarded as necessary, and life without these services was viewed as barbaric. Americans demanded extensive municipal facilities in 1900, and if the central city did not act to provide these facilities, then suburbanites would have to incorporate and provide the services for themselves. The result would be still more municipalities.

The creation of this multitude of new municipalities did not occur, however, without considerable feuding and friction. The metropolis was growing rapidly and it was fragmenting just as rapidly. Yet no one was overseeing this proliferation of governmental units, and townships were subdividing into municipalities without blueprint or plan. Since no central authority supervised or coordinated the development of local government units in the metropolitan area, a general melee ensued among adjoining municipalities, each struggling for supremacy in its particular fragment of the urban area. The state had relinquished to the local citizenry control over the creation of government bodies, with legislatures either rubber-stamping incorporation petitions or authorizing county officials to do so. It was the responsibility of the residents in the metropolis to redraw the map of America, and in the late nineteenth and early twentieth centuries they dissected metropolitan America in a free-for-all for territory. Repeatedly incorporation efforts marked the clarion call to battle among suburban residents, as local citizens partitioned Cook, Milwaukee, and Los Angeles counties.

In 1888–89 such a conflict broke out between suburban Edgewood and Swissvale along the eastern city limits of Pittsburgh. Residents of Edgewood petitioned for incorporation, proposing that the boundaries of their borough include the Union Switch and Signal Company works located virtually in the center of the distinct but unincorporated village of Swissvale. Swissvale's citizens immediately protested this attempt to usurp their township's most lucrative source of tax revenue and argued that since company workers lived in Swissvale and Braddock Township the company should pay taxes to their township. According to these critics, Edgewood's efforts would impose "on the School District of Braddock township the burden of schooling the children of the workmen ... while depriving it of the taxes which ought justly to go to the maintenance of its schools." Thus burdens and benefits would be distributed inequitably among Pittsburgh's eastern suburbs, with Edgewood collecting the revenues and Braddock paying the expenses. The Pennsylvania Supreme Court decided the issue, upholding Edgewood's imaginative drawing of the borough limits.[72] In Pennsylvania, as elsewhere, equity did not govern the incorporation process. Instead, a policy of first come first served prevailed.

During the 1890s the multiplication of municipal corporations in northeastern New Jersey also led to friction in the suburbs. In 1893 the residents of Lodi Township in Bergen County attempted to create a new municipality that would include within its bounds the existing incorporated villages of Carlstadt and New Carlstadt. An appeal to the state supreme court was required to untangle this confusion, but the two original villages did survive.[73] Two years later Bloomfield, New Jersey, lying immediately north of Newark, petitioned for incorporation as a city under the state's general laws. Included within the boundaries described in the petition was all of the existing borough of Glen Ridge with the exception of a small portion which contained only seven residents. This time two appearances before the New Jersey Supreme Court were necessary before the web of suburban boundaries was unraveled. Glen Ridge remained an independent municipality, but the incident revealed the confusion and conflict that could result from a system that valued local self-rule over central coordination.[74]

Likewise, in Colorado during the 1890s, two suburban municipalities claimed the same territory. In 1891 forty-three residents in the western suburbs of Denver petitioned for the incorporation of the town of Brooklyn. The proposed corporation contained only sixteen acres, and foes of incorporation claimed "that the lines of the proposed town were so run as to fraudulently leave out many interested parties doing business within the limits of the proposed town but residing adjacent to it." These critics obtained an injunction halting any further proceedings on the Brooklyn incorporation, and they then petitioned for the incorporation of an area known as Colfax, which comprised the entire western suburban district, including Brooklyn. Voters approved the incorporation of Colfax, but meanwhile sponsors of the Brooklyn petition had appealed to the state supreme court. This court further complicated the situation when it dissolved the injunction and seemingly authorized Brooklyn, now a section of Colfax, to proceed with its incorporation election. No one knew whether the Colfax incorporation remained valid, and one Brooklyn leader cried: "We are now in a state of anarchy. This is 'No Man's Land.'" Chaotic Colfax did survive, only to be annexed by Denver during the next decade.[75]

Elsewhere similar feuds divided the metropolitan area further. From 1900 to 1902 the proposed municipalities of Dover and Bay to the west of Cleveland clashed over which would govern the northern third of Dover township.[76] Residents of Brook Park, south of Cleveland, fought the nearby municipality of Berea in a struggle for independence. In the Chicago metropolitan area, Waukegan and North Chicago battled for control of the north shore, while Gary, Whiting, Hammond, and East Chicago vied for supremacy along the southern coast of Lake Michigan.[77] As in the case of Brooklyn and Colfax, it was often a question of survival on the basis of primacy and speed. In the partitioning of metropolitan America the successful suburbs were those that laid their stakes to the richest territory first. No central legislature protected the losers, for the states had assumed a laissez-faire stance toward municipal incorporation, sacrificing order and planning for the sake of local self-determination.

During the late nineteenth and early twentieth centuries, then, lawmakers had deferred to the wishes of residents in the emerging suburbs, offering them a decisive voice in their community's political destiny. Pliant legislators handed out acts of incorporation with no questions asked and enacted general incorporation measures that gave localities a carte blanche. Suburbanites had exploited this privilege because a climate of social and economic diversity made political separatism seem increasingly desirable. Moreover, a desire for municipal services heightened the demand for the creation of new suburban municipalities. Both the legal means and the social and economic motives for fragmentation existed, and outlying residents thus initiated an often chaotic dissection of the metropolis. In Edgewood, Colfax, and Dover, local residents sparred for tracts of suburban acreage and battled over whether an industrial plant would lie in one municipality or another. Throughout the nation, particularistic communities vied for resources, wealth, and advantage as state legislatures abdicated supervision over the creation of cities and villages. By the early twentieth century suburbanites had begun carving up the metropolis, and the states had handed them the knife.

3

THE CONSOLIDATION OF THE METROPOLIS, 1850–1910

By 1890 Bostonians were flooding into the outer reaches of Dorchester and West Roxbury, and builders were erecting row after row of frame dwellings to house the urban overflow. In Chicago the streetcar lines were carrying passengers as far as Seventy-ninth Street, as mile after mile of the Illinois prairie fell victim to the developer's grid of avenues and houses. In the boom town of Denver real estate salesmen were advertising the sylvan beauty of lots in suburban Montclair, far removed from the hectic city center. Throughout the East, Midwest, and West, the American metropolis was expanding, pushed ever outward by waves of new citizens. The combined population of the twenty most populous cities of 1900 grew 286 percent during the period from 1870 to 1900 as millions invaded urban areas from the farms of America and from the nations of Europe. Chicago approximately doubled in population every decade from 1860 to 1890. Cleveland's population almost quadrupled between 1860 and 1880, then more than doubled again between 1880 and 1900. With the typical American city doubling in population every twenty years, anything less was regarded as stability.

In response to this wave of new settlements, the legal structure for making local boundary adjustments also changed. Not only were outlying municipalities springing up, but a system of annexation and consolidation was developing that allowed the central city to absorb much of the expansion. The realities of urban growth demanded that city limits remain flexible and alterable, and lawmakers were prepared to meet these demands. The law adjusted to the realities recorded by the census bureau, and the result was pages of annexation statutes and volumes of judicial decisions on boundary adjustment. Nineteenth-century American legislators created the legal means for metropolitan fragmentation, but these same lawmakers also created the legal instruments for consolidation.

Basic to this new structure of boundary adjustment was the same

concern for local self-determination that was evident in the incorporation laws. Gradually, during the period from 1850 to 1910, state legislators surrendered much of their central authority over annexation, permitting local officials, the courts, and the general electorate to assume
an increasingly prominent role in the determination of municipal limits.
Questions of boundary adjustment were decided by the local community,
not by the central legislature or any other central coordinating body.
As in the case of incorporation, lawmakers sacrificed coordination and
planning by assuming a laissez-faire stance toward the mapping of
municipal limits.

This hands-off attitude, a product of the second half of the nineteenth
century, was in marked contrast to the interventionist policies of earlier
legislatures. In 1816, through an act of the Maryland legislature, the
city of Baltimore annexed twelve square miles of adjoining territory.
In 1836 Pennsylvania's legislators united the city of Pittsburgh and
Northern Liberties Borough without a referendum being held in either
municipality. Five years later Missouri's legislature extended the Saint
Louis city limits despite protests from residents of the annexed region,
and the Missouri Supreme Court vigorously upheld the legislature's
action.[1] In 1854 the state of Pennsylvania united the city of Philadelphia
and twenty-eight other local governments in Philadelphia County without asking the consent of local voters. The resulting municipality encompassed 129 square miles and 500,000 people.[2] Repeatedly during these
early decades of urban expansion, state legislators mapped and remapped
the limits of local government units, exercising central control over
municipal organization.

By the 1840's and 1850's, however, opposition to state intervention
in local matters began mounting, and delegates to state constitutional
conventions criticized the growing number of special privileges granted
certain localities. For example, at the New York Constitutional Convention of 1846 Henry C. Murphy of Brooklyn complained about the un-
equal privileges awarded various municipalities, urging instead "the
propriety of an uniform organization of cities" within the state. Murphy
argued that legislatures enacted local laws embodying special privilege
because no one in Albany "except the representatives from the locality
cares what it contains" and such measures "are passed without examination because they affect only a particular community."[3]

Farther west, lawmakers not only feared special privilege but also
objected to the amount of time legislatures wasted on a myriad of local
measures. In 1850 delegates to Indiana's constitutional convention
argued that "there is no necessity for this local legislation—none whatever" and sought "to prevent the Legislature from spending its time
in legislating upon these little matters."[4] One year later the drafters of

Ohio's new constitution expressed a similar concern about special municipal legislation, with one delegate claiming "that there was no necessary difficulty about legislating by general law upon the subject of municipal corporations."[5] Likewise, in 1857 delegates to Iowa's constitutional convention complained "that a great portion of many sessions of our Legislature is spent in local legislation;" they contended "that we should provide against special and local legislation" especially since "we propose to provide for biennial instead of annual sessions of the legislature."[6]

Repeatedly delegates denounced corporate privileges, referring most often to the privileges of business corporations. But some felt special grants to municipal corporations also produced inequities and consumed an unnecessary amount of the legislators' time.[7] Equitable, inexpensive government was the American ideal, and the passage of special and local laws was contrary to this ideal. Such legislation extended legislative sessions, keeping the lawmakers from their farms and offices, and it enabled corrupt characters to take advantage of the hurried amateurs governing the state. General laws seemed the solution, but general laws would mean an end to direct legislative supervision of municipal expansion.

The state constitutions of the mid-nineteenth century reflected this growing preference for general legislation. Ohio's constitution of 1851 required that the "General Assembly shall provide for the organization of cities and incorporated villages, by general laws."[8] Indiana's constitution of the same year included a provision that "corporations, other than banking, shall not be created by special act, but may be formed under general laws."[9] In 1857 Iowa adopted a constitution that forbade the passage of special laws "for the incorporation of cities and towns" and required the enactment of general laws "in all other cases where a general law can be made applicable."[10] The first constitution of Kansas closely resembled that of Ohio with regard to municipal organization, and in 1867 Nebraska copied the Ohio model too.[11] Illinois' constitution of 1870 asserted that "the General Assembly shall not pass local or special laws . . . incorporating cities, towns, or villages"; California's constitution of 1879 also required general laws for municipal corporations.[12] In state after state, it was clear that the framers of the fundamental law no longer wanted state legislators to devote their energies to drafting one law that would add 200 acres to Cincinnati and another that would enlarge Cleveland by 600 acres. The framers believed that legislatures could establish general procedures for such minor local questions and thereby relieve the state government of troublesome and time-consuming tasks.

In response to these constitutional changes, legislators soon established general procedures for annexation and for municipal consolidation. Under Ohio's general law of 1852, residents of an unincorporated area could initiate annexation proceedings by submitting a petition to the county commissioners. The commissioners would determine whether a requisite majority of the residents in the outlying area had signed the petition and would then submit the boundary question to voters of the annexing municipality. The municipal council could also initiate annexation proceedings by submitting a boundary alteration proposal to the city's voters. If the voters approved the proposal, then the council would petition the county commissioners for annexation. When extension of municipal boundaries involved the consolidation of two or more adjoining municipalities, then it was necessary for the electorate in both cities to sanction the change. Basic to the Ohio statute, then, were the ideas of popular referendum and local self-determination. The county commissioners would supervise the procedure and judge the validity of petitions, but the individual voter would also play a part in redrawing the map of urban Ohio.[13]

Other states followed the example of Ohio, allocating responsibility for boundary adjustments to local officials and to the local electorate. Indiana's act for the incorporation of cities, enacted in 1852, granted county commissioners the powers to conduct hearings with regard to annexation and to approve or disapprove alterations in municipal limits. Five years later Indiana's legislature specified the general procedure for the consolidation of adjoining municipalities and required the approval of voters in both cities prior to consolidation.[14] Illinois' general annexation law of 1872 also required a referendum prior to the union of two incorporated areas, but the county circuit court was to determine whether unincorporated territory should be annexed.[15] By the 1870s, then, the most populous states in the Midwest had adopted new methods for determining municipal boundaries. By doing so they had bolstered the power of local officials and of the local electorate.

Two basic annexation procedures developed in the states west of the Mississippi, one in which municipal and county officials determined boundary questions and a second in which the electorate enjoyed a voice in the proceedings. In Kansas, Nebraska, and Missouri the first procedure governed the alteration of boundaries. Under annexation statutes enacted during the 1880s, Missouri cities, with the exception of Saint Louis, could annex unincorporated territory through passage of a simple ordinance and without the consent of those residents of the area to be annexed.[16] Likewise, a series of Kansas laws enacted during the late 1860s stated that "the city council . . . shall in every case have power to increase or diminish the city limits, in manner as in their judgment and discretion may redound to the benefit of the city," though annexation of unplatted land required "the consent in writing of the owners of a majority of the whole number of acres . . . in the territory proposed to be added."[17] Similarly, in Nebraska annexation generally required only a municipal ordinance and the approval of the district court, there being no provision for popular referendum.[18] In Nebraska and Missouri a referendum was necessary for the consolidation of adjoining municipalities, but cities could annex unincorporated territory without appeal to the citizenry.[19]

Elsewhere, in the years following the Civil War, consent of the electorate became a vital element in the annexation process. Under Arkansas' general statute of 1875, residents of an unincorporated area could initiate annexation proceedings by submitting a petition signed by a majority of the voters of that area. If the city council petitioned the circuit court for a boundary change, according to Arkansas law, "it shall be lawful for the council to submit the question to the qualified electors."[20] Iowa and Colorado adopted almost identical procedures, requiring the assent of the voters except in the case of platted contiguous territory.[21] And the California Municipal Corporations Act of 1883 authorized the city council to judge the validity of petitions for annexation but specified that a majority of voters in both the city and the area to be annexed must consent to the change in boundary.[22]

Thus, in most of the states west of the Appalachians, constitutional restraints had resulted in general annexation measures by 1890. These annexation measures shifted the focus of control over boundary adjustment from the state government to the county or municipal authorities and to the electorate. These laws governed the expansion of some of America's largest cities during the nineteenth and twentieth centuries, determining in part the nature of their growth. The city of Cleveland annexed ninety percent of its present area in accordance with the general procedures prescribed by the state of Ohio. Los Angeles expanded from 28 square miles in 1890 to 441 square miles in 1930 as a result of annexations and consolidations conducted in accordance with the general statutory procedure. These general statutes, arising from constitutional restrictions of the mid-nineteenth century, were to mold the growth of many American cities as the idea of local and popular self-determination gradually supplanted that of central control.

Yet constitutional restraints on special legislation did not eliminate legislative interference in states such as Ohio, Illinois, or California. Instead, legislators often overlooked the new provisions in state constitutions, enacting measures that were either blatantly local in nature or thinly disguised as general laws. Thus they composed legislation that applied "generally" to all cities having a population between 100,000 and 125,000 on a certain date when in fact only one city in the state fit that definition. In many states legislatures divided municipalities into first-class, second-class, and third-class cities and enacted a separate set of general laws for each class. This also served as a mask for local legislation in a state such as Nebraska, where only Omaha qualified as a metropolitan-class city and Lincoln was the sole municipality in the first-class category. In Nebraska and elsewhere state legislators often succeeded in their subterfuge, but at times they did not. Since their success or failure rested on the judgment of the courts, the judiciary also assumed a prominent role in the annexation process of the late nineteenth century. The courts were called upon repeatedly to determine the exact bounds of legislative authority and to halt legislative invasions of forbidden territory.

The state courts were not wholly consistent on the question of special annexation laws, but they did present another obstacle in the increasingly complex path of boundary adjustment. This was first evident in the case of *Ohio* v. *City of Cincinnati*, decided in 1870. In April 1870 the Ohio General Assembly passed an act that described the procedure whereby the city of Cincinnati could annex six suburban municipalities and sixteen square miles of rural land. The act specifically charted the proposed boundaries of the enlarged city, and there was no pretense that the law would apply to any other area in the state. The Ohio Supreme Court recognized the special nature of the legislation and declared "that the act is clearly in contravention of the restrictive provisions of the constitution, and therefore of no binding force and validity." Thus the court stymied Cincinnati's expansion at this time, and the city failed to annex the bulk of the suburban territory until legislation phrased in general terms was passed twenty-three years later.[23]

During the following three decades, other state courts also invalidated special annexation and consolidation schemes. In 1870 the Kansas Supreme Court voided a special act adding territory to the city of Wyandotte, and fourteen years later this same court invalidated an annexation law that applied only to the cities of Topeka, Lawrence, and Atchison.[24] Likewise, in 1893 the highest court in Colorado struck down special legislation that sought to alter the boundaries of Denver by consolidating that city with thirteen adjoining municipalities.[25] And three years later the Iowa Supreme Court invalidated an act that authorized the city of Des Moines to extend its boundaries two and one-half miles in each direction from its existing limits and to absorb eight other cities and towns.[26] In Ohio, Colorado, and Iowa the state legislators sought to reorganize the fragmented local governments of their states' largest urban areas. Yet in each case the state courts deemed the legislation to be special, thereby reinforcing the constitutional barrier to central coordination of boundary adjustments.

Thus the judiciary represented one further obstacle to be surmounted if annexation or consolidation were to be achieved. In their efforts to adjust boundaries in accord with the rapid urban growth of the period, municipal leaders in Ohio, Illinois, Colorado, or California not only had to run the gauntlet of county officials and the local electorate, they also had to expect a possible court contest that could delay or void their plans. Repeatedly disgruntled residents of annexed territory called upon the state courts to examine the procedural or constitutional defects of an expansion scheme, and the aggressive judges of the late nineteenth century were not reluctant to check the actions of overzealous state and local officials.

By the turn of the century the movement to check state action accelerated as home rule advocates joined the battle against central authority. In the 1890s Minnesota adopted both a constitutional amendment prohibiting special legislation and a home rule amendment. In accordance with the new constitutional provisions, the legislature enacted a general annexation measure.[27] In 1906 the home rule amendment to Oregon's constitution prohibited special legislation and ended state dictation of municipal boundaries within the Portland metropolitan area. Likewise, the Michigan home rule act of 1909 included general rules for annexation and delegated responsibility for boundary adjustment to urban and suburban voters.[28] Since home rule meant rule by the local authorities and local electorate, it also meant a halt to any broader efforts at reorganizing the expanding American metropolis.

By 1910 home rule and special legislation provisions in twenty-seven of the forty-six state constitutions prohibited special acts relating to cities.[29] In the urban states of Massachusetts and New York, state lawmakers retained the power to legislate specifically for New York City and Boston, but these states represented a deviation from the norm. Elsewhere classification schemes often enabled legislatures to avoid constitutional restraints, but the state courts would not necessarily tolerate these classification disguises. In 1902 the Ohio Supreme Court held that classification of cities was unconstitutional, and three years later the Indiana Supreme Court struck down a law that provided for an alteration in the boundaries of cities having a population "of between six and seven thousand" residents.[30] In the future Ohio's numerous urban centers would have to adhere to general procedures created for all cities, and Indiana's municipalities would likewise have to conform to more general rules.

Between 1850 and 1910, then, the procedure for municipal boundary adjustment had changed radically as lawmakers acted to limit the power of state legislatures. In the 1850s and 1860s, framers of state constitutions had deemed state interference in local government inequitable and inefficient. By the turn of the century, drafters of constitutional provisions were complaining of outside control and of violations of the right to local self-government. But during both periods the complaints would result in a check on central state authority and a dispersion of decision-making power.

To understand the legal structure of boundary adjustment better, it is useful to examine the application of that structure in the various annexation contests of the late nineteenth century. In Cleveland, Chicago, Denver, Indianapolis, Boston, and New York City, expansionists engaged in vigorous campaigns to extend municipal limits, and in each case the influence of the principle of local self-determination was present. From New England to the Pacific Northwest, state legislators deferred to the right of the local unit to determine its own fate, and a new annexation procedure developed. The procedure was not always simple; and local voters, village councils, and judges wrestled tirelessly with the complex problem of boundary adjustment and the need to mollify often conflicting interests. In some of these cities years passed before annexationists achieved success. Referendum followed referendum, and court battles, council fights, and general free-for-alls often disrupted the peace of suburbia. But Cleveland, Chicago, Denver, Indianapolis, Boston, and New York City did succeed in acquiring new territories, for lawmakers had fashioned a means whereby the citizenry could adjust boundaries in accordance with the realities of massive population growth. These examples demonstrate the actual operation of the new procedures.

In each of these cities, the new procedures resulted in repeated triumphs for the annexationist cause. The cities were allowed to expand, and this expansion was largely a result of the suburbanite's desire for superior central-city services. Hyde Park, Elyria, West Cleveland, and South Omaha incorporated to obtain municipal services, but by the close of the second decade of the twentieth century each had chosen to consolidate with the central city to achieve still better services. In the late nineteenth century, the rising expectations of suburbanites proved not only a motive for incorporation but also a motive for annexation. The forces of separatism may have been pulling the metropolis apart, but in the nineteenth century the desire for improved services was a countervailing force for unity. So long as the central city had an advantage over the suburbs in the provision of public services, then the rising material expectations of Americans would act as a force on the side of consolidation. Throughout the later decades of the century the central city maintained this advantage, and throughout this period the central city could bribe suburbanites into sanctioning wedlock between city and suburb. Thus in Cleveland, Chicago, Denver, Indianapolis, Boston, and New York City, the means for consolidation existed as did the motive. And, with both means and motive, expansionists proved victorious, fashioning extensive urban empires.

Cleveland's crusade to extend its boundaries during the period from 1870 to 1910 typifies the struggle of an expanding city to achieve unified urban rule. The battle began in 1872, when Cleveland sought to expand eastward by consolidating with the independent municipality of East Cleveland.* To achieve this, first a majority of voters in each municipality had to approve the merger, then commissioners appointed by the two municipal councils negotiated the terms of consolidation, and finally each council had to approve the scheme. Consolidation forces easily topped the first hurdle in April 1872 when the electorate of both cities approved union by handsome majorities. One exuberant Cleveland newspaper proclaimed, "Come in East Cleveland. Henceforth you are 'one of us.'"[31]

The rejoicing, however, proved a bit premature, for the city fathers still had to negotiate the terms of merger, including such ticklish issues as the assumption of the East Cleveland municipal debt. East Cleveland's commissioners demanded that Cleveland assume the $75,000 debt, but Cleveland's representatives refused. By July differences between Cleveland and East Cleveland had deadlocked negotiations, and suburban residents were seriously reconsidering the merits of merger with the central city.[32]

At a series of heated meetings East Cleveland residents debated the merits and shortcomings of annexation. As many as 300 citizens gathered to discuss the future of their community, and, according to reporters present, "the remarks of nearly all were received with cheers, showing that there were strong sympathizers on both sides."[33] Foes of consolidation minimized the importance of promised water from Cleveland by noting that "it would be a long time before the water would be extended to the side streets."[34] Moreover, if East Cleveland residents had to pay the village debt, the total tax rate for suburban property owners would soar to 27 1/10 mills, "an increase of 14 1/10 mills on their present tax."[35] Critics of the proposed merger also "touched on the liquor question, and spoke of the free range which would be given rum sellers" if the East Cleveland temperance measures yielded to Cleveland's more tolerant attitude toward alcohol.[36] Finally, one outspoken opponent of consolidation "wound up by vehemently declaring that the vote which was taken last spring was a fraud, and a swindle, and he could prove it."[37]

Suburban supporters of consolidation retaliated by observing that "there is no natural division between the city and East Cleveland" to

---

*This East Cleveland is not the same municipality as a second East Cleveland, which survives today and is mentioned in chapters 5, 7, and 8.

justify the political separation of the two communities.[38] Furthermore, East Cleveland needed more businesses and factories, "and this it will never have until it annexes to the city and enjoys the advantages of water, etc., which the city would give it."[39] Advocates of the merger argued that East Cleveland's tax rate "for the present year is inadequate to meet the expenses of the corporation, and denounced it as having been ... put thus low for the purpose of strengthening the arguments of the opposers to annexation."[40] One leading citizen summed up the feelings of many when he announced that he "considered life in the city, with a fire and police department, schools, etc., better than in a village where these advantages cannot be enjoyed."[41] Few could question that Cleveland had much to offer suburbanites eager for the comforts and conveniences that only highly developed municipal services could provide.

In August the city of Cleveland agreed to assume part of the East Cleveland debt, but to allay doubts about the validity of the spring election, officials chose to call a second election on the merger question. At this point members of the East Cleveland village council momentarily stalled the annexation campaign by refusing to pass the necessary ordinance calling for an election. Consideration of such an ordinance was on the agenda of the September 3 council meeting, but before the council could discuss the issue "a motion was made to adjourn, and the chair put the question with an eager haste that was touching in the extreme."[42] According to one newspaper reporter, "there was just one voice that rang out in startling accents, in favor of adjournment," but "the chair declared the meeting adjourned, grabbed his hat, and struck a bee line for the door, followed by the expeditious clerk."[43] Thus foes of consolidation delayed the proposed union until finally, on September 18, the East Cleveland council passed the necessary ordinance.

During the next three weeks friends and foes of consolidation dedicated themselves to winning the upcoming consolidation election. One suburban council member reported that "both sides are working like beavers to further their respective interests; each positively averring that they have a majority, and can show it at the polls."[44] The Ohio legislature had abdicated central responsibility for boundary adjustment and accepted the principle of local self-determination. Now the people of Cleveland and East Cleveland were exercising the right to determine their local destiny and doing so with a vengeance.

In East Cleveland consolidation carried by an even larger majority in October than it had in April, and both the village and city councils passed final ordinances approving annexation. Yet the merger process was not complete, for after the city council and electorate had spoken, disgruntled citizens retained one final recourse, and that was appeal to the courts. On October 25 seven citizens of East Cleveland obtained an injunction halting merger of the two municipalities. Cleveland's city solicitor moved that the injunction be dissolved, and the friends and foes of municipal union fought one last battle in the Cuyahoga County Court of Common Pleas on October 28.[45]

Annexation foes failed to present sufficient reasons for delay of the merger, and on October 29 the court ordered the injunction dissolved.[46] At last Cleveland and East Cleveland were united—after debates and discussion, appeals to the electorate, approval by the two city councils, and final action by the judiciary. The experience of 1872 demonstrated the multiple obstacles to unified urban rule and the role that voters, local officials, and the courts might play under this system of local self-determination.

The Cleveland-East Cleveland merger was just the first in a long list of consolidations in Cuyahoga County between 1870 and 1910. Independent municipalities hugged the boundaries of Cleveland throughout this period, and consequently the central city expanded primarily through mergers with surrounding villages rather than through annexation of unincorporated territory. In 1894 the villages of West Cleveland and Brooklyn succumbed, while in 1905 the municipalities of Glenville and South Brooklyn joined the city, and in 1909 Corlett followed suit as did the village of Collinwood in 1910. Residents of some unincorporated tracts also petitioned for union with the city. In December of 1873 the property owners of a large section of Newburgh township went before the country commissioners who, hearing no objections, approved annexation. In each of these cases a similar pattern of decision making prevailed, a pattern that emphasized the role of residents, local officials, and often the judiciary.

The annexations of both Brooklyn and Glenville resulted in court battles, and the absorption of South Brooklyn entailed a form of Machiavallian scheming common to the suburbs. In 1905 the citizens of South Brooklyn had voted more than two to one in favor of consolidation, and the Cleveland electorate had expressed almost unanimous approval of the merger. Four of the six South Brooklyn council members, however, opposed union with the central city, and before the municipalities could merge the village council was required to pass an ordinance of consolidation. To avoid confronting the issue, the four opponents boycotted council meetings so that a quorum was never present. Village residents protested at mass meetings, and proconsolidation leaders began legal proceedings to oust one of the uncooperative councilmen from office. Supporters of consolidation claimed that the foreign-born councilman was not a citizen of the United States, and the court upheld these claims, removing him from office. If those favoring merger could remove one more opposition councilman and fill both vacancies with men friendly to union with Cleveland, then the battle would be won. They achieved this goal when one of the nonattending councilmen peeked into a council meeting to see what was happening. The proconsolidation mayor caught sight of his truant foe and cried: "Mr. Williams, I see you are present . . . and I now declare a quorum present for the transaction of business." In a fit of anger, Williams answered, "Mr. Mayor I resign as councilman of the village." The mayor immediately accepted his resignation, and two promerger councilmen were chosen to fill the vacancies.[47] Consequently, South Brooklyn joined Cleveland despite obstacle and delay.

Local officials also delayed the annexation of Collinwood, attempting to preserve that municipality's independence despite voter support for consolidation. In November 1907, the citizens of Collinwood voted four to one in favor of joining Cleveland and ousted the antimerger mayor and councilmen from office.[48] However, the new village council members reneged on their promised support for consolidation and refused to ratify a merger ordinance.[49] Collinwood's residents wanted to enjoy the lighting, paving, and police services offered by the city of Cleveland, and now these suburban citizens felt betrayed. According to one newspaper, "charges of treachery were hurled at the councilmen and angry denunciations of the action were heard all over the village."[50] But Cleveland city solicitor, Newton Baker, admitted that "the council was acting within its power," and consequently union was not possible until a new council was elected.[51]

Two years later, in November 1909, Collinwood's voters expressed their dissatisfaction, defeating the incumbent councilmen and electing a proannexation slate.[52] With this last obstacle removed, Collinwood finally merged with Cleveland in early 1910, adding nine thousand people to the central city's population.[53] In Collinwood, as in South Brooklyn and East Cleveland, local officials had delayed the unification of urban governments, but eventually the will of the local electorate had prevailed.

During the period from 1870 to 1910, Clevelanders thus grappled with the new procedures of annexation that required approval by the local electorate and local officials and that permitted appeal to the courts. There had been delays as expansionists were forced to conform to the principle of local self-determination, but they had surmounted the obstacles. Suburbanites wanted Cleveland's water; they wanted street lights, pavements, and fire and police protection. And to achieve these ends they were willing to join with the central city. Consequently, in the annexation referenda of the late nineteenth and early twentieth centuries, they repeatedly sanctioned union.

To the west, the city of Chicago was also expanding its limits in accord with the principle of local self-determination. Between 1851 and 1869

Chicago had absorbed approximately twenty-six square miles, the municipal boundaries being successively altered by simple acts of the state legislature.[54] In 1872, however, lawmakers in Springfield enacted a general annexation law providing for local referenda, and in 1887 the legislature approved a second statute that described the means by which cities could absorb outlying townships. The township act was a complex measure well suited to the grotesque complexity of local government in Illinois. But it clarified the procedure for the assumption of debts and for the retention of prohibition ordinances, and it included the increasingly standard elements of popular approval and mediation by county officials.[55]

Those eager to extend Chicago's boundaries soon sought to apply this township statute to Cook County in order to annex parts of the suburban towns and municipalities of Hyde Park, Lake, Lake View, Jefferson, and Cicero. Residents of these villages and townships petitioned for annexation, and the county circuit court scheduled a popular vote on the issue in November 1887. There ensued a fiery campaign with a series of enthusiastic mass meetings and long processions led by "Cummings Brass Band" with banners proclaiming "Hurrah for Annexation!" and "Annexation Will Increase Our Industries."[56] Suburban supporters of annexation argued that their communities "needed a share of Chicago's perfect police, fire, postal systems, and all the other blessings of civilization that a big city can avail itself of."[57] In the village of Hyde Park annexationists reminded voters that the suburb owned only two steam fire engines to serve its forty-eight square miles, and in time of fire "it was impossible to get water into the second story of your houses."[58] Moreover, they argued that "we now sewer into Lake Michigan and draw our water from the same lake one mile out" so that soon "the water will become unfit for use."[59] Annexation, in contrast, would provide Hyde Parkers with "the best water works in the United States, the best police, the best fire department and you become a part of the best city in the United States."[60]

On election day in 1887 the voters generally favored an expanded city. In Hyde Park, Jefferson, and Cicero townships annexation carried by handsome majorities, while in Lake and Lake View annexationists suffered defeat.[61] At this point, however, suburban officials advanced to the next stage in the annexation process—the court battle. The Hyde Park trustees hired a corps of distinguished lawyers, including the future United States Chief Justice Melville Fuller. Fuller and his colleagues argued that annexation of one part of Hyde Park would leave the remaining section of the town with a heavy debt burden and little taxable property; they also claimed that twenty-three of those who signed the petition for annexation were not registered voters. Further, they believed that the annexation was null and void because only a majority of the 4,200 who had voted in November favored annexation and not a majority of the 6,400 registered to vote. Finally, the attorneys argued that Chicago had attempted to extend its boundaries "by means of a big sized sneak," the annexation legislation having "been carried through under guise of an act in relation to township organization." A provision of the Illinois constitution required that the title of legislation adequately describe the content of the measure, and, according to counsel for Hyde Park, annexation "was so far from being germane to the title of the act that it had defeated itself by making the whole act unconstitutional."[62]

Armed with these contentions, Hyde Park's battery of attorneys appealed to the judiciary for a restoration of independent municipal rule. The Superior Court of Cook County upheld annexation, but in March 1888 the Illinois State Supreme Court ruled that the legislation of 1887 was in fact unconstitutional. According to the justices, the township law violated the section of the state constitution that provided "no act hereafter passed shall embrace more than one subject, and that shall be expressed in its title." The drafters of the Illinois constitution intended that this provision, like those prohibiting special legislation, would prevent lawmakers from sneaking measures through the legislature by disguising them with misleading titles. In an effort to honor the intentions of the framers, the supreme court ordered the separation of Hyde Park and Chicago.[63]

However, this setback did not halt the growth of the city permanently. Annexationists boasted that "they can't keep us out on small technicalities."[64] Likewise the *Chicago Tribune* argued that the Supreme Court decision "should not be considered a permanent bar," for "if the suburban voters wish to ... get rid of the multitudinous petty boards, rings, and cliques that prey on them they will send to Springfield ... men capable of drafting a law which can stand the test of a technical Supreme Court."[65] This is what happened, and in 1889 the state legislature drafted a new general law describing consolidation procedures; they gave this law an appropriate and accurate title.[66]

Again annexation and consolidation depended on the approval of suburban voters. Consequently, in 1889 the citizens of Lake, Lake View, and Hyde Park confronted the issue of boundary alterations for the second time in two years. As in 1887, annexationists held mass meetings "at Spetz Hall, Gross Hall and Germania Hall located in different parts of Lake View" complete with a brass band and speakers who "laid down the gospel of annexation in a convincing way."[67] Suburban residents who favored annexation complained that "we are being taxed to death and ground down by a lot of petty officials who care no more for the town than a hog does for the opera."[68] Others argued that the suburban

"water supply was so filthy as to be positively unfit for drinking purposes"; they claimed that union with Chicago would mean that "we will
no longer be obliged to drink our own sewage."[69] Residents of Lake
View were especially critical of suburban water, and one claimed "to
know of several persons who have died from typhoid fever caused by
drinking Lake View water."[70] In this gentleman's household, he claimed,
"my wife boils all the water we use." A public health survey of the municipalities along Lake Michigan found that in fact Hyde Park water
was "the most impure of them all and that of Lake View the next."[71]
Others observed that "the government of the suburbs is very weak" and
claimed that Lake View had only one policeman and that "same old
fellow is always in the same old place."[72] According to the *Chicago
Herald*, "the Lake View Fire Department was never known to put out a
fire" and conditions were not much better in Hyde Park or Lake.[73]

Foes of annexation mobilized in opposition to this flood of unionist
sentiment and attempted to answer annexation charges. One leading
meat packer from suburban Lake claimed that "we have ample water
facilities now," and "everything is just as we want it."[74] A Hyde Park
resident admitted that "my principal objection to annexing Hyde Park
... is that our taxes must necessarily be increased and I don't care to
pay anymore taxes than can be avoided."[75] And the city attorney of Lake
View sought to frighten his constituents when he "raised a hue and cry
about the heavy taxation" that would result from annexation.[76] Various
factions again appealed to the suburban electorate in a lusty and emo-
tional annexation campaign, with the separatists warning of higher costs
and the unionists promising better services.

In 1889 the annexationists were even more successful than they had
been in 1887, for they won handsome majorities in each of the suburban
townships. There was, however, one further step in the annexation process, since the possibility for judicial interference persisted. The mayor
of Lake View protested the voters' decision, claiming that the people
"don't know what they are about" and John True, Lake View's treasurer,
brought suit challenging the validity of consolidation.[77] True and his
counsel argued that Chicago was already indebted beyond the constitutional limit and that the city of Chicago should not be permitted to
assume further liabilities by annexing debt-ridden Lake View. Again
the case went to the Illinois Supreme Court, but this time the court
ruled in favor of the annexationists and against True and the municipality of Lake View.[78] The court's decision was the final word on the
issue, and, after two years of contention, those seeking the unification of
urban government had won their victory.

But Chicago's experience simply exemplified the tangled process of
boundary alteration that prevailed by the late nineteenth century. An-

nexationists had achieved their goal in Illinois only after the passage of two annexation statutes, the conduct of two annexation campaigns, a double victory at the polls, and two appeals before the state supreme court in Springfield. Whereas in the early nineteenth century legislators had drawn municipal boundaries, now the courts, the legislature, and the electorate shared in the mapping of Chicago's limits. Despite the occasional complexities of this procedure, Chicago's expansionists did achieve their ends, for in the Chicago area as in metropolitan Cleveland, suburbanites wanted the relatively clean city water, the professional central-city fire fighting services, and the general amenities of urban life that only a giant such as Chicago could provide in the 1880s. In Chicago as in Cleveland, superior city services were the charm that lured suburbanites into the central city.

This same dedication to local self-determination and concern for improved services is evident in Denver's annexation campaign of the 1890s. In Denver as in both Cleveland and Chicago, the city fathers wanted to absorb a group of small outlying incorporated towns. And, in Colorado as in Ohio and Illinois, the process proved complex and lengthy, for legislators, judges, and state and city voters all shared in the determination of boundary alterations.

The campaign for consolidation began in 1893 when the Colorado legislature proposed annexing thirteen outlying towns by simply redefining Denver's boundaries in the city's new charter.[79] Many suburban residents reacted strongly against this effort to usurp their communities and draw them into the central city, and these malcontents expressed their feelings at a series of protest meetings. At one mass gathering, a leader from suburban South Denver summed up the attitude of separatists in that community when he urged "that our present boundary lines remain intact, and that we have full local option on what affects our district."[80] The council of Highlands made similar demands, and the municipality of Valverde presented a strong petition against "being arbitrarily annexed to Denver by means of the ... charter unless the question is submitted to popular vote."[81] Likewise, Denver's *Rocky Mountain News* attacked the measure, claiming that if suburban residents "do not wish to be annexed, they should not ... be compelled to come in against their will."[82]

Moreover, some legislators doubted the constitutionality of this involuntary procedure, and Colorado's House of Representatives asked the state supreme court to rule on the validity of the measure. According to the Colorado court, some forms of special legislation might be permissible under the state constitution, but "the power of the legislature to annul the corporate existence of the adjoining towns by an amendment to the special charter of the city of Denver ... must be denied." The court claimed that "if the proposed legislation can be upheld, then it is difficult to conceive of any legislation with reference to . . . corporate boundaries . . . that cannot be enacted as an amendment to the present charter." Such special legislation was not acceptable under the constitution of Colorado, and state lawmakers would have to choose an alternate mode for consolidating the governments of metropolitan Denver.[83]

The alternative chosen was an annexation measure that was phrased in general terms and that included a consolidation procedure similar to those of Ohio and Illinois. Residents of outlying towns could petition the county court for annexation to Denver, and in response the county court would order the board of trustees or council of the outlying municipality to submit the issue of annexation to the voters. If the voters in the outlying towns approved annexation, then the court would order the consolidation of the town and the city of Denver. Again an appeal was made to the state supreme court, but this time the scheme was upheld.[84]

During the following four years, consolidation proposals appeared on the ballots in many of the suburban municipalities. For example, in February 1894 South Denver, Colfax, and Harman voted on the issue. Annexation sentiment was strong in South Denver, where it was claimed that "annexation will give the suburb excellent fire and police protection; that the value of real estate will increase . . . , and that taxes will be greatly reduced."[85] But those opposed to annexation were also active, organizing an antiannexation club and holding mass meetings in the Odd Fellows Hall.[86] In Colfax the ruling Populist party urged union with Denver, and in Harman debates over consolidation disrupted the usual tranquility of the town.[87] Expensive water rates in the suburbs troubled outlying residents, and the appeal of Denver's police, fire, and sewage services was attractive to voters in each of the communities surrounding the central city. Throughout the suburban towns people discussed, argued, and fought over the issue of consolidation in accord with the emerging American pattern of local, popular rule, and in each they evaluated and reevaluated the merits of Denver's services. On election day, South Denver's citizens voted almost three to one in favor of merger, while in both Colfax and Harman the voters rejected consolidation.[88]

The will of the suburban electorate, however, did not remain unchallenged, as Colfax residents would soon discover. In November 1894 citizens of the town of Colfax reconsidered the comforts and conveniences that Denver's services might provide and again cast ballots on the merger issue. This time the appeal of superior services was too great for the separatists, and the suburb voted seventy-seven to sixty-four in favor of consolidation. Those favoring an independent Colfax now turned to the courts, charging that unqualified persons had voted, that the pro-merger town trustees had appointed a biased board of election judges, and that the format of the ballot had been contrary to that specified in the consolidation law. The Colorado Court of Appeals agreed with the dissidents, ruling that "the election was irregular and void."[89] But in 1898, after four years of controversy, the Colorado Supreme Court overturned the court of appeals decision, ruling that the intermediate-level appellate court had no authority to hear appeals in annexation contests.[90] Finally the union between Colfax and Denver was confirmed.

By the close of the century, residents in seven of the outlying municipalities had voted in favor of annexation, but in the case of North Denver the state supreme court had exercised the power it denied the court of appeals, thereby blocking entry into the city.[91] Moreover, in the case of a second suburb, the town of Fletcher, the judiciary, state legislature, and Denver's officialdom all joined in an effort to subvert the will of the suburban electorate. Fletcher was the municipal pariah of the Denver area, and lawmakers spared no energy in segregating it from the city.

Under the consolidation scheme as enacted by the legislature in 1893, the annexing city had no voice in the consolidation process. When the heavily indebted town of Fletcher sought union with Denver, the Denver City Council opposed any merger with this financial burden and rushed to the state legislature with demands for an amendment to the annexation procedure. The Colorado legislature acceded to Denver's demands and required assent of the annexing city prior to annexation. Fletcher appealed to the state supreme court, which upheld the retrospective application of this law to the debt-ridden community. Consequently the town of Fletcher remained an independent if impoverished municipality.[92]

Within seven years, then, Denver had annexed five suburban communities, but only after the drafting of three state laws, repeated appeals to the courts, and numerous annexation campaigns and elections in a variety of municipalities. Yet those favoring consolidation originally had proposed the annexation of thirteen outlying municipalities to the city of Denver, and they had only partially achieved this end. Previous court decisions had voided special legislation that disincorporated existing municipalities, holding it to be unconstitutional. Thus forcible consolidation of the remaining towns would require constitutional amendment, and Colorado lawmakers set about to achieve this change in the fundamental law of the state.

In 1901 Colorado's legislature drafted a home rule amendment that redefined Denver's boundaries, including within the reorganized city six additional municipalities. Since this boundary alteration was a provision in a constitutional amendment, it required not simply the approval of local voters but the assent of a majority of the state's electorate. And in 1902 the voters of the state approved the adjustment by a vote of fifty-nine thousand to twenty-five thousand.[93] Finally Denver had absorbed eleven of the thirteen suburban communities and had excluded bankrupt Fletcher. But Denver had achieved final consolidation only after a statewide popular referendum. Decision-making authority over urban boundaries had moved outward from the former locus of power in the state legislature, and by 1902 even lowly voters in Durango, Grand Junction, and Fort Collins exercised a direct voice in the organization of metropolitan Denver.

In Ohio, Illinois, and Colorado state lawmakers had abdicated much of their authority over the drawing of municipal boundaries, and suburban voters had won a veto in the consolidation struggle. Likewise, in the state of Indiana, legislators had yielded central control and enhanced local power. But Indiana's solons did not grant such a decisive voice to the outlying residents. Instead, in Indiana central-city officials would play the chief role in fixing municipal boundaries. Suburbanites had some power to limit central-city aggression, yet it was basically the big-city councils and mayors that mapped the metropolitan area. Boundary adjustment was the primary prerogative not of the local electorate but of the local officials. Referenda did not play a role in Indiana's process of drawing city limits, but still there was no state coordination of annexation and consolidation.

Under Indiana's statues of 1891 and 1895 any city with a population of over 100,000 could annex adjoining territory through a simple ordinance of the city council. If the territory to be annexed included an incorporated town or city, then aggrieved citizens of the territory could present a remonstrance to the county circuit court. This court would then review the grievances. If it found that the remonstrance enjoyed the support of less than two-thirds of the voters of the municipality to be annexed, then the court would approve the annexation. If more than two-thirds remonstrated, then the annexation would be void, "unless the Court shall find from the evidence that the prosperity of such city and territory will be materially retarded and the safety of the inhabitants and property thereof endangered without such annexation."[94] In other words, the central city determined its own boundaries through passage of a simple ordinance, and suburbanites could only override this ordinance with a two-thirds veto and approval of the circuit court.

Yet Indiana law did make some concessions to recalcitrant suburbs, most notably the suburb of Woodruff Place. In 1895 Indianapolis engaged in one of its many attacks on the autonomy of this residential park, and it chose the chambers of the state legislature for its battleground. Business leader and former Democratic vice-presidential nominee William English testified at a state legislative hearing that the town of Woodruff Place was hampering his efforts to develop real estate on the east side of Indianapolis. Mayor Denny of Indianapolis claimed that there was "no question that at least nine-tenths of the people of Indianapolis favored the annexation of Woodruff Place."[95] Both demanded special legislation, clad in the constitutionally required garb of a general law, that would permit annexation of the suburb to the city. Suburbanites argued "that to annex Woodruff Place meant to rob a number of people of their homes." Moreover, they challenged the probity of the distinguished William English, and one unkind suburbanite referred to the "many unpainted houses in the city belonging to Mr. English."[96]

These suburban defenders were to prove successful, and Woodruff Place would not only survive but also win a concession from the legislature. Under the statute of 1895, a city of 100,000 or more population (Indianapolis) could contract with any incorporated town surrounded by the city (Woodruff Place) for the provision of fire, police, sweeping, sprinkling, and sewage services to that enclave, and the central city would have to accept as compensation a figure fixed by the county circuit court.[97] Indianapolis could not, then, blackmail the residential park of Woodruff Place and demand exorbitant fees for its services. Instead, the county court would act as a mediator between city and suburb and protect the interests of Woodruff Place.

While Woodruff Place bolstered its suburban battlements, Indianapolis's other suburbs dedicated themselves to policies of municipal suicide. Suburbanites in Brightwood, Haughville, Mount Jackson, West Indianapolis, and Irvington yearned for Indianapolis's municipal services and demanded consolidation. Gas rates in Brightwood were 50 percent higher than in the city, and annexation would save residents thousands of dollars.[98] Under the new streetcar franchise the fare from Brightwood to West Indianapolis would be thirteen cents, but if the two suburbs entered the city, then the fare would be only 3 cents.[99] Suburban sewage and water facilities did not equal those of the city. Despite these inadequacies, the tax rates in West Indianapolis, Haughville, and Brightwood were $1.76, $1.90, and $2.13, respectively, as compared with only $1.65 in the city.[100] Law enforcement in the suburbs was inadequate, and according to the Indianapolis police superintendent "the toughs and roughs . . . have all gone out to the suburbs" where "they have a snap."[101] Mount Jackson was known as an area of "questionable resorts," and working-class Haughville and West Indianapolis were also far from pristine in their morals.[102]

In contrast, Irvington was a residential community of retired missionaries, ministers, lawyers, doctors, and professors. Surrounding the campus of the church-operated Butler University, it was a haven of true

Victorian virtue with gingerbread verandas, lace curtains, and prayer meetings. There was no whiskey in Irvington, but unfortunately there was also very little water. Since the town had no waterworks, fire remained a serious danger.[103] Questions of drainage, paving, and street lighting divided the community as some complained of increased expenditure while others demanded further improvements. During the late 1890s the local Citizens' Home Rule party commended the town board of trustees for its efforts to lift Irvington "from the condition of a muddy, dark, unprotected weed patch to a well organized community with passable roads and walks, with public lights and with enlarged school facilities."[104] But still some "complained that they must pay for a sewer that did not carry off the water at the time of the recent rains," and others urged "the strictest economy in the administration ... of the town in order that the heavy rate of taxation, now the highest in the county, may be reduced."[105]

By 1897 suburban demands for annexation were mounting, and the mayor and council of Indianapolis were ready to take action. The city council announced its intention of absorbing the outlying municipalities, and Mayor Taggart concurred with the council's views though he only favored annexing those areas whose residents supported entry to the city.[106] In order to understand suburban views better, the council finance committee held a hearing on the annexation issue. Nearly one hundred people were present, including some suburban consolidationists who proudly wore "white ribbons bearing the words, 'Haughville Annexation.'" The representatives from Haughville reported that "there was ... so little opposition to annexation" in their suburb "that no organized effort against it could be made." Councilman McKain of the city of West Indianapolis said that "90 percent of the people in West Indianapolis favored annexation," and "he was willing to be annexed and legislated out of office." No one from Mount Jackson or Brightwood voiced any complaints as each of the municipalities eschewed the course of separatism.[107]

Everywhere the enthusiasm for consolidation was rising. The *Indianapolis Sentinel* reported that annexationist "agitation in the suburbs has been growing hotter," and the *Indianapolis News* observed that the temperature of annexationist fervor in Irvington "is 120 Fahrenheit."[108] Irvington consolidationists submitted a petition favoring annexation that was signed by 225 of the suburb's 280 voters, and Mayor Taggart quipped that he was going to look up the word *annexation* in the dictionary and "see if it can ever be a fever which becomes contagious."[109] The town trustees of Mount Jackson postponed improvements in that municipality because they "did not want to put any obstacle in the way of annexation," and in none of the municipalities did officials organize to block consolidation.[110] Suburbia would gain cheaper gas, safer water, improved drainage, and better police protection from union with Indianapolis, and residents in the drab subdivisions of West Indianapolis or Haughville did not fear the philistine aesthetics of Indianapolis as did their refined counterparts in Woodruff Place.

On 15 March 1897 the Indianapolis City Council answered the petitions of the suburban annexationists and approved the absorption of Haughville, Brightwood, Mount Jackson, and West Indianapolis.[111] Irvington did not enter the city at this time. According to the *News*, merger with Irvington "would make the eastern outline of the city appear on the maps like a gigantic proboscis"; furthermore, many felt that Irvington was still too far from the mass of urban settlement to merit annexation.[112] Though the territory along "the National road between the city and the suburb is moderately settled," the *Sentinel* observed, "there are large tracts of vacant land lying between the two places south of the National road that would make admission of the suburb undesirable at this time."[113] The Indianapolis City Council enjoyed the right to exclude whatever territory it wished, and as yet it was not willing to accept the burden of providing services to Irvington.

In 1902, city officials did approve annexation of Irvington, but four years later it again exercised its discretionary authority to exclude the suburban municipality of Broad Ripple.[114] Broad Ripple's residents, like those of Irvington, suffered from inadequate police and fire protection. Moreover, the streetcar fare from the suburb to the city was ten cents, whereas if the city annexed Broad Ripple, this fare would drop to only three cents. By 1906 the sources of municipal revenue in Broad Ripple were also diminishing. In Indiana incorporated villages were subject to township liquor laws, and Washington Township had chosen to close the five saloons that had provided Broad Ripple with substantial revenue. Without the saloons, taxes would rise and suburban autonomy would prove increasingly burdensome.[115]

Consequently, in January 1906 Broad Ripple annexationists submitted a petition signed by virtually all of the suburb's eligible voters with "only five or six holding out."[116] The Indianapolis City Council approved annexation but the mayor, who opposed absorption of a community so far north of the city, vetoed the ordinance.[117] Broad Ripple was forced to remain independent until the central-city authorities decided to remap the metropolitan boundaries, for in Indiana the mayor and city council, not the legislature or a state agency, determined municipal boundaries.

Again, then, in Indianapolis as in the cities examined previously, the locality had determined political boundaries while the state legislature attended to other business. And again the pattern of suburban support for annexation prevailed. In Irvington, Brightwood, and Haughville as in South Denver, Hyde Park, Lake View, or East Cleveland, suburban residents backed entry into the city and were among the most enthusiastic sponsors of expansionism. Citizens in Broad Ripple and Irvington urged the creation of a giant, misshapen Indianapolis, an imperial city that included miles of rural territory, for an imperial Indianapolis would shower services on the suburbanites, providing water, inexpensive streetcar fares, lower gas rates, and other comforts and conveniences. Unlike Chicago and Cleveland, Indianapolis had the power to force its suburbs into a metropolitan union. But the city used its extensive authority not to force suburbanites into the city but to keep out the overeager annexationists.

Constitutional restraints on legislative authority seriously limited the potential for central coordination in Indiana, Colorado, Illinois, and Ohio. On the other hand, the constitutions of Massachusetts and New York allowed broad state interference in local questions; they neither prohibited nor limited special legislation. In both of these eastern states the central authorities enjoyed virtually unlimited power over the governmental organization of the metropolitan area. Although the state constitutions did not prevent legislators from adding ten square miles to Boston or forty square miles to New York City, popular dedication to the principle of local self-determination did impose restraints on lawmakers in Boston and Albany. By the late nineteenth century, suburban citizens and local officials in the American metropolis expected some voice in the boundary adjustment process regardless of whether their constitutions guaranteed such a voice. In 1900 central lawmakers could not operate with the cavalier disregard for local opinion that was possible in 1820. Instead, consultation with the general electorate often seemed a necessity. Thus, even in Massachussetts and New York, the new pattern of dispersed power affected the structure of urban rule and the struggle for metropolitan consolidation.

As early as the 1850s, the Massachusetts legislature had accepted the principle of local self-determination and had introduced the popular referendum as a prerequisite for annexation. In 1804 the town of Boston annexed South Boston simply through an act of the Massachusetts General Court, without popular vote or judicial interference. But in 1854 Massachusetts legislators authorized the consolidation of Charlestown and Boston on the condition that the electorate of both cities approve the merger. Citizens of Charlestown had long debated the issue of consolidation, and proponents of the merger pointed to Boston's abundant water supply and the increase in property values that would result from annexation.[118] In the referendum, the voters of both cities approved union. Again, however, the judiciary would decide the question of municipal consolidation, for foes of the merger appealed to the Massachusetts Supreme Judicial Court, which held that the act authorizing consolidation was unconstitutional. According to the court, the consolidation measure violated a provision in the state constitution that forbade the legislature to alter the bounds of legislative or congressional districts until the next decennial census. The merger legislation had included such a change, so the union between the two cities was void.[119]

Two years later, those favoring unification of the Boston metropolitan region again sought to extend the city's boundaries through annexation of the northern suburb of Chelsea. Again popular approval by the voters of both Boston and Chelsea was necessary prior to consolidation, and this time Boston's voters foiled the scheme by rejecting the merger proposal. Chelsea was the municipal headache of the Boston region, with a rapidly growing population in need of expensive public services. The provision of water and sewage facilities in Chelsea would have depleted Boston's treasury, and Boston's citizenry refused to accept this suburban parasite just as Denver was to reject Fletcher. Due to the constitutional scruples of the courts and the thrift of the populace, by the close of the 1850s Boston had failed to annex any adjoining town.[120]

During the 1860s the legislature took further steps to consolidate the region. In 1867 Massachusetts lawmakers enacted a measure requiring the merger of Roxbury and Boston without any provision for referendum. But the idea of local self-determination was by this time an entrenched principle, and Massachusetts's governor vetoed the measure because it failed to require voter approval. The legislature then attached a referendum provision, and an annexation campaign ensued.[121]

In Roxbury as in East Cleveland, Hyde Park, and South Denver, annexationists and antiannexationists organized mass meetings and traded charges. According to proponents of consolidation, union with Boston was the only means by which to solve the suburb's serious sewage and drainage problems. Referring to the muck and mire of the suburb, one speaker observed that "Roxbury literally slops over, and he was totally opposed to slopping over."[122] Another claimed that "those low lands that now breed pestilence and death would be taken after annexation and made healthy and valuable."[123] Moreover, Roxbury "will not only be raised out of the mud . . . , but be benefited by wide streets" and "those grand and beautiful avenues" that Boston would extend through the suburb.[124] Others assured Roxbury voters that annexation not only enjoyed the support of "aristocrats and capitalists" who would profit from increased land values, but that it also had the backing of all but one of Roxbury's former mayors.[125] Foes of annexation claimed that the former officials "had gone to seed" and that Roxbury "was provided with better drainage than it would be should annexation take place."[126] But most seemed to agree that the suburb "would be benefited through annexation by having water and all the conveniences that a large city could afford."[127] And on election day in September 1867 Roxbury citizens voted three to one in favor of union while Boston voters endorsed the proposal by a four-to-one margin.[128]

There followed a wave of annexation elections between 1869 and 1873, with the voters of Dorchester, Brighton, Charlestown, and West Roxbury all expressing their support for consolidation. In Dorchester both friends and foes of annexation gathered at local "velocipede" rinks and reenacted the pageant of claims and counterclaims so common in American annexation contests. Annexationists argued that, through union with Boston, "Dorchester would have her streets laid out in a systematic manner and all well lighted," and they further claimed that "a vote for annexation was a vote for progress; a vote against annexation was a vote for high taxes in a sleepy town or a one horse city."[129] Opponents of consolidation retorted that "Dorchester now was one of the best-governed towns and most free of crime of all in the state," and they also predicted that "the men that would be brought from Boston" as a result of annexation would be from the Irish Catholic Fort Hill district and "would not make very desirable neighbors."[130] Again such arguments carried little weight, for on election day in 1869 Dorchester residents chose by a vote of 928 to 726 to unite with Boston.[131]

Meanwhile, in West Roxbury the need for urban services and improvements also drove suburbanites into the arms of the central city. In 1871 a special committee appointed by the West Roxbury town meeting investigated the dire need for new sources of water due to "the gradual deterioration of wells as the districts in which they are situated become more thickly settled." The committee reported that "our people are ready for and desire the introduction of an ample supply of good water, at reasonable cost," but warned that the city of Boston might "forestall us in securing sources of supply now available to us."[132] Two years later the Massachusetts Board of Health reported that among West Roxbury residents there was "more and more complaint of wells and also increasing need of sewers," and many citizens looked "for relief from these evils in annexation to Boston."[133] That same year these yearnings for consolidation resulted in union between the troubled suburb and the well-serviced central city.

The suburban town of Brookline likewise suffered problems with sewage and water. But it would successfully remedy its water shortage by 1875, and during the 1870s only Brookline and Winthrop among the Boston suburbs would vote against union with Boston.[134] Boston extended its domain handsomely, yet Brookline would remain an independent enclave in accordance with the will of the local community. In the future Massachusetts lawmakers would assume direct control over Boston's metropolitan commissions, but they would continue to defer to the local electorate on questions of consolidation.

Few states intervened so frequently or aggressively in the affairs of local units as did New York. In 1874 the New York state legislature doubled the area of New York City without seeking the approval of the residents of the annexed territory, and that same body periodically remapped the boundaries of Buffalo, Rochester, and Syracuse. At the close of the century, however, New York legislators did concede somewhat to local opinion. For in the 1890s the state consolidated the multitude of governments in the New York City region, and metropolitan voters were granted some voice in the creation of the massive new municipality.

When the question of unifying the governments of metropolitan New York City was brought before the legislature in 1894, lawmakers expressed their concern for local public opinion. In the assembly debates legislators demanded that the state "give the people a chance to be heard," and the lawmakers enacted a measure that "submitted to a vote of the duly-qualified electors ... the question of ... consolidation under one municipal government." The legislators in Albany believed that a popular referendum "was simply in the line of home rule and was but a question of fundamental principle."[135] Even in New York, then, ideas of home rule had undermined central control of urban organization and broadened the decision-making role of the metropolitan electorate.

Though the legislature had not promised specifically to adhere to the results of the referendum, New Yorkers assumed that voter consent was a prerequisite for consolidation. Consequently, consolidationists were elated when in November 1894 the voters expressed their support for metropolitan union. Each of the municipalities, with the exceptions of the towns of Westchester and Mount Vernon, voted in favor of consolidation. Especially vital was the small majority received in the city of Brooklyn. Consolidation proved especially popular in the poorly serviced towns and villages of Queens County and Staten Island where the citizenry was much in need of inexpensive, safe water and of the general battery of amenities that New York City could provide. Exploiting these needs, expansionists were able to garner a total majority of forty-four thousand in the metropolitan area, and the legislature now felt authorized to proceed with the creation of a charter for "Greater New York."[136]

However, the road to consolidation was not without further obstacles, for under the "home rule" provision of the New York Constitution of 1894, the mayors of both New York City and Brooklyn enjoyed a suspensive veto over special state legislation dealing with the two cities. Though the voters of both New York City and Brooklyn had approved consolidation, both mayors vetoed the consolidation bill that passed the legislature in 1896. The legislature could override the vetoes by a simple majority vote, and it did so that same year. A state-appointed commission then drafted for the united city a charter which the mayor of Brooklyn signed and the mayor of New York City vetoed.[137] Again the obstinacy of local authorities delayed consolidation, but the legislature overruled the mayor, and Greater New York became a reality on 1 January 1898.

Urban leaders had thus achieved their dreams of consolidation in Cleveland, Chicago, Denver, Indianapolis, Boston, and New York City, but even in the centralized state of New York, lawmakers made some concession to local sentiment. Local officials and voters had become the most vital actors in the annexation drama, and their veto could stymie the expansion of the central city. Local self-determination had gained the upper hand in the annexation process, and the desires for unified government and for metropolitan efficiency would have to yield to this higher consideration.

During the late nineteenth century, however, those who played a role in the annexation process generally favored annexation and consolidated government. The local electorate, both urban and suburban, repeatedly voted in favor of annexation while the state legislatures worked within their newly restricted sphere of powers to achieve this same end. The courts and local officials represented the chief obstacles to annexation, but even the judiciary often interpreted constitutional restraints liberally, upholding suspect annexation laws.

Prior to 1910, then, fragmentation did not seem an inevitable consequence of the legal structure. Instead, in suburb after suburb voters chose to unite with the central city in order to enjoy the public services that the larger municipality could offer. Among the citizens of East Cleveland, Collinwood, South Denver, Charlestown, Roxbury, and a mass of other communities, the lure of superior municipal services was too great to resist. They may not have approved of Cleveland's liquor policy or Boston's Irish population, but generally the danger of impure water was of greater concern that were the evils of whiskey, and sewage in the cellar seemed a more pressing problem than did ethnicity. If it was choice between saloons and damnation in the next world and contaminated water and typhoid in this world, considerations of the present usually prevailed. Thus, when the forces of social segregation came into conflict with the desire for improved municipal services, the latter was preeminent. Dorchester's residents may not have relished associating with the shanty Irish of Boston's Fort Hill district, but they relished even less the mud, mire, and disease of their underdeveloped community. East Clevelanders abhorred the central-city saloons, but they were willing to accept the threat of whiskey if it was mixed with the promise of water. The forces of social and economic segregation were pulling the metropolis apart, but as yet they were not powerful enough to overcome the unifying fear of fire, sickness, and crime that troubled the residents of poorly serviced suburbia.

Throughout the nation, few suburbs could equal the central cities in provision of public services. In 1890, the Long Island municipality of Jamaica was without sewers, while neither Flushing nor College Point had franchises for electric lights. Although many New York sururbs had a piped supply of water, in suburban Flatbush the water rate per family was $40.00, in College Point it was $24.50, and in the Staten Island municipalities of New Brighton and Port Richmond households paid $42.00 for water. In contrast, the rate in New York City was only $15.[138] New York City had sewers, electric lights, and cheap water, and in 1894 Jamaica, Flatbush, College Point, New Brighton, and Port Richmond each voted to abandon the extravagance and deprivation of independence and to join the much-blessed central city.

Likewise in 1890 the suburban municipality of West Cleveland had neither sewers nor electric lights, and the same was true for the Chicago suburb of Rogers Park. Moreover, the water rate in Rogers Park was $23.50, compared with $15.00 in Chicago. East Portland, the leading suburb of Portland, Oregon, also lacked a sewage system, and the average East Portland family paid an astounding $87.00 for water, compared with $51.00 in Portland itself.[139] The advantages of amalgamation were obvious to voters in each of these suburbs, and between 1890 and 1894 the citizens of West Cleveland, Rogers Park, and East Portland all elected to merge with the central city. Many of the suburbs originally had incorporated in order to obtain municipal services, and this same desire for public improvements led to the demise of these towns and villages.

The story was similar in the Denver metropolitan area. In 1890 Denver's largest suburb, the city of Highlands, had neither sewers nor electricity, and during the early 1890s community leaders complained of the "extortionate sum" paid for water.[140] According to the water committee of the Highlands City Council, "the present conditions under which we are now securing our water supply are not only burdensome but outrageous in the extreme."[141] Meanwhile, in 1894 Colorado's State Board of Health reported that the suburb of Colfax had "no sewerage," while in the town of South Denver the wells were "subject to seepage pollution." There was "but little" sanitary inspection of the water supply, no sewers existed, and in answer to the question, "How are the contents of privies finally disposed of?" the South Denver health officer replied simply, "Leave it alone."[142] In contrast, the central city of Denver had an ample supply of relatively cheap, clean water and an extensive sewage system.

Not only was life in the unimproved suburbs inconvenient and expensive, it also could prove dangerous. In the consolidation campaign of 1889, Lake View residents complained bitterly about their contaminated water system and local drainage problems, and their complaints were well founded. In 1889 Lake View's death rate from diseases associated with polluted water and inadequate drainage soared above that of the central city. The mortality rate for typhoid fever was 20 percent higher than that for the city of Chicago as a whole, and the rate for malarial fevers was 120 percent greater.[143] Lake View was becoming a residential haven for wealthy Chicago businessmen, but there was little future for the community if it earned a reputation as a suburban death trap.

Fears of yellow fever underlay the annexation movement in Memphis. The dread disease had killed almost 10 percent of the Memphis population in 1878–79, and residents did not want to witness such slaughter again. Consequently, they devoted a considerable amount of money to sanitation, and within the next twenty years the city constructed approximately forty-five miles of sewers. But by 1898 about thirty thousand people lived in suburban regions without sewer lines, and another epidemic was expected. Threatened by this scourge, suburbanites voted overwhelmingly to enter the city. The area of Memphis increased by twelve square mile, or 322 percent, and within the next three years the city laid an impressive eighty-eight miles of sewer lines.[144]

The numerous suburbs of Birmingham, Alabama, were also cesspools of pollution and sources of disease. In 1907 an estimated fifty thousand suburban residents in Alabama's greatest metropolitan area were without any sewage service. Physicians in the Birmingham region recognized the consequent danger to the public health and informed the state legislature that "we are now afflicted with a local epidemic of typhoid fever, and unless all this territory is put under our city government and the sanitation is urgently enforced we may suffer terrible consequences in the future from the ravages of said epidemic."[145] Moreover, the County Medical Society officially endorsed union of city and suburbs and resolved that metropolitan amalgamation "is a sanitary necessity."[146] In Birmingham as elsewhere, death and disease were powerful lobbyists for the cause of consolidation, and few suburbanites could resist their devastating message.

Faced with the dangers and discomforts of suburban autonomy, voters in outlying communities across the nation elected to merge with the central city. Between 1850 and 1880 residents in eight Boston suburbs voted on the issue of consolidation, and in six of the eight they approved union. Moreover, in the 1890s the inadequately serviced towns of Chelsea, Somerville, and Revere seemed interested in consolidation with Boston, but Bostonians proved reluctant to assume these municipal liabilities.

Expansionists in Baltimore were less successful, and in 1874 suburbanites defeated an annexation proposal by two to one. Yet fourteen years later voters in two of the three suburban districts elected to enter the city of Baltimore. From 1850 through 1909 residents in eight suburban municipalities in the Cleveland area cast ballots on consolidation proposals, and in all eight the majority approved of merger with the central city. In the Chicago metropolitan area, the win-loss record of annexation forces was only slightly less impressive. Of the sixteen annexation contests between 1887 and 1898, consolidationists won twelve and lost only four. To the north, suburban residents of Bay View, Wisconsin, voted in 1886 to enter the city of Milwaukee though Milwaukee Democrats resisted annexation of the Republican suburb. South of the Mason-Dixon line, 59 percent of Birmingham's suburbanites voted in 1909 for consolidation, and in six of the ten suburban municipalities a majority favored union with the central city. Annexationists in the Los Angeles area were even more successful, winning eleven of the twelve annexation contests from 1895 to 1910, including the vital election that merged Los Angeles with the harbor city of San Pedro. Voters in East Portland and Albina likewise approved merger with Portland in 1891, and between 1900 and 1910 residents of eight suburban municipalities surrounding Seattle elected to abandon autonomy and consolidate with the central city.[147]

The amalgamation of Cincinnati's fragmented metropolitan area was typical. In 1893 a majority of voters in the municipalities of Avondale, Linwood, Westwood, and Riverside all favored union with the central city.[148] Ten years later a merger proposal won the favor of 89 percent of those casting ballots in the village of Bond Hill, 86 percent of the voters in the municipality of Hyde Park, 80 percent in Evanston, and 55 percent in Winton Place.[149] In 1909, 90 percent of the electorate in the village of Delhi endorsed union with the central city, and during the entire period from 1880 through 1909 only one municipality rejected annexation to Cincinnati.[150] Delhi had no water, no sewage system, no gas or electricity; if annexed, the city of Cincinnati would agree "to furnish water to the inhabitants of the annexed territory," "to take such steps as are in its power towards compelling The Union Gas & Electric Company to supply gas and electricity for light, heat and power purposes," and "to devise and carry into effect some proper sewerage system" for the village.[151] Winton Place and Bond Hill had long desired sewage systems, and each expected the city of Cincinnati to realize plans for waste disposal.[152] Evanston had generally good services, but it had made these civic improvements at great expense, and Evanston's mayor admitted that "burdens had been assumed that might in the future become onerous on the taxpayers."[153] Moreover, Delhi, Winton Place, and Evanston all relied on volunteer fire fighters and were deprived of the advantage of Cincinnati's professional force.[154] Abandonment of autonomy seemed a small price to pay for gas, electricity, water, sewage disposal, debt assumption, and a trained fire department.

Permissive incorporation laws and the principle of local self-determination thus did not bar the expansion of America's cities prior to 1910. From 1850 to 1910 suburban voters generally seemed to favor union with the central city, and only the minority regretted suburbia's loss of autonomy. In fact, the rate of territorial expansion increased in most cities after the state legislatures abdicated authority to determine boundaries, thus enabling the local electorate to assume a role in the annexation process. As seen in table 1, in five of the seven most populous cities located in states adhering to the principle of local self-determination, the rate of territorial growth was greater during the thirty years after the legislatures yielded power to the local electorate than it had been during the previous thirty years. Large cities such as Chicago, Los Angeles, Detroit, Cleveland, and Boston with their impressive public improvements had something valuable to offer the suburbanite. And so long as consolidation was a bargain rather than a burden for the suburban resident, the central city would have little difficulty in winning further conquests.

Annexation procedures had changed during the late nineteenth century, with many state legislatures abandoning forcible annexation and yielding decision-making authority to the local unit. The result was a sometimes cumbersome system of boundary adjustment involving

TABLE 1. Territorial Growth before and after Acceptance of the Principle of Local Self-determination

City	Increase during 30 years before	Increase during 30 years after
Chicago	236%	433%
Los Angeles	0%	1,146%
Detroit	172%	241%
Cleveland	185%	423%
Boston	0%	721%
Milwaukee	34%*	26%
Minneapolis	575%	0%

SOURCES: Roderick McKenzie, *The Metropolitan Community* (New York, 1933), pp. 336–337; Richard Reading, comp., *Municipal Manual of the City of Detroit* (Detroit, 1928), pp. 276–277; Calvin F. Schmid, *Social Saga of Two Cities: An Ecological and Statistical Study of Social Trends in Minneapolis and St. Paul* (Minneapolis, 1937), pp. 387–391; Goff, "Governmental Integration in Milwaukee," pp. 82A, 82B.

*Some of this growth is the result of a referendum. Milwaukee annexed Bay View in 1887 after voters in the suburb approved union with the central city. At that time, however, Wisconsin had not abandoned the idea of the state legislature mapping local boundaries.

county, village, and city officials as well as the judiciary and the local voter. Yet the change in law had not slowed the pace of central-city expansion. Local self-determination and central-city growth were not inconsistent, and the suburban veto did not preclude further annexation. Suburban voters voluntarily elected to unite with the central city if it was to their advantage, and during the period from 1850 to 1910 union was advantageous in most areas. Suburban units could not yet compete as purveyors of water, sewage disposal, or fire and police protection; the central city provided superior services at a lower cost. Suburbanites were not obstinate opponents of big government at all costs; they abandoned their suburban governments when there were good reasons for doing so. During the late nineteenth century these good reasons were all too obvious to the residents of such suburbs as East Cleveland, Lake View, Highlands, Irvington, Roxbury, and Flatbush.

4

THE BRITISH ALTERNATIVE

In the United States, suburban doctors, lawyers, plumbers, and merchants debated the destiny of metropolitan government in scores of town halls and Odd Fellows lodges from Brookline to San Pedro. Amid boos and applause, cries of fraud and wailing over water, whiskey, sewage, and sin, the "people" were fashioning the future of the nation's largest cities. This was the American way, a system of bickering and bargaining among the metropolitan fragments that produced referenda battles, litigation, and with luck some solutions. Under the American system, the locality was the determining unit, and the parts decided the nature of the whole.

Yet this was not the only means by which a nation with a representative form of government could mold the metropolitan future. In Great Britain a different system was developing, a system that placed less emphasis on local self-determination and more on central control. Lawmakers in London refused to yield responsibility for local governmental organization or decision-making authority to the local populace. Instead, Britons conceived of local government as a national concern; agencies of the central government should therefore determine questions of boundaries and incorporation. The destinies of metropolitan Britain did not rest in the hands of the suburban electorate but depended on the will of the nation's administrators and legislators.

Britain's Parliament had not always exerted such firm control over that nation's municipalities. Before 1835 the lawmakers in Westminster had refused to tamper with the chartered privileges of municipal corporations. As a result, the powers, functions, and boundaries of most boroughs had remained unchanged for centuries. The passage of the Municipal Corporation Act of 1835, however, marked the beginning of a new era in English local government, an era characterized by increasing central intervention and coordination. While American legislators were gradually assuming a laissez-faire attitude toward the organization of local government units, British lawmakers were abandoning their past policy of neglect and exercising their power to restructure the confused pattern of grass-roots rule.

This centralization is evident in Britain's procedure for municipal incorporation. In late-nineteenth-century England incorporation was a privilege bestowed on relatively few communities, not a right available to all. In order to obtain a municipal charter, householders of the proposed borough had to petition the nation's Privy Council, a body consisting primarily of the prime minister and leading cabinet officers. A committee of the Privy Council would then investigate to determine whether the applicant met the standards for incorporation. The Privy Council generally did not recommend a charter for any town having less than ten thousand inhabitants, and the community also needed to demonstrate a history of sound administration and a financial base capable of supporting a municipal government.[1] Not every community met the requirements, and though the council received fifty-five applications for incorporation between 1888 and 1902, only thirty-five charters were granted.[2] By 1907 England and Wales could claim only 324 municipal boroughs, whereas the single state of Illinois boasted more than 1,000 municipalities.[3] In England and Wales there was only approximately one municipality for every 100,000 inhabitants, but in Illinois this ratio was one to 5,000.

Under the Local Government Act of 1888, however, smaller communities in Great Britain could organize as urban districts and enjoy most of the powers of a municipality, including the power to maintain such facilities as waterworks and sewage disposal plants. To organize an urban district, a majority of voters from the area had to petition the county council for the county in which the district was located. The county council would investigate the application, and if it perceived a need for a new district, it would then issue the necessary order establishing one. If one-sixth of the voters from the proposed district protested the county council's decision, then an agency of the central government known as the Local Government Board would review the county council's decision.[4] The Local Government Board was a full-blown administrative bureaucracy with eleven departments, 350 clerks, and an army of inspectors, all commanded by the president of the Local Government Board, who was a member of the national cabinet.[5] This central agency had the power to veto a county council's order and would do so if it deemed the creation of an additional district contrary to the public interest. By 1907 818 such urban districts existed in England and Wales, the products of both local initiative and central scrutiny.[6]

Though urban districts were generally less populous than incorpo-

TABLE 2. British Urban Districts and American Municipalities as Distributed by Population

	0–3,000	3,000–10,000	10,000 and over
England and Wales (1901)	22.8%	49.0%	28.2%
New York (1900)	77.5%	13.8%	8.8%
Illinois (1900)	91.2%	6.2%	2.6%
California (1900)	70.7%	20.7%	8.6%

SOURCES: British figures based on Josef Redlich and Francis Hirst, *Local Government in England* (London, 1903), 2: 119. American figures based on U.S. census of 1900.

rated boroughs, they were considerably larger than most American municipalities. Few communities of less than one thousand residents acquired the status of urban district, and, as seen in table 2, in 1901 77 percent could claim a population of three thousand or more.[7] In contrast, only 9 percent of all Illinois municipalities had populations over three thousand, and in New York, California, and the other states the pattern was much the same. Throughout America, local self-determination had spawned a myriad of puny municipalities. In Great Britain, however, the Privy Council and Local Government Board sought to limit such fragmentation, encouraging the creation only of larger units.

In its annual report for 1904–1905, the Local Government Board stated its objections to small units specifically when it explained its refusal to permit the creation of two urban districts with only 1,600 and 3,200 residents. According to the Board, "the sub-division of administrative districts often leads to increased expenditure, and in the case of areas having a small population and low assessable value, this increase of expenditure is not generally accompanied by a corresponding increase of administrative efficiency."[8] In other words, efficiency and economy were the preeminent concerns, not the desire of two small areas to exercise governmental powers.

During the early twentieth century, then, the British pursued a policy aimed at restricting the number of local units, whereas American lawmakers generally ignored the subject and allowed localities to fragment in whatever manner they desired. As indicated in table 3, in 1901 the combined number of municipal boroughs and urban districts in England and Wales totalled 1,119, and by 1921 this figure had risen to only 1,128.[9] In contrast, in America the states did not attempt to halt the proliferation of municipalities; as a result, in 1920 as compared to 1900, there were 77 additional cities and villages in New York, 181 in Illinois, and 138 in California.

Britain's central authorities regulated not only the creation of districts and boroughs by also the enlargement of these units through annexation or consolidation. Under the Local Government Act of 1888, muni-

TABLE 3. Increase in Number of Urban Districts and Municipalities

| | Numerical Increase | | |
	1900–01	1920–21	Percentage Increase
England and Wales	1,119	1,128	0.8
New York	457	534	16.8
Illinois	930	1,111	19.5
California	116	254	119.0

SOURCES: Redlich and Hirst, *Local Government*, 1: 224, 2: 119; *The Municipal Year Book of the United Kingdom for 1922* (London, 1922), p. 239; U.S. Censuses of 1900 and 1920.

cipalities could annex territory either through special parliamentary legislation or by means of a provisional order of the Local Government Board confirmed by an act of Parliament. Between 1888 and 1907 there were 154 alterations in municipal boundaries, 112 of them the result of provisional orders. [10] In 1892 the borough of Leicester increased in area by one-third and added thirty-three thousand people to its population; three years later the borough of Liverpool tripled its domain. [11] Parliament extended the bounds of Sheffield in 1900, enhancing the area of that corporation by 20 percent. [12] In 1904 the outlying districts of Fenham, Benwell, Walker, and a portion of Kenton joined the borough of Newcastle Upon Tyne, and in 1907 the Local Government Board fostered the amalgamation of four Midland pottery towns that combined to form the borough of Stoke-on-Trent. [13] Britain's boroughs were expanding, but the central authorities were guiding this expansion without fear of a veto from local voters.

Moreover, the Local Government Board did not simply rubber-stamp the requests of municipal councils but sought to ensure equity in the adjustment of borough limits. During the late nineteenth and early twentieth centuries the board rejected over 20 percent of the annexation proposals submitted by those larger municipalities known as county boroughs. Especially crucial to the board's decision was the quality of existing services within the borough, and the inspectors who investigated annexation proposals were members of the board's engineering inspectorate and knowledgeable about the faults and shortcomings of sewers and waterworks. Thus, in 1893 the Board reviewed a request by the borough of Shaftesbury but "declined to entertain any proposal for extension while the town remained without an efficient system of sewerage, scavenging, and public lighting." [14] Five years later the Board refused to consider an annexation request from Bewdley "owing to the defective sanitary condition of the borough." [15] In 1908 the board received an annexation petition from Bath, but "the condition of the city as regards sewerage, sewage disposal and water supply precluded us from making a provisional order for the extension of the city at the present time." [16] And in 1909 the borough of Worcester received a similar reply when it proposed extension of its municipal limits. [17] If the councillors of Shaftesbury, Bewdley, and Worcester were unable to govern the existing territory within their jurisdiction adequately, then the Local Government Board was not willing to approve further additions to their domain.

Likewise, the Board blocked attempts by municipalities to annex large tracts of rural land. For example, they rejected an annexation proposal submitted by the borough of Wakefield because "we do not consider . . . that large areas of an essentially rural character which are not likely to be developed for building purposes in the near future should be brought within municipal limits." [18] They denied Rochester's request to annex "323 acres of land covered almost entirely by woods," and Dover's proposal to absorb "a very large area in the Dover rural district" also failed to win approval. [19] This form of grandiose expansion may have been acceptable in the United States, where Los Angeles was annexing hundreds of square miles of orange trees, but in Britain the Local Government Board sought to ensure that municipal boundaries would conform to the boundaries of urban settlement.

To understand the centralized system of Great Britain better, it is useful to examine the expansion of the borough of Birmingham during the period 1888 to 1911. Birmingham was the Chicago of Great Britain, the municipal Horatio Alger, the embodiment of nineteenth-century industrial growth and development. At the time of its incorporation in 1838, Birmingham contained 170,000 inhabitants, but by 1888 the population had risen to 440,000, with an additional 160,000 in its suburbs. Its metropolitan population had overflowed traditional governmental boundaries and spread into the three adjacent counties of Warwickshire, Worcestershire, and Staffordshire. Birmingham, like so many American cities, was an expanding, growing metropolis, and extensive boundary adjustments were necessary if local government was to adapt to the rapid rate of change.

The Birmingham Town Council recognized this and in January 1888 proposed the absorption of 160,000 residents in outlying districts. Birmingham's mayor argued that "it was a question whether Birmingham was to be hemmed in on every side by a number of small local boards ... or whether these outlying ... districts should join hands with and become part of the larger authority." One Birmingham alderman observed that "these surrounding districts were really part of Birmingham," and their suburban residents "used the shops in the borough, ... they traversed the streets, they came to the town for their amusements, and in considerable part for the education of their children." Moreover, "but for the borough they would have to pay more than they did for their water and gas," and "they used the borough parks, and did not pay for them" and "the municipal Art Gallery, and did not pay for it." [20] To rectify this discrepancy in cost and benefit, the town fathers now applied to the central government for an alteration in the borough limits.

Suburban residents and authorities viewed Birmingham's proposal as an act of aggression, however. In suburban Moseley and Aston Manor those opposed to annexation held public meetings to denounce extension of the city limits. [21] The Lord Lieutenant of Worcestershire likewise castigated the proposal, describing it "as a large scheme of spoliation." [22] In Aston Manor and Worcestershire, as in Lake View and East Cleveland, many officials and residents would not yield to the city without a struggle. Authority in Great Britain may have been centralized, but this did not mean that suburban citizens would remain mute or play a negligible role in the reorganization of metropolitan rule. The people would speak, but the central authorities would decide.

In 1888 the central authorities postponed action on the boundary question and not until three years later did the Local Government Board order a change in Birmingham's limits. By provisional order, the board annexed to the borough not only the urban districts of Balsall Heath, Harborne, and Saltley but also the hamlet of Little Bromwich, increasing the area of Birmingham by approximately six square miles and adding 45,800 to its population. [23] A Birmingham newspaper celebrated the occasion by proclaiming the merits of union with the city. The newspaper argued that as a result of consolidation "the blameless inanity characteristic of local life at Harborne will be changed for the fierce and purifying excitement of municipal warfare." [24]

However, some citizens of the outlying regions were not so enthusiastic about the cleansing militancy of life in the big city. Most notably the school boards of Aston, Harborne, and King's Norton opposed the terms by which the Birmingham School Board now assumed their debts. Thus, when the Local Government Board's order appeared before Parliament for confirmation, these school boards protested and secured alterations in the provisions for debt settlement. [25] In Great Britain, as in the United States, local agencies refused to surrender without a struggle. But, in contrast to the American system, in Britain central legislators intervened in negotiations regarding annexation and they supervised the arbitration of differences.

Despite the alterations of 1891, the majority of Birmingham's suburbs remained independent of the central city. Suburban Birmingham, however, was not as fragmented as the Chicago metropolis, for in Great

Britain, the county councils and central authorities would not grant powers of self-government to one-hundred-acre suburban enclaves containing only 200 people. During the first decade of the twentieth century, suburban Birmingham consisted of only three urban districts, one borough, and one rural district; these five units ranged in population from twenty-nine thousand to eighty-two thousand. The one suburban borough, Aston Manor, had only achieved incorporation in 1903, after having been denied that privilege in 1876 and 1888. English law did not allow every race track promoter, tax-evading industrialist, or community of teetotalers to create its own municipality. As a result, in order to achieve metropolitan union, consolidationists in Birmingham had to cement fewer fissures than did their counterparts in Chicago or Cleveland. Whereas consolidation of metropolitan Chicago required annexation of scores of small governmental units, each one having a veto over merger proposals, the unification of Birmingham required the absorption of only a few large units, none of which had the power to block action by the Local Government Board or Parliament.

By 1909 Birmingham's Town Council had again assumed an aggressive stance, and the members voted unanimously in favor of annexing the five suburban units. [26] The councillors then applied to the Local Government Board for such an alteration, but meanwhile the suburbs began preparing to defend their autonomy. The Handsworth Urban District Council rejected Birmingham's proposal by a vote of seventeen to one, and the Aston Manor Town Council also voted to oppose the merger scheme. [27] Suburban residents favoring annexation formed unification committees, while those opposing the plan answered with public rallies. [28] In Handsworth an antiannexation speaker proclaimed the motto "Handsworth for Handsworth people," and he compared Birmingham's overtures to "a thrush addressing an objective worm upon the advantages of losing its humble form and becoming part of the anatomy of a beautiful bird." According to this foe of metropolitan union, "there might be worms in Handsworth, but they preferred to retain their humble identity than be part of the magnificent anatomy of Birmingham."[29]

Faced with local movements both for and against consolidation, the suburban governments conducted special polls to determine popular sentiment. The Erdington District Council polled local taxpayers and found that 1,529 people opposed the merger whereas 1,174 supported it. In a similar poll in King's Norton, suburban taxpayers voted two to one against union with Birmingham, but in Aston Manor the vote was 3,782 for consolidation and 2,401 against. [30] A Birmingham newspaper observed, however, that "there is no machinery yet devised by which the will of the people can be discovered," and "petitions, polls and even elections ... each in turn is shown to be hopelessly misleading."[31] In

Britain journalists and lawmakers alike placed less faith in the popular referendum than did their brethren in the United States, and consequently it was not a part of the legal procedure for determining local government organization. Yet in Great Britain, as in any democracy, the authorities could not ignore popular opinion completely, and the local polls exemplify this concern for the will of the people.

The Local Government Board opened its inquiry into the Birmingham boundary issue in December 1909, and for more than three weeks the board heard the pros and cons of consolidation. Birmingham's Town Council called thirty-eight witnesses to support its case, while the anti-annexationist county councils of Worcestershire, Warwickshire, and Staffordshire presented sixteen witnesses. During the lengthy inquiry, twenty-four thousand questions were asked, and the total testimony filled two thousand printed pages. Friends and foes of the proposal devoted much time and money to the inquiry. The Erdington District Council alone spent £2,000 in attacking the merger scheme, while the borough of Birmingham allocated £19,000 for lawyers and lobbying.[32] After considering the case, in May 1910 the Local Government Board finally issued a provisional order for the consolidation of Birmingham and its suburbs.[33]

Before the order became law, Parliament had to confirm the board's action, and some suburban leaders were eager to appeal their case to the nation's lawmakers. Two weeks after the issuance of the provisional order, the Worcestershire County Council decided unanimously to oppose any scheme involving the annexation of a portion of that county.[34] Handsworth, King's Norton, and Yardley likewise maintained their opposition, though Erdington and Aston Manor were now willing to negotiate the terms of the merger.[35] At this point the scene of conflict shifted to London and the Houses of Parliament.

In July 1910 a select committee of the House of Commons began hearings on the question, with counsel for each of the suburbs present and representatives of both the Staffordshire and Worcestershire County Councils. At the hearings Birmingham's Neville Chamberlain defended the annexation scheme, arguing that "the present separation of the districts was purely artificial" and that consolidation would allow "more economical administration."[36] Likewise Birmingham's city engineer described the borough's drainage systems and "the difficulties that had arisen from divided jurisdictions," and the chairman of the Birmingham council's boundaries committee testified that "the Bill was not promoted in the financial interest of Birmingham or any part of the area, but in the general interest of the whole."[37] On the other hand, Handsworth's counsel described consolidation as the "milking of the Handsworth milch cow into the Birmingham pail," and an accountant testifying on behalf of King's Norton observed that "experience did not show that administration of large areas tended to economy."[38] The chairman of the Worcester County Council claimed that annexation would deprive the council of 33 percent of its taxable property, leaving the county government impoverished.[39] And the spokesman for Staffordshire argued that dismemberment of the rural counties through annexation resulted in "disintegration of finance, the lowering of the prestige of county councils" and "tended to destroy that sentiment of pride in one's county that made for good government."[40]

The counsel for suburban King's Norton assailed the central authorities bitterly and argued for local self-determination in words that would have earned applause in America. He castigated "the belief of gentlemen in Whitehall that they knew better what was good for a district than the people living in it." According to this gentlemen, "there was a strong, genuine desire of the majority of the people to keep the form of administration best suited to their needs, and why should this be overruled to gratify the ambitions of Birmingham?" He claimed that "the only reason . . . for hauling in King's Norton was the desire to advertise Birmingham as in population the second city in the Kingdom."[41] Suburbia was, then, to sacrifice its independence for the sake of chamber-of-commerce boosterism.

Despite these protests, the Birmingham bill passed through the committee favorably only to face criticism on the floor of the Commons in July 1910 and February 1911. Much discussion centered on the issue of compensating Worcestershire, Staffordshire, and Warwickshire for losses in tax revenue, and the County Councils Association threw its weight behind the protests of the three threatened counties. Stanley Baldwin, a member from Worcestershire, spoke on behalf of that county, describing how "this rupture in our county will bear with it very serious consequences."[42] Another defended the interests of Warwickshire and warned that "we will oppose the Bill unless we get some real justice."[43] And Mr. Staveley-Hill, the representative from Staffordshire, joined the chorus of spokesmen asking for remuneration to the counties.[44]

Other members of the Commons attacked the annexation scheme as a threat to small-town existence. One critic protested "against this centralisation in the hands of officials in large centres" and attacked efforts to divorce "the people . . . from that intimate association which they have under the urban district councils."[45] Another lambasted those who sought to "efface all that activity of local life which has hitherto prevailed in the smaller communities" through "the creation of these huge, bloated, apoplectic corporations."[46] And still another argued that "the larger the authority the more dogmatic and tyrannical are the officials" and expressed "astonishment to find some members of my party be-littling urban district councils." [47]

Proponents of the plan responded with praise for the efficiency of unified rule. The president of the Local Government Board cited statistical proof "that in the sphere of municipal management, from the point of view of cheaper electric light, cheaper gas, and cheaper tramways, the larger unit is better than the smaller one." [48] Others favored the absorption of tax-rich suburbs because it was only through acquisition of additional revenues "that municipal authorities can deal with the pressing and crying evils existing in the slums of cities." [49] According to these members, annexation "will enable the richer district to help the poorer in a manner which it would not be able to do otherwise." [50] Annexationists thus cited the benefits of efficiency and social equity, whereas separatists praised the merits of small-town intimacy. A majority of Parliament was to find the arguments for amalgamation more convincing, for in February 1911 the House of Commons approved the Birmingham annexation measure, and in May the Lords did likewise.

Meanwhile the suburbs prepared for approaching doom by negotiating the terms of consolidation with Birmingham. The city agreed that for a limited number of years it would tax the suburbs at a lower rate than the remainder of the borough. Birmingham also agreed to pay £140,000 to Worcestershire, £60,000 to Warwickshire, and £43,500 to Staffordshire as compensation for loss of taxable property. This mollified suburban officials sufficiently that four of the five suburban councils had approved consolidation by February 1911. [51] Thus the suburbs reconciled themselves to their fate, and Birmingham expanded from 12,639 acres to 43,537 acres. By the close of 1911 the newly consolidated borough contained 845,000 people, and Birmingham boasted of being the second largest city in the kingdom.

Birmingham, however, won its battle in a much different manner from Chicago, Cleveland, or even Boston. In Britain suburbs could make no last minute appeals to the courts, for no constitutional restraints bound Parliament, and the will of the legislature was final. Moreover, metropolitan union did not depend on the will of local officials as it had in the annexations of Collinwood, East Cleveland, or South Brooklyn. Councillors in Erdlington, King's Norton, and Aston Manor might reject Birmingham's overtures unanimously, but this would not necessarily halt consolidation. And, most importantly, the passage of unification schemes did not depend on the will of the local majority. Lawmakers would consider local opinion and weigh the views of the suburban citizenry, but the residents of Birmingham's fringe areas exercised no legal authority in the determination of metropolitan boundaries. Instead, authority rested clearly with the central government's Local Government Board and ultimately with the nation's legislators. British law encouraged not a dispersion of decision-making authority but rather a concentration of power in the hands of Parliament.

In a few of the smaller American states, the legislatures continued to exercise an authority similar to that of the British Parliament. States such as Maine, Vermont, and New Hampshire were compact and homogenous in population, and their legislatures were not swamped with business. Consequently, in these states lawmakers saw no reason to refrain from interfering in the affairs of local units. Likewise Delaware's lawmakers continued to incorporate municipalities and to alter boundaries solely through special legislation, but then Delaware could only claim one urban center worthy of being called a city.

During the early twentieth century Maryland's legislators followed the example of their neighbors in Delaware by altering boundaries without local referenda. In 1874 and 1888 Maryland lawmakers had deferred to the will of voters in suburban Baltimore, but in 1914 they doubled the size of Hagerstown without voter consent and four years later they added twenty-two square miles to Baltimore without seeking local approval. In the Baltimore annexation battle of 1918, suburban officials "emitted loud and heart-rending calls for rescue from the greedy clutches of a cruel city" and secured a plank in the platform of the state Democratic party calling for "the consent of the majority of the qualified voters of the territory proposed to be annexed, as required by the principles of self-government and home rule always dear to a free people."[52] But most Marylanders seemed to disagree with such principles. One of Baltimore's most respected judges announced that "I not only believe that annexation without a referendum is constitutional, but I believe just as fully that if the members of this Legislature believe that the citizens ... require annexation ... it is the duty of ... this Legislature to settle it without a referendum."[53] Annexationists argued that in Maryland as in Britain the central legislature should map municipal boundaries, and in the Baltimore boundary dispute of 1918 this position prevailed.

This same issue disrupted the tranquillity of Birmingham, Alabama, during the years 1907 to 1910 when Birmingham legislators introduced a bill to annex sixteen independent communities. The bill failed to provide for a referendum on the question, and many legislators immediately attacked this attempt at forced amalgamation, claiming that suburbanites "are entitled to be heard on this question."[54] As a sop to critics, proponents of the bill agreed to an amendment providing that a referendum be held throughout the metropolitan area. If a majority of the metropolitan voters favored union, then the proposed measure would take effect. Consolidation would not depend on approval by voters in each of the suburbs or in the surburban zone as a whole. Even in the New York City consolidation contest, New Yorkers viewed the approval of Brooklyn voters as a prerequisite to union. But in Birmingham no suburb would exercise such a veto.

This did not satisfy some Alabama legislators who noted that "it is possible for the people of Birmingham to vote this territory into the city, although every vote in the outlying districts is against it."[55] Despite such protests the measure passed, and the result was Greater Birmingham, a city of 132,000 residents. Alabama solons had nodded in deference to the American ideal of local self-determination. But the central legislators were primarily responsible for the enlargement of Alabama's Birmingham just as Britain's Parliament determined the fate of that nation's Birmingham.[56]

The experiences of Baltimore and Birmingham, Alabama, however, were exceptions to the American rule, for British-style central coordination and control were alien to the United States. In Great Britain Parliament, aided by an administrative agency of the central government, supervised the creation and expansion of local government units, accepting or rejecting the petitions presented by the locality. The continued existence of Aston Manor or King's Norton depended on the Local Government Board and the lawmakers in London, not on the suburban councillors or voters. In contrast, most American lawmakers and civic leaders conceded the right of the nation's small towns and suburbs to determine their own destinies, choosing either independence or amalgamation. In the United States legislators did not create state administrative agencies to investigate the merits of incorporating Munhall, Oak Park, or North Randall, nor did they allow state boards to veto the expansion of Cleveland, Chicago, or Los Angeles. The British model emphasized rational coordination of local government units and established a system of legal eugenics that sought to maximize efficiency by aborting the birth of unviable municipal runts. But American lawmakers did not pursue a policy aimed at rationalizing local government organization, eliminating undersized units, and requiring consolidation. Instead, they deferred to the judgment of the voters and officials in each metropolitan fragment, allowing suburbia to seal the fate of urban America.

5

THE SUBURBAN ASCENDANCY, 1910–40

In 1920 New York City covered 299 square miles, and in 1970 it covered 299 square miles. In 1920 the city of Baltimore governed an area of 79 square miles, and in 1970 it governed an area of 79 square miles. The nineteenth-century boom town of Chicago spread over 199 square miles in 1920, and fifty years later it included 224 square miles, the addition being largely O'Hare Airport. Denver, Colorado, had absorbed 41 square miles between 1890 and 1910, but during the next sixty years it would annex less than 13 additional square miles. In metropolitan areas across America, the territorial conquests of the central city were diminishing in number, and the suburban battlements, which consolidation forces had perforated in the nineteenth century, were now becoming impregnable. The city of Miami failed to extend its boundaries after 1925; Detroit reached its full growth in 1926; and Minneapolis annexed its last piece of territory in 1927. In some states such as Texas permissive annexation laws created a favorable climate for continued expansion of the central city.[1] But an age of expansion was coming to a close for many of the nation's largest municipalities, and an era of suburban supremacy appeared imminent.

In city after city this slowdown in territorial growth was evident. As is evident in table 4, the nation's twenty most populous cities in 1940 had won their greatest conquests during the late nineteenth century; in every decade from 1870 to 1900 the combined areas of these twenty giants had increased by at least 18 percent. After 1900, however, the total areas of these cities increased at a much reduced pace, matching the nineteenth-century figures only between 1910 and 1920, when Los Angeles was winning its vast empire. Despite a rapid increase in urban population during the 1920s, the combined areas of these cities increased by only ten percent, and during the 1930s there was virtually no change

TABLE 4. Increase in Combined Area of Nation's Twenty Most Populous Cities

1870-80	1880-90	1890-1900	1900-10	1910-20	1920-30	1930-40
18.2%	25.5%	31.6%	11.0%	26.3%	10.6%	0.5%

SOURCE: McKenzie, *Metropolitan Community* (New York, 1933), pp. 336-37.

in boundaries, for economic depression discouraged city officials from embarking on campaigns of conquest that might necessitate costly extensions of municipal services.[2] Thus, by the second quarter of the twentieth century, most of America's major cities had stopped growing, either momentarily or permanently.

As the territorial expansion of the central cities slowed, the percentage of the metropolitan population living in the central city dropped. In 1940 63 percent of the residents of the metropolitan areas containing the twenty most populous cities lived in the central cities (see table 5), whereas forty years earlier 77 percent had resided in the core municipality of these metropolitan districts. During each decade from 1900 to 1940 the proportion of suburban residents increased as central cities failed to absorb fringe areas. In 1900 only 9 percent of the residents of Cleveland's metropolitan district lived outside the city limits, but by 1940 28 percent did so. At the beginning of the century 8 percent of the residents of metropolitan Chicago lived in the suburbs, whereas in 1940 25 percent lived beyond the central-city limits. In 1900 11 percent of the metropolitan population of Saint Louis resided in the suburbs, and 12 percent of Milwaukee's metropolitan citizenry were suburbanites. Forty years later these figures had risen to 40 percent and 26 percent, respectively.[3] In Cleveland, Chicago, Saint Louis, and Milwaukee the metropolitan inhabitants were moving far beyond the central-city boundaries, as thousands of urbanites became suburbanites.

Underlying this decline in central-city expansion was an increasing appreciation of the advantages of suburban rule. During the nineteenth century, suburban residents had sought annexation or consolidation because of the superior municipal services offered by the central city.

TABLE 5. Proportion Living in Central Cities in Nation's Most Populous Metropolitan Areas

1900	1910	1920	1930	1940
77.2%	76.3%	69.0%	64.8%	63.2%

SOURCES: U.S. censuses of 1910, 1920, 1930, and 1940. The figures are for only nineteen metropolitan areas, since two of the twenty largest cities (New York City and Newark) shared the same metropolitan area.

Charlestown's residents had envied Boston's water supply; East Cleveland's citizens had longed for the water, fire, and police services of the big city; Lake View's consolidationists had spoken of the suburb's polluted water and unhealthy sewage systems. But by the twentieth century, many of the larger and older suburban municipalities could match the central city's services, for improved technology, know-how, and a strengthened municipal bond market had allowed suburbs to serve their citizens more fully than in the past. High income taxes during World War I and in the early 1920s enhanced the attractiveness of tax-exempt interest from municipal bonds, and an increasing number of loopholes in municipal debt restrictions in a state such as Ohio had allowed the expanding suburbs of Cleveland to borrow and spend to an unprecedented extent for sewers, streets, and lighting. Moreover, many of the smallest and poorest municipalities, those least capable of servicing the public, had disappeared through consolidation with the central city or with their larger suburban neighbors, leaving the more populous and wealthier domains of Lakewood, Evanston, and Pasadena to rebuff the expansionist forays of the central city. In the suburban jungle, only the fittest survived—those that could equal Cleveland, Chicago, or Los Angeles in the provision of water, lighting, and police protection.

Throughout the country outlying municipalities were developing increasingly sophisticated public services. In 1890 only 29 percent of the outlying municipalities in Cook County, Illinois, enjoyed a piped supply of water, whereas by 1915 45 percent of the suburban cities and villages could claim this advantage.[4] And by 1934 83 percent of the municipalities within a fifty-mile radius of Chicago enjoyed a public water supply.[5] During the period from 1890 to 1896 the Cook County communities of Chicago Heights, Des Plaines, Harvey, Kenilworth, LaGrange, LaGrange Park, Maywood, River Forest, Western Springs, Wilmette, and Winnetka all constructed their first waterworks, as did Highland Park, Highwood, and Lake Forest immediately to the north in Lake County.[6] As safe, clean water flowed into suburban homes, interest in consolidation waned. By 1900 annexation sentiment was on the decline in Cook County, and it would become gradually weaker with the improvement of suburban services.

Elsewhere, the same change was evident. Only two of the thirty-four outlying municipalities in Cincinnati's Hamilton County had water supplies in 1890, but twenty-five years later almost 40 percent enjoyed piped water. In Pittsburgh's Allegheny County, waterworks supplied 34 percent of the suburban municipalities in 1890 but 64 percent in 1915.[7] Moreover, the number of places in the United States served by sewage systems soared from 450 in 1890 to 3,000 in 1920.[8] In suburb after suburb the storm sewer supplanted the open ditch, mud yielded to asphalt, and the volunteer fire corps surrendered its duties to a paid body of trained fire fighters. By the 1920s typhoid and yellow fever no longer made suburban living hazardous to one's health, and electric street lights now illuminated the suburban drive as well as the city boulevard.

Metropolitan cooperation during this period also enhanced the quality of services available to the suburbs, leaving them less vulnerable to central-city attack. For example, in 1889 the Illinois legislature created the Chicago Sanitary District, which included the city of Chicago and its nearest suburbs. Created at the behest of the city of Chicago, the district assumed responsibility for sewage disposal in the metropolitan area and sought to ensure that waste from Chicago and its suburbs would float down the Illinois River toward the Mississippi rather than pollute Lake Michigan and the city's water supply. Among the provisions of the act, however, was a section requiring all municipalities that bordered on the lake to sell water to all municipalities within the district but not bordering on the lake at the same price that they charged consumers within their own city limits. In other words, Chicago would have to sell city water to its western suburbs at a moderate cost, and safe, clean water would no longer be a benefit derived solely through annexation.[9] In 1904 the city of Chicago tried to cut off water to the town of Cicero, but the Illinois Supreme Court ordered the central city to comply with the provisions of the Sanitary District Act.[10] Cicero residents paid taxes in support of the sanitary district, thereby helping Chicago protect its supply of pure water. Chicago, in return, had to reward Cicero by sharing this water with the suburb.

In the Boston area, special-purpose metropolitan districts also aided the suburbs and bolstered their chances for survival. The seriously fragmented Boston metropolis had suffered from an inadequate water supply throughout the last half of the nineteenth century, and in the 1890s state lawmakers recognized the need for action on a metropolitan scale. According to the chief engineer for the state board of health, the central city needed "an additional water supply as soon as it can be obtained." Water in suburban Arlington, he noted, contained "abundant growths of minute organisms which give ... (it) a disagreeable taste and odor," and the source of water in suburban Hyde Park and Milton "will always be regarded with suspicion."[11] Responding to this problem, the Massachusetts legislature in 1895 created the Metropolitan Water District, a regional authority charged with the responsibility of supplying water to Boston and to eighteen surrounding suburban towns. Earlier in the century Charlestown, Roxbury, and West Roxbury had viewed annexation to Boston as the only solution to their water problems. Now metropolitan cooperation offered an alternative solution that obviated the necessity of unification through annexation.

In Southern California cooperation between city and suburb came later than it had in the Chicago and Boston areas, for Los Angeles's abundant water supply from the Owens River Aqueduct allowed it to pursue an independent course until the mid-1920s. During the period from 1913 to 1920, residents in hundreds of square miles of adjacent territory sought admission to the city in order to avail themselves of the Owens River water, but by 1924 it was obvious that the Owens River was no longer adequate to supply the needs of the booming city. During that year city officials met with representatives of thirty-six adjacent communities to form a lobbying group to campaign for construction of an aqueduct from the Colorado River. Once the cities had obtained authorization for the new aqueduct, the California legislature incorporated the Metropolitan Water District to govern distribution of the water supply throughout the metropolitan area.[12] Since Colorado River water would flow into Pasadena and Santa Monica as well as Los Angeles, the central city would no longer hold a monopoly on the necessities of life and could no longer lure suburban voters with promises of water.

Throughout America metropolitan agreements brought improved services to suburbia. In 1905 a state law creating the Board of Water Supply of the City of New York required the board to provide water to a dozen or more Westchester County communities located near the path of the proposed Catskill Aqueduct. At the behest of the city of Newark, New Jersey's legislature created the North Jersey District Water Supply Commission in 1918, and by 1924 Newark and seven suburban municipalities were cooperating to complete a massive water project. In an effort designed primarily to satisfy the area's pressing need for water, Oakland, California, joined with eight surrounding municipalities in 1923 to form the East Bay Municipal Utility District.[13] From New York to California, central cities as well as suburbs needed water, and metropolitan cooperation seemed the best means of acquiring the valuable liquid.

Yet cooperation undermined the competitive advantage that the central city traditionally had enjoyed with regard to public services. The central city may have suffered at times from a lack of safe water or a need for improved drainage, but due to its size the central city could command the resources necessary for a solution to these problems more readily than could the individual suburb. Metropolitan cooperation eased the financial burden on the central city somewhat by spreading the costs between city and suburb. But it did much more for the suburb. It permitted the suburb to enjoy a quality of service that it could never have attained singly. Through cooperative effort, suburban governments could raise the level of public services to a standard of quality that would satisfy suburban residents, and as a result those residents would look less longingly at the advantages of the central city. The year in which Illinois' legislature enacted the Sanitary District Bill was the last year in which Chicago would make massive additions to its territory. Boston would annex only one town following the creation of the Metropolitan Water District, and Los Angeles's expansionist heyday came to an end just as water from the Owens River was running short. New York City, Newark, and Oakland would not expand their boundaries again, and one of the reasons was that they no longer had as much to offer the suburbanite.

Special-purpose metropolitan districts were not the only instruments of metropolitan cooperation that developed during the early twentieth century. Between 1900 and 1930 the state legislature of Ohio enacted twenty-five measures providing for intergovernmental contractual relations, including statutes that allowed municipalities to construct joint sewage systems and joint waterworks. Moreover, states were authorizing counties to assume municipal functions and to provide services to suburban units. In 1917 Ohio's legislature authorized counties to cooperate with municipalities in the creation of joint sewage disposal works, and in 1923 it passed a similar measure with regard to water supply. Beginning in 1907, Los Angeles County contracted with individual municipalities to provide services, and between 1909 and 1930 the California legislature authorized the creation of county library, health, and sanitation districts in order to provide urban amenities to suburban municipalities and unincorporated areas.[14] Expanded county functions and intermunicipal agreements thus enabled suburbanites to improve the quality of their public services, and as a result the appeal of amalgamation with the central city again diminished.

Throughout the nation the changing role of county government was especially noteworthy. Though only two states had authorized county libraries prior to 1898, between 1898 and 1930 twenty-eight states enacted laws empowering counties to provide library services. The first county park was founded in 1895, but by 1928 there were an estimated forty-five such parks in the nation. Urban and suburban counties were especially active in the creation of recreation facilities typically associated with cities. Bergen, Essex, and Union counties in metropolitan northeastern New Jersey were among the first to create park systems, as was Camden County, New Jersey, in the Philadelphia metropolitan area. In New York, urban Erie County (Buffalo) and suburban Westchester County maintained parks in 1928, and in Michigan, Wayne County (Detroit) did likewise. By the close of the 1920s, Milwaukee County, Los Angeles County, and the counties containing Chicago, Houston, Fort Worth, Saint Paul, and Kansas City all were administering parks.[15] In 1930 seven metropolitan counties were engaged in sewer projects, and three provided water supplies to suburban residents. Three metropolitan counties were also involved in regional planning and controlled the platting of subdivisions, and two provided fire protection. Suburban Baltimore County performed most of the functions of a municipality, as did Westchester County, and Los Angeles County's functions had increased in number from 22 in 1852 to 784 in 1934.[16]

The growing importance of county government in metropolitan areas is evident from the county's increased share of combined county-municipal expenditures. In 1913 in ninety-six metropolitan areas, the county governments spent 16 percent of the combined county-municipal expenditures, but by 1932 the urban county spent 21 percent of this combined total. Of the total expenditure on recreation, in 1913 the county spent only 6 percent, but in 1932 the county spent 21 percent. The urban county's share of total expenditures on health rose from 4 percent to 13 percent.[17] In urban areas from New York to California the county was extending its governmental functions and responsibilities more rapidly than the municipality, and the county's share of local government expenditures was rising.

Thus suburbanites throughout the nation were able to obtain an increasing number of services from their county governments, and many no longer needed to resort to union with the central city in order to obtain the advantages of urban life. In the nineteenth century, suburbanites had only two choices when confronted with the question of services. They could either rely on the limited resources of the suburb and receive inferior fire and police protection, a substandard water supply, and no sewer services; or they could elect to consolidate with the central city and enjoy an improved standard of living. By the 1920s and 1930s, however, their options were more numerous. They could create special metropolitan districts, assign new responsibilities to the county government, or draft intermunicipal agreements. By each of these means they could obtain the quality of service found in the central city. County governments and special districts had not yet supplanted the municipality in the American metropolis, but they did offer an alternate source of services in many areas, and they precluded the necessity of suburbanites sacrificing themselves to the central city.

While suburban services were improving, a wave of unfavorable publicity was dampening the citizen's enthusiasm for central-city government and politics. During the first decade of the twentieth century, thousands of suburban subscribers to *McClure's Magazine* read Lincoln Steffens's muckraking exposés of corruption in big-city government. *Colliers, Century,* and the local metropolitan newspapers all carried similar accounts of chicanery and irresponsible rule. Tales of thievery in New York City were current as early as the 1870s, but by the 1900s the stories of corruption focused on Pittsburgh, Saint Louis, Minneapolis, and cities across the entire nation. The prestige of central-city government had been challenged in the late nineteenth century, but at the beginning of the twentieth century it dipped to new depths, offending suburbanites and bolstering their opposition to consolidation.

Urban reformers of the late nineteenth and early twentieth centuries had attempted to cleanse city hall by tinkering with municipal charters and by inventing new schemes for ending corruption, but even their efforts proved abortive. In the 1870s and 1880s, some had suggested limiting the electorate to taxpayers, thus excluding the unworthy mass of vagabond foreigners from casting ballots in support of the venal political machines. Then the fashion in reform had turned to the idea of the strong mayor with authority concentrated in his hands and out of the grasp of greedy saloon-keeping aldermen. Bipartisan boards also became a fad because such commissions would not be so subject to insidious party influence. Nonpartisan elections, the short ballot, home rule, the commission form of government, and finally the city manager plan were all proposed as solutions for the urban dilemma. By the third decade of the twentieth century, a vast array of experiments, schemes, and panaceas had disappointed those who sought honest, efficient government. To some the big city seemed beset by insoluble problems, and many felt a revulsion at the idea of being swallowed whole by this monster of graft and corruption. Thus, as the repute of suburban government rose, there was no corresponding increase in the reputation of the central-city regime.

In city after city the mood of the populace leaned toward continued separatism. In the 1870s or 1880s suburban annexationists could speak convincingly of the blessings of civilization to be derived from the cities of Chicago or Cleveland and complain of suburban hacks and their incompetent governments. By 1910, however, such rhetoric had disappeared from the annexation contests. No one spoke of the central city as the model of good government, and city hall now seemed a distant den of unresponsive politicians. Reform administrations might sweeten the smell of big-city politics momentarily, but the odor of corruption would linger, irritating the senses of suburban voters. After 1910 some might still be able to argue that the central city excelled in the quality of its fire department, sewage system, or water, but no one was to challenge Lord Bryce's condemnation of city government as the greatest failure in the American system. During the second decade of the twentieth century Chicago suburbanites cited suburban Brookline, Massachusetts, not their own central city, as the best-governed city in America. This was an indication of the changed attitude of the times. Journalists and reformers had revealed the shame of the cities, and suburban municipalities had no desire to wed themselves to a tarnished bride.

By 1920, then, the material expectations of Americans and their desires for superb public services and for improved government were no longer necessarily factors that benefited the cause of central-city expansionists. The reputation of central-city government was damaged almost beyond repair, and the quality of suburban services was improving. Some suburban areas still might find central-city services appealing, and some suburban municipalities were governed by individuals whose actions would outrage the sensibilities of the most amoral urban boss. But a parity was developing between central-city services and services in the wealthier, larger suburbs; the demands for water, sewers, pavements, and police that previously had cemented many of the fissures in the metropolis did not act as such a binding force in the 1920s.

While the forces encouraging unity were weakening, the forces of separatism and disunion remained powerful. During the period from 1910 to 1940, the trend toward social and economic segregation persisted, and the class and ethnic barriers between neighborhoods rose even higher. In the twentieth century, as in the late nineteenth century, the metropolis contained many interests, each wanting a government tailored to its own particular desires. Industry wanted low-tax havens. Middle-class Americans wanted good schools, attractive surroundings, and freedom from saloons. Each fragment of society sought a political fragment suitable to its needs, and this did not bode well for those seeking the annexation of suburbia. The appeal of consolidation was diminishing, but the lure of particularism continued to be attractive.

The advent of zoning ordinances between 1910 and 1930 added legal imprimatur to the segregation of earlier decades. Throughout the nation, city and village councils formalized the informal divisions of the past by outlawing commerce and manufacturing in some areas, reserving them for residence. Zoning was especially popular in fragmented suburbia, where municipalities could reinforce the particularism of their community through the passage of exclusionary ordinances. Posh suburbs from Scarsdale to Beverly Hills excluded manufacturing and the less seemly aspects of commerce, ensuring their strictly upper-middle-class residential status. Twentieth-century law bolstered and helped perpetuate the late-nineteenth-century trend toward separatism, further diminishing the likelihood of a united and integrated metropolis.

Meanwhile, ethnic rifts widened during the years from 1910 to 1925, with white nativist feelings reaching a new peak during the period of World War I. As immigrants from southern and eastern Europe continued to flood the nation, demands rose for restrictions on entry into the country. These demands culminated in the 1921 and 1924 quota laws which seriously curtailed the influx of foreigners. Antiblack sentiment also mounted during these years, resulting in the vicious urban race riots of 1917 and 1919. Moreover, from 1920 to 1925 the Ku Klux Klan attained the pinnacle of its power in both city and country. Social segregation was becoming increasingly popular as Americans sought to isolate themselves from people of differing backgrounds and viewpoints. And this persistence of social and ethnic particularism did not facilitate the consolidation of the nation's municipal units.

At the same time the moral question of alcohol continued to divide the metropolis, and dispute over the issue reached a peak between 1910 and 1919. Slavic and south European Roman Catholics were pouring into the central cities, and their tolerance for alcohol strongly offended enclaves of suburban sobriety such as Oak Park and Evanston. Under the spell of the Anti-Saloon League and her sister organizations, suburban abstainers dreaded the invasion of saloons and sabbath breakers from the city and viewed consolidation as a sure path to hell. With the advent of national prohibition in 1919, the issue diminished in significance, although certain of the suburbs soon found they had developed reputations as dens of sin and corruption. Men like Al Capone quickly discovered that it was easier and cheaper to buy the mayor, council, and police force of suburban Cicero and Stickney than their counterparts in Chicago. The police of suburban Hamtramck convoyed bootlegger's trucks through their city to the exasperation of Detroit's bluenosed authorities; and in Cleveland's suburbs of Linndale and Newburgh Heights stills and roadhouses were as much symbols of suburbia as were happy homes and cheerful children.[18] Suburbia remained divided between the "wets" and "drys," the tarnished and the chaste, and this moral heterogeneity perpetuated political divisions.

The advent of women's suffrage and increased female participation in the political process also may have proved detrimental to consolidation efforts, contributing to the further segregation of the metropolis, for suburban women were particularly hostile to saloon rule and intolerant toward central-city political bosses. In Chicago's "dry" suburb of Oak Park, women played a major role in the annexation referendum of 1910. According to a reporter for the *Chicago Record-Herald*, "all day long" on election day "Oak Park women, acting as their own chauffeurs and in their own machines," drove around town waving placards reading "Oak Park for the Oak Parkers" and urging "indifferent and feeble voters to the polls in the interest of 'home rule.'"[19] Illinois women won the right to vote in 1914, and they soon exercised this privilege in annexation contests. The fear of invasion by Chicago saloons had been an issue in recent Cicero annexation battles, and in 1914 75 percent of

Cicero's female voters opposed merger with the central city, as compared to only 66 percent of Cicero's male voters.[20] In the Morgan Park annexation contest that same year, there was little difference in the voting patterns of the two sexes.[21] But generally when liquor and morals were at issue, women seemed more likely to side with the forces of suburban sanctity rather than the proponents of metropolitan union.

During the period from 1910 to 1940, then, separatism appeared on the rise, unabated by the unifying appeal of superior central-city services. The social and economic forces that underlay earlier fragmentation persisted, but the factors that had encouraged amalgamation in the late nineteenth century no longer prevailed. Centripetal force did not balance centrifugal pull as it had in an earlier era. No longer was there as much rhetoric about services that only the big city could offer. Instead, there was more talk about the advantages of life in a small community, a homogeneous hometown where one could make one's influence felt. Americans wanted to separate into communities that would suit their particular purposes and where they would not confront opposition from people with different interests. They wanted to live in communities where everyone believed in green lawns and white picket fences, in sobriety, and in chastity. They did not want to live in communities where they would have to vie with conflicting viewpoints or battle manufacturers and their soot, ward heelers and their saloons. Fragmented suburbia offered them the opportunity to realize this peculiar paradise, and with the improvement of suburban services they no longer had to sacrifice comfort and convenience to attain this end. The central city was a hodgepodge of battling interests, and the unitary rule of the central city was ill suited to the preservation of particularism. Fragmented suburbia, in contrast, was well adapted to the segregated society of twentieth-century America.

The year 1910, however, did not mark an absolute halt to annexation efforts. Some areas still did accept union with the central city, voluntarily submitting to consolidated rule. But these accessions were rarely choice conquests, for central cities proved most successful in absorbing poorly governed areas, many of which lacked tax revenue and all of which demanded services. The quality of services in the largest, wealthiest suburbs approached that of central-city services, and in some metropolitan areas special districts and counties could satisfy suburban needs. Yet there were still suburban areas that were unable to offer services and thus unable to survive as independent units in the metropolitan arena. These suburban failures, the losers in the game of government, were the ones most willing to accept union with the central city. The largest and wealthiest suburbs and those areas with unusually fine services provided by special district and county governments could afford to pursue the separatist course, but in tax-poor and ill-governed fragments the price for separatism was too high.

Thus Pittsburgh was not able to merge with wealthy Mount Lebanon or pristine, middle-class Wilkinsburg (nicknamed the "Holy City" because of its reputation for good, clean government), but it did assume the burden of lower-class Saint Clair. Detroit did not annex Hamtramck with its massive Dodge plant, Highland Park with its huge Ford factory, or the string of Grosse Pointes with their handsome mansions. Instead it absorbed miles of open country to the northwest with a low tax valuation and with no water mains, paved streets, or street lights. Indianapolis extended its boundaries to include the amusement-park community of Broad Ripple and moderate-income University Heights with its tax-exempt college campus. But the town of Beech Grove, with its extensive Big Four Railroad Shops, remained an independent municipality. Miami did not merge with the municipality of Miami Beach, absorbing its potentially tax-rich beach property; nor did it annex the new subdivision of Coral Gables with its expensive homes. Instead it acquired acres of interior swamp. Expansion in the 1920s was to mean red ink on the municipal ledgers and, in the cases of Detroit and Miami, near bankruptcy in the 1930s.

In the 1880s and 1890s, the central cities might not have been willing to assume such burdens. In the nineteenth century Boston repeatedly had refused to annex liabilities. Denver had connived to exclude debt-ridden Fletcher, and at the beginning of the twentieth century Indianapolis had refused Broad Ripple's overtures for annexation. During the period from 1850 to 1910, central cities still felt they could afford to be selective in their acquisitions. Central cities at this time still had the upper hand because their superior municipal services were a talisman that could charm the suburbs into submission. Consequently, the nineteenth-century city excluded unwanted burdens and yet continued to grow.

By the 1920s, however, central cities abandoned discretion and succumbed to unthinking expansionist fervor, for the decade was one dedicated not only to particularism but also to bigness and growth. Many Americans may have yearned for the insulated homogeneity of the small town, but at the same time they admired the contradictory notion of expansion and imperial size. The 1920s was an era of unprecedented boosterism, an age that worshiped big business, the giant corporation, and soaring stock market prices. It was an age that admired quantity above quality, that thought more of the production figures of Henry Ford's assembly line than the hand-tooled work of the master craftsman.

In the 1920s growth was considered good, stagnation bad. And this mentality governed the actions of the cities. A city must grow and expand no matter the consequences.

The guardians of this philosophy of growth were the local chambers of commerce. In this age when America's business was business, the chamber of commerce was at the peak of its power and a chamber-of-commerce mentality pervaded the nation. Business leaders in every city used the chamber of commerce as the chief instrument for boosting the city's fortunes and reputation. Census rank seemed one of the vital factors in any city's future success. Pittsburgh business leaders claimed that their city had lost the opportunity of serving as headquarters of the Federal Reserve branch because Cleveland had risen more rapidly in census rank and had assumed the honor of becoming the largest city in the region. The bigger city was supposedly the better city, since size was a source of growth potential. Business leaders may have been flocking to the dry suburbs to enjoy home life in these small but exclusive outlying municipalities, but they still believed in central-city expansion and remained its prime boosters. Their moral and aesthetic sensibilities may have recognized the advantages of the small suburb, yet their business judgment was forthrightly on the side of bigness. Chamber of commerce moguls admired the suburb, but they knew as an article of faith that the city must grow, for in the decalogue of sins listed by the chamber of commerce, stagnation was the first and foremost. Annexation was a means of redeeming Pittsburgh, Cleveland, and Milwaukee from this sin.

Although growth was considered essential, the ring of suburban municipalities had begun to choke off opportunities for future central-city expansion. Therefore many central cities took advantage of every chance to expand. When any weakness appeared in the suburban ring, the central city moved in and annexed. But the conquests were not comparable to Chicago's acquisitions of 1889 or Boston's annexations of Dorchester and Roxbury. More often, the central city reaped a bounty of problems. The tax base of the annexed territories was frequently poor, and the need for services was generally great. The cities wanted to become bigger and therefore better, and they were willing to accept acquisitions that they would have rejected earlier. In the imperialistic eyes of the central city, towns such as Fletcher no longer appeared as pariahs but as prizes.

An examination of the major municipal consolidations of the 1920s reveals the nature of the communities willing to surrender their corporate autonomies. From 1920 through 1929 ten municipalities with populations of 2,500 or more merged with cities having 100,000 or more residents, and generally these ten were working-class dormitories with little or no industrial wealth. The census of 1920 provides little data on socio-economic status, but perhaps the best indicator available from that census is the percentage of persons sixteen to twenty years old attending school. Education traditionally has been a symbol of status in the United States as well as a privilege most readily available to those in the upper ranks of society. Consequently, those communities with a high percentage of their citizenry seeking a high school or college degree generally rank at the top of the socio-economic scale. However, as seen in table 6, in eight and possibly nine of the ten suburbs that yielded autonomy, a smaller percentage of the inhabitants sixteen to twenty sought an education than were doing so in the metropolitan county as a whole. And in seven of the ten the percentage was lower than it was in the central city itself.[22] The central city was, then, acquiring a population with lower-than-average educational aspirations, not absorbing the "better elements" of suburban society.

Moreover, these communities were not primarily industrial suburbs, rich with taxable manufacturing plants. Of the fifty-three Pennsylvania municipalities with populations of between ten thousand and fifty thousand in 1920, the borough of Carrick ranked fifty-third in terms of value added by manufacture; it had only five industrial establishments employing 23 workers.[23] Of the thirty-nine Ohio municipalities in this population category recorded in the census of manufacturing for 1920, Kenmore ranked thirty-eighth with seven establishments and 153 employees.[24] Of the eighteen California cities with populations between ten thousand and fifty thousand, Venice ranked eighteenth in value added by manufacture, claiming only nine manufacturing concerns with a total of 64 em-

TABLE 6. Persons Aged Sixteen to Twenty Attending School in Central City, Metropolitan County, and Annexed Suburbs, 1920

Central city	Metropolitan county	Annexed suburbs
Pittsburgh 22.5%	Allegheny County 21.2%	Carrick 18.6%
		Knoxville 26.0%
		St. Clair 12.4%
Akron 14.9%	Summit County 16.5%	Kenmore 11.0%
Cleveland 21.4%	Cuyahoga County 23.9%	West Park 53.8%*
(5.3% illiterate)	(4.8% illiterate)	(9.8% illiterate)
Milwaukee 28.1%	Milwaukee County 27.1%	North Milwaukee 12.7%
Kansas City,		
Kansas 19.3%	Wyandotte County 20.3%	Rosedale 15.6%
Spokane 40.7%	Spokane County 41.1%	Hillyard 35.2%
Los Angeles 33.0%	Los Angeles County 36.1%	Venice 33.3%
		Watts 20.4%

SOURCE: U.S. census of 1920.
*Almost certainly an error

ployees.[25] And Kansas labor statistics for 1920 reveal that Rosedale, with a population of 7,674, was equally lacking in industry, having only five manufacturing concerns with a total payroll of 110 workers.[26] Pittsburgh did not absorb adjoining McKees Rocks, with factories employing 3,592 workers, nor did Akron annex suburban Barberton, with industries employing 5,829. Instead, they were able to merge only with the less handsomely endowed of their neighbors.

To understand better the problem confronting the central cities between 1910 and 1940, it is necessary to examine specific annexation battles in Chicago, Pittsburgh, Cleveland, Milwaukee, and Los Angeles. In each of these cities members of the chambers of commerce and city clubs continued to seek unification of the metropolis through traditional annexation and consolidation procedures. In each case annexationists met with some success, but their conquests were often Pyrrhic victories. Each city faced the problem of recalcitrance by tax-rich industrial suburbs, wealthy residential communities, and well-governed outlying municipalities. Though many suburbanites may have applauded any advance their central city made in census rank, they were not willing to sacrifice the advantages they enjoyed in the suburbs in order to achieve this advance. Consolidation in a unitary municipal behemoth seemed too high a price to pay for a boost in central-city prestige. Yet if the suburb was replete with shortcomings, the price might seem a bit more reasonable. Thus residents in the weak and needy suburbs or in those suburbs that were simply poorly managed did vote to abandon independent rule. It was in these trouble-ridden communities that central-city expansionists would triumph. Central cities were greedy for growth, and they satisfied their hunger for expansion by gobbling up a string of municipal failures and burdensome liabilities.

Chicago's annexationists found their task increasingly difficult after the turn of the century, as the suburbs repeatedly rejected offers to join the city. Between 1909 and 1914 Evanston vetoed a merger proposal, Oak Park defeated consolidation schemes twice, and voters in the town of Cicero rejected annexation measures in four separate elections. In Evanston supporters of the merger proposal argued that "men who accumulate great wealth in Chicago should live in Chicago, be interested in Chicago's welfare, vote in Chicago, and take an active part in Chicago's social and political affairs."[27] Moreover, one annexationist accused Evanston's leaders of "frittering away your time here on the petty peanut politics of Evanston when you might be applying your power and influence and intellect to the solution of the tremendous problems that confront Chicago."[28] In Cicero consolidationists claimed that "annexation to Chicago means ... a great reduction in gas, water, and telephone rates, as well as better transportation services."[29] But one Cicero politician articulated the majority viewpoint when he observed that "the people here ... do not care to help pay Chicago's taxes."[30]

In Oak Park the annexation contests were heated with the typical exchanges of warnings and promises. Annexationists claimed that Oak Park taxes were too high, as were water and gas rates, and residents of Oak Park's south side complained of inadequate water and sewage services while arguing that "the millionaires north of us are exclusive and looked down upon the home-makers to the south."[31] Moreover, those favoring merger with Chicago attacked Oak Park schools where "the three R's are being lost sight of and their place taken by poetry and ethics."[32] According to one critic, Oak Park's "first grade pupils were taught to say 'Twinkle, twinkle, little star,' and ... the sixth grade pupils spent the arithmetic hour on the day of the big snow storm in reading Whittier's 'Snow Bound,'" while "open mutiny on the part of the larger boys was not uncommon" in the suburb's schools.[33]

Such arguments, however, won few votes, for Oak Park's services were adequate and its schools were the pride of the community. Annexation foes claimed that, in fact, "our taxes ... are no higher than are paid on Chicago property" because "the assessed valuation of our properties is only about 55 to 60 per cent of the full value, while Chicago's is fully 90 per cent."[34] Moreover, they observed that "there has not been a suggestion of scandal or dishonesty in our political affairs" while Chicago's "police department is rotten to the core" and "its public service department is corrupt."[35] They asked, would Chicago's police department "permit gambling houses, houses of ill repute, and disorderly amusement resorts in our midst?"[36] Oak Park's separatists believed it would, and consequently they demanded continued autonomy.

Antiannexationists viewed the attacks on Oak Park's schools as especially ludicrous, claiming that "most of our newer residents moved to Oak Park on account of the excellence of our schools."[37] According to the separatists, "the average number of pupils in Oak Park to the grade teacher is 31, while in Chicago it is 45," and "Oak Park spent $165,000" on its school district of 18,000 residents while "Chicago's school authorities spent only $67,000 for each 18,000 of its population."[38] The interior walls of Chicago's schools were "cleaned but once in seven years," but "in Oak Park there is an annual school house cleaning."[39] Chicago had "over forty portable school houses and over 9,000 pupils who can attend school only half of each day for the want of school rooms."[40] Yet "the Oak Park schools were known everywhere among educators for their excellence," and "our schools are Oak Park's chief pride."[41]

On election day voters rallied around these foes of annexation in each of Chicago's three major suburbs. Cicero's electorate repeatedly chose independence by a margin of two to one, and according to the *Chicago*

Tribune, the annexation proposal of 1911 "was considered largely a joke." [42] Likewise, Oak Park's voters rejected union with the city by a three-to-one edge, and Evanston's residents backed autonomy by a ratio of four to one. [43] By 1915 it was evident that further attempts to absorb these major suburbs were futile.

Meanwhile Chicago was absorbing a few small fragments that could not cope with the burdens of independence as capably as Cicero, Oak Park, or Evanston. In 1914 the village of Morgan Park merged with Chicago after the local citizenry rebelled against that municipality's long history of high tax rates and inadequate services. Though the residents were primarily middle class, the village was small, lacked industrial wealth, and suffered under an undistinguished government that could not handle the trials of autonomy. Morgan Park's village tax rate exceeded those of Chicago and Evanston and was usually double that of the village of Oak Park. [44] Moreover, by 1913 the per capita bonded debt in Morgan Park exceeded those of Chicago, Oak Park, and Cicero and was almost double that of Evanston. [45] When a new administration assumed charge of Morgan Park in 1907, it "found floating debts in [the] shape of time warrants and unpaid bills amounting to over $14,000.00." [46] Of the 143 Illinois municipalities of 2,500 or more inhabitants, Morgan Park ranked fifth in per capita interest payments on the municipal debt. Neither Chicago, Cicero, Oak Park, nor Evanston suffered the burdens of such heavy per capita debt charges. [47] At the same time, per capita outlays for fire and police protection and for health and sanitation were less in Morgan Park than in Chicago, Cicero, Oak Park, or Evanston. [48] Morgan Park's citizenry paid higher taxes than did residents in other municipalities, but their money went to bond holders rather than to policemen, firemen, or health officials.

Annexationists in Morgan Park recognized these grim facts and complained bitterly about the problems confronting their community. The village was not originally within the Chicago Sanitary District as were Cicero and Oak Park, and it had constructed its own independent but inadequate waterworks. According to local residents, Morgan Park water contained "a large percentage of lime and magnesia salts, which render it undesirable for use as a beverage and for cooking, almost useless for bathing and laundry purposes, harmful to grass and other vegetation, and rapidly and completely destructive to heating pipes, radiators and boilers." [49] One Morgan Park annexationist claimed that "water is scarce, and is growing scarcer every day," and what water exists is "unfit to wash your hands or sprinkle your lawn" and "is certainly not fit to put into your stomach or bladder." [50] Still another warned that "our artesian lime water may in time turn us all into limestone monuments." The proponents of merger also observed that "the typhoid death rate of Morgan Park exceeds that of Chicago."[51] Other complaints centered on Morgan Park's "semi-volunteer" fire company, which compared badly to Chicago's fire department. Some criticized the suburb's four-man police corps, predicting a force of twenty-four policemen for the area once it had entered Chicago.[52] Annexationists added to their list of advantages the promise of better schools, improved library facilities, more extensive street lighting, food inspection, and cheaper street car fares.[53] Union with Chicago supposedly meant "anti-appendicitis, anti-rheumatism soft lake water," "policemen who will walk at least once around your home" each night, "whole lots of electric lights everywhere," and "last, but not least, lower taxes."[54] Faced with such promises, the people of Morgan Park chose to surrender autonomy for the less costly prospect of Chicago city rule.

The small village of Clearing found independent municipal rule an even more onerous burden. Incorporated in 1909, this working-class suburb could not meet the demands of a growing population, and in 1915 the citizens voted to join Chicago. The tax-rich Clearing Industrial District, however, had remained in unincorporated Stickney Township, and the village of Bedford Park annexed this area in 1940.[55] Thus Chicago absorbed a municipal failure with its inexpensive working-class homes but lost the more valuable industrial property to the suburbs.

Chicago's two chief accessions of the 1920s were also of dubious value. In 1927 the residents of Mount Greenwood voted to enter the city, and the following year Dunning united with Chicago. Both were among the poorest suburban areas, and in real estate surveys for 1930, 1934, and 1939 the average rents in Dunning and Mount Greenwood consistently ranked below the median for the city.[56] By the close of the 1930s both communities likewise ranked below average among the city's neighborhoods in terms of condition of the housing structures, and pockets of blight were already evident.[57] Mount Greenwood was the poorest neighborhood in southwestern Chicago, and Dunning was the poorest neighborhood in northwestern Chicago. But that was their only distinction. Otherwise they were simply monotonous tracts of cheap frame houses uninterrupted by tax-rich industrial plants or by property of high valuation. Both demanded Chicago's municipal services, but neither could pay much in return.

Thus Chicago's annexationists were no longer matching the city's nineteenth-century record of expansion. Referenda victories had far outnumbered defeats in the 1880s and 1890s, but between 1910 and 1940 defeats would mount, and the spoils of victory generally consisted of only a few stray tracts of little value. Separatism was triumphing over consolidation; a supposedly corrupt, rum-soaked, foreign-dominated Chicago no longer attracted suburbanites who enjoyed exemplary municipal services in such outlying communities as Evanston and Oak Park.

The story was similar in Pittsburgh. Throughout the early twentieth century annexationists in Pittsburgh engaged in an active expansion campaign highlighted in 1907 by the absorption of the twin city, Allegheny, against the will of a majority of Allegheny's citizens. This was the last time Pennsylvania's legislature would authorize an involuntary merger in the Pittsburgh region; consequently the city's further growth depended on the sanction of the suburban citizenry. Yet the most affluent suburbanites consistently refused to consider annexation. None of the twenty-one tracts annexed to the city of Pittsburgh from 1920 through 1931 ranked among the finest residential districts of the metropolis. According to a real estate survey conducted in 1934, the average value of homes in these recently annexed areas was $5,400 as compared to an approximate average of $7,000 for the city as a whole.[58] Moreover, none were areas of significant industrial wealth. Some of the annexed areas, such as Knoxville and Overbrook, were respectable middle-class residential districts. But the acquisitions also included the impoverished shanty districts of Mifflin and Chartiers, townships which sought the advantages of central-city services and demanded heavy expenditures for public improvements.

Annexation thus imposed many burdens on the city of Pittsburgh, and as early as 1927 Pittsburgh's mayor complained that "the financial experience of the city with many of the boroughs annexed in recent years has not always been a happy one." According to the mayor, "the paving and sewering of the unimproved territory has absorbed each year almost all the two per cent borrowing power vested in the city council," and consequently the city labored "under constant embarrassment in connection with the maintenance and replacement of public works of a more general utility."[59] Urban boosters dreaded the prospect of a drop in census rank and therefore believed annexation a necessity. But for Pittsburgh and other cities it proved a costly necessity.

Despite complaints from the mayor, Pittsburgh was willing to pay the cost of growth; like Chicago, Cleveland, Milwaukee, and Los Angeles, it reaped its share of suburban failures. One such acquisition was the borough of Hays, a grim, dingy, working-class town, one of the many that formed a sooty rim along the Monongahela River. In Prohibition-era Hays, reform-minded councilmen expected no more from the police than "to see that all slot machines were removed from the borough and that the saloons ... did not keep open at night."[60] Political feuding was bitter, and the riotous council meetings attracted large crowds desiring a diversion from the local taverns. Such wrangling, however, would lead to the demise of the borough in 1928.

In January of that year, a new borough administration assumed control, winning a slim four-to-three majority on the borough council. On gaining power, the new rulers fired the borough's two policemen and hired two replacements, Chief of Police Frank Tobasco and motorcycle officer Clyde Kearns.[61] Three weeks later the police issue again disrupted local politics when the mayor, W. T. Adams, found Tobasco and Kearns lounging in his office at one o'clock on Sunday morning. Adams ordered them to leave and either shoved or slapped Kearns, whereupon Kearns arrested Adams and asked Tobasco to lend him a blackjack to use on the mayor.[62] Adams then suspended Kearns, but the following Tuesday the police committee of the borough council ordered Kearns reinstated.[63] Then Adams again suspended Kearns, and the council again reinstated him; this was followed by another round of suspensions and reinstatements.[64] Adams argued that Kearns "has six indictments standing against him in the court house for hijacking, blackjacking, robbery and numerous other crimes and his picture is in the rogues gallery."[65] But the council ignored him.

Certain citizens, however, were fed up with such nonsense and now petitioned for annexation to Pittsburgh. The local suburban newspaper admitted that "unquestionably the political rottenness that has held sway... is causing more persons to lean towards annexation," and considering the district's "share of questionable office holders and peanut politicians ... you can't blame the citizens very much for wanting change."[66] Advocates of merger also argued that the tax "rate is exorbitant considering that the majority of the people are working people ... and only make an ordinary wage."[67] Admitting failure, even Adams and a majority of the borough councilmen signed the annexation petition. Hays had failed as a municipality, and in April 1928 a majority of the borough electorate chose union with Pittsburgh.[68] Thus the central city assumed responsibility for the municipal losers while the winners maintained their independence.

Meanwhile the city of Cleveland was harvesting its own crop of losers. During the early twentieth century Cleveland repeatedly failed to annex the large, well-to-do residential suburbs of Lakewood and East Cleveland, although it did absorb areas with few assets and great liabilities. In 1910 and 1922 Lakewood voted against merger proposals, and local residents claimed that "Lakewood now provides ample school facilities, police, fire, city planning, zoning, and sanitary protection to its inhabitants and uniformly good street paving and improvements."[69] Moreover, the municipality "is ready, able and willing to enlarge these facilities as the population increases, according to a standard of excellence which Cleveland cannot afford."[70] East Cleveland's residents opposed consolidation schemes in 1910 and 1916 "because our schools would be hurt by coming in contact with the Cleveland educational institutions" and "saloons might be established in East Cleveland also if we came into Cleveland, and we could not endure bar-rooms next to our homes."[71] For prosperous Lakewood and East Cleveland, union with the central city could offer few advantages and much danger in the form of saloon rule.

Smaller, less developed municipalities, however, continued to merge with the city of Cleveland. In 1912 the villages of Nottingham and New-burg both elected to join the central city in order to take advantage of its facilities. Leading the Nottingham annexation campaign were the village's municipal officers, individuals who recognized the village government's shortcomings. For fire protection Nottingham relied on a volunteer fire department with a "hose cart ... which citizens dragged to fires by hand."[72] Moreover, the mayor and council had discovered "that of the $8,000 raised by taxation, more than half went for what was called 'overhead charges', leaving only $3,000 or $4,000 for village improvements."[73] This was not enough, and village leaders realized that the only hope for adequate public services was through union with the city. Newburg also suffered from inadequate facilities, and village residents had been forced to pay tuition for the education of their children in Cleveland's public schools.[74] Furthermore, Newburg was not a neighborhood of which the Cleveland Chamber of Commerce could boast. Its chief business was the Luna Amusement Park, though Newburg's twenty-four saloons provided some employment and much recreation for village residents.[75] Moreover, the village was reputed to be the stronghold of the Socialist party in Cuyahoga County.[76] Instead of the fine schools, modern firefighting equipment, and paved streets of Lakewood and East Cleveland, the central city absorbed a mecca of saloons and Socialists, with roller coasters and sideshows but a shortage of educational institutions.

In 1922, however, annexationists won a major contest in the Cleveland region when the municipality of West Park chose to enter the city. West Park encompassed twelve square miles, much of it still rural. It had a heterogeneous population of middle-class whites, working-class Slavic immigrants, and a substantial poor black minority. In 1920 it had an average density of only one person per acre as compared to twelve per acre in Lakewood and fourteen per acre in East Cleveland, and its large tracts of undeveloped land would require expensive municipal improvements in the near future.[77] The suburb already suffered from a lack of streetcar transportation despite serious efforts by the suburban council to obtain extension of the Cleveland Railway Company lines. Annexationists argued "that by joining Cleveland, extensions of Cleveland car service could be obtained," and the promise of public transportation was the chief motive for merger.[78] In 1922 the city of Lakewood also voted on the annexation question. But Lakewood had streetcar service, and suburban municipalities only united with the central city to achieve necessary benefits.

Cleveland's last merger with a suburban municipality occurred in 1932, when it united with the village of Miles Heights. A working-class suburb with large foreign-born and black populations, Miles Heights had a government notorious for its corruption and incompetence. The village incorporated in 1927, and when the state auditor's office made its routine examination of municipal records and accounts the following year, it found "many errors in the payment of bills, the lax use of special funds for purposes other than those specified in the law; the collection of larger special assessments than were needed, ... the illegal transfer of the surplus to the sinking fund instead of returning it to the rightful property owners," and many other errors and questionable practices. [79] The auditor's report for 1929 revealed an even greater host of irregularities, and by 1930 the village leaders seemed dedicated to surpassing the venality of legendary Boss Tweed. Between 1928 and 1930 the mayor's salary rose from $600 to $2,000, the clerk's salary soared sevenfold from $500 to $3,400, and the assistant clerk's pay increased from $1,000 to $3,600. Moreover, the assistant clerk was the wife of the clerk, and brothers, cousins, and old friends constituted the bulk of the village's employees. [80] To pay for this chicanery, the council raised the tax rate from $1.96 in 1928 to $2.53 in 1930. [81] By 1932 the situation was intolerable, and residents voted to abandon autonomy and unite with Cleveland. If a municipality failed, the punishment was union with the central city, and Miles Heights, even more than West Park, Nottingham, and Newburg, was a decided failure.

Cleveland had made some notable acquisitions, but its conquests were fewer and less impressive than in the nineteenth century. Whereas before 1910 Cleveland annexationists had never lost a referendum battle, between 1910 and 1940 they won four and lost five, and the four that they won did not compensate for the losses. By 1930 West Park did include some of the finest residential tracts within the city, but these never rivaled the havens of suburban wealth. And Miles Heights could contribute almost nothing to the central city except problems. At the time of its annexation, all four of the inhabited census tracts in Miles Heights ranked below the central-city median in terms of value of homes and monthly rentals, and the most populous tract ranked 202d out of a total of 206 Cleveland census tracts in value of homes and rentals. [82] Few areas in the metropolis were as impoverished or as corrupt as Miles Heights, yet this was to be Cleveland's sole prize from the 1930s.

Urban boosters in the city of Milwaukee were conducting an even more ambitious annexation campaign than their counterparts in Cleveland. Milwaukee had absorbed only four square miles between 1900 and 1920, but in 1922 the annexation committee of the City Club of Milwaukee initiated an aggressive program to consolidate the governments within Milwaukee County. [83] Gradually, Milwaukee annexed a few hundred acres at a time, until by 1926 it had acquired 8.5 square miles, a 33 percent increase in area in four years. Among the chief acquisitions was an unattractive community with the appropriately unattractive name Piggsville. The streets of Piggsville resembled a hog wallow, and annexation would prove a definite advantage to residents in this outlying district. [84]

Aggressive Milwaukee leaders, however, envisioned greater gains; they sought total conquest of the county through consolidation of the city and county governments. In 1923 representatives of the city club appeared before the Wisconsin legislature to urge the appointment of a special committee to investigate unification of the Milwaukee metropolis. Although the legislature of 1925 complied with this request, [85] two years later the same legislative committee reported that consolidation of the entire county under one city government was impractical. [86] Consequently, the city of Milwaukee would have to absorb the suburbs bit by bit through the traditional annexation and consolidation procedure.

This procedure did not result in a harvest of the choicest suburban areas, however. The chief fruit of the campaign was the city of North Milwaukee, the municipal failure of the metropolitan area. In 1922 the people of this working-class community, with its drab rows of frame houses, had voted to enter the central city. Under Wisconsin law the suburban city council also had to approve consolidation and North Milwaukee's councilmen refused to do so. Yet merger efforts continued, for North Milwaukee's residents had ample reason for shedding their vaunted autonomy. The tax rate in North Milwaukee was 15 percent higher than in Milwaukee, the cost of water was 50 percent higher, and electricity cost 20 percent more. [87] Moreover, North Milwaukee had no high school, and parents had to send their children to Milwaukee schools and pay a tuition of approximately $80 a year. [88] Milwaukee also enjoyed garbage collection, street lighting and sewage systems that were superior to those in North Milwaukee. In addition, North Milwaukee lacked an attractive tax base. Although consolidationists observed that "we have been waiting for the development of the territory in and around North Milwaukee as a great industrial center," sadly "the boom never came." [89] The city of North Milwaukee, in other words, had little to offer the central city yet much to gain from merger. Consequently, in 1928 the suburb and central city joined, following the defeat of recalcitrant North Milwaukee officials.

In contrast, voters in the city of Wauwatosa and village of Whitefish

Bay defeated merger proposals decisively, and murmurs of consolidation ruffled the tranquillity of elite Shorewood only slightly. Both Whitefish Bay and Shorewood were havens for professionals and business executives whose homes lined the shores of Lake Michigan and who enjoyed lower tax rates than did residents of the central city. Wauwatosa was a middle-income dormitory with a controversial and archaic system of tax assessment and problems with water service. But the city of Wauwatosa generally fulfilled its civic functions, and annexationists lost in that municipality by a margin of three to one.[90] West Allis, South Milwaukee, and West Milwaukee all were heavily industrialized working-class communities that enjoyed tax revenues from giant manufacturing concerns such as Allis-Chalmers and Bucyrus-Erie. In none of these favored communities was there vigorous agitation for merger during the 1920s. Only in North Milwaukee, the municipality with the highest tax rates and the least prospects, and in areas such as Piggsville, did union with the central city appear attractive.

During the 1930s, Milwaukee boosters stepped up their campaign for further consolidation, trying again to win support for unification of the entire county. In January 1934 the Milwaukee City Council passed a resolution requesting passage of a constitutional amendment authorizing the consolidation of "all existing governmental units within the county into a single government."[91] And the Milwaukee County Board of Supervisors ordered an advisory referendum asking voters whether they "favor effecting ... consolidation of municipal service and governments in Milwaukee County."[92] Expansionists had taken the initiative, and now the electorate in all of the suburbs would be able to express their views on metropolitan union.

Though some proponents of consolidation claimed that the county should only assume certain limited municipal functions, suburban leaders viewed the proposal as a giant annexation scheme aimed at imposing central-city tyranny. The *Wauwatosa News* advised voters how to cast their ballots, warning: "Unless you want to pay higher taxes on a higher assessed valuation of your property; ... unless you are satisfied to have less voice in your government and give up the advantages you now enjoy, VOTE 'NO'!"[93] According to the Wauwatosa editor, "Consolidation will save money all right, but only for Milwaukee! The suburbs would pay and pay and pay for Milwaukee's delinquencies."[94] A "pioneer West Allis resident" argued that "we located our home outside of Milwaukee to better our living conditions and to obtain more comforts and lower taxes," and he did "not now care to yield to some fancy schemes Milwaukee has concocted."[95] The suburban *West Allis Star* claimed that "Milwaukee ... is faced with financial difficulties" and "with eyes of greed they look upon West Allis and other suburbs to pay their obligations and in return receive less service at a greater cost."[96] And the chief lobbying group for suburban interests, the Milwaukee County League of Municipalities, distributed a pamphlet that argued "a consolidation government would be far removed from the direct control of the people" and would be dominated by "boards, bureaus and commissions with armies of employes that would burden the people with taxes."[97] Throughout suburban Milwaukee the argument was the same. Consolidation would mean dictatorship by the central city, higher taxes, and reduced services.

Suburban voters believed these prophets of doom, and the outlying electorate in every suburb but one vetoed consolidation.[98] Milwaukee city voters, however, endorsed merger by an overwhelming margin, and central-city officials proceeded to present a plan for merger before the state legislature. The Socialist-dominated city administration asked for a constitutional amendment that "would authorize counties of over 500,000 population to consolidate all local governmental units into one county government."[99] According to the party's newspaper, "the Socialists favor complete city and county consolidation, but they do not look with favor upon piecemeal or functional consolidation."[100] But Wisconsin's rural-dominated Progressive party controlled the state legislature, and this group of dairy farmers traditionally had viewed schemes of metropolitan consolidation in much the same way as they regarded oleomargarine: city-county union would be a radical step that might threaten rural interests in the state by enhancing the power of Milwaukee. Consequently these Progressives squelched the Socialist plan and saved the suburbs. Between 1920 and 1940, Milwaukee was to annex eighteen square miles, but complete consolidation and absorption of the wealthiest residential and industrial areas remained an elusive goal.

To the west, the city of Los Angeles had achieved its greatest municipal conquests in the decade from 1910 to 1920, when it had absorbed the vast open spaces of the San Fernando Valley. Between 1920 and 1930 the city's expansion continued, albeit at a reduced pace, with the annexation of a number of areas thirsting for the city's water. The parched little municipalities of Sawtelle, Hyde Park, and Eagle Rock joined the city in 1922 and 1923, having failed to provide basic services to their residents. Moreover, Los Angeles acquired the unincorporated and uninhabited wilds of the Santa Monica Mountains, thereby adding little to the city's tax rolls. And in 1925 Los Angeles assumed responsibility for laundering dingy suburban morals when it merged with the amusement-park city of Venice. Suburban supporters of the merger believed that union was the only means by which to "drag, dear blessed Venice out of the gutter," and they looked forward to the application of Los Angeles's blue laws and an end to Sunday and all-night dancing along the Venetian amusement piers.[101] Foes of consolidation attacked Los Angeles as "that juggernaut monster neighbor of cannibalistic tendencies," ignoring the rampant corruption of Venice's government and the recent theft of municipal funds by the Venice city treasurer.[102] The majority of the Venetian citizenry, however, sided with the cause of righteousness, so that Los Angeles was able to absorb the suburb and assume the heavy cost and burden of policing its nightspots.

Meanwhile, the central city was consummating a marriage with that grimy collection of cheap bungalows known as the city of Watts. Divided by constant political bickering, Watts's leaders believed that merger was the only solution to the municipality's problems. Lacking any tax base, the lower-class community had struggled to survive, but in 1926 Watts's voters, with the approval of the municipal board of trustees, chose by a margin of two to one to enter the central city.[103]

Finally, in 1927 Los Angeles joined with still another problem community, the municipality of Barnes City. This community was the winter quarters of the Al G. Barnes Circus, which opposed merger because of fears that Los Angeles would outlaw elephants within the city limits. Many local residents, however, favored union as a means of ridding their suburb of menageries and sideshow freaks. These consolidationists proved victorious, and Los Angeles inherited the dilemma of disposing of the circus.[104]

Meanwhile, in 1923 that developing haven of movie stars and millionaires, Beverly Hills, defeated a merger proposal. In Beverly Hills Douglas Fairbanks, Mary Pickford, Tom Mix, Rudolph Valentino, Harold Lloyd, Will Rogers, and Conrad Nagel all joined hands to defeat annexation, thereby guarding against Los Angeles's higher tax rates while preserving the Beverly Hills police force with its tolerant attitude toward stellar peccadillos. Supporters of annexation envied Los Angeles's supply of water, and one real estate man claimed that "there's more water in the swimming pool at Pickfair than I have on two large tracts I can't sell."[105] But swashbuckler Fairbanks retorted that annexation "is the most serious crisis we've ever faced" and rallied the forces in favor of independence.[106] Ranged against the celluloid heroes of bunkhouse, boudoir, and shipboard, the lowly real estate men had little hope for success, and Beverly Hills's residents voted 507 to 337 against consolidation.[107] Thirty-six years later a grateful suburb would remember the efforts of cinema's separatists and erect a monument "in tribute to those celebrities of the motion picture industry who worked so valiantly for the preservation of Beverly Hills as a separate municipality."[108]

In 1924 the large and prosperous suburb of Santa Monica also rebuffed a merger attempt, and the suburbs of Burbank and Alhambra did likewise. Los Angeles was still expanding, but its conquests were the problem children of the metropolis. Dance halls, elephant pens, and shacks cluttered the newly annexed regions of the city, while the mansions of Beverly Hills as well as the heavy industries of suburban Vernon remained beyond the city's limits.

Throughout the nation the story was the same. Akron annexed Kenmore, a community that "has hobbled along on crutches from year to year so far as its financial setup has been concerned" and that devoted 65 percent of its city budget to debt payments.[109] Columbus, Ohio, annexed East Columbus at a time when 38 percent of the suburb's residents were on relief.[110] And Spokane annexed Hillyard, a municipality torn by labor strife but almost devoid of taxable industrial property.[111] In contrast, Akron failed to acquire the tax resources of Barberton or Cuyahoga Falls; voters in the gilded residential suburb of Upper Arlington voted ten to one against union with Columbus; and the tax-rich Great Northern Railway Shops remained beyond the grasp of the city of Spokane. In Ohio and Washington, in Pennsylvania and California, the central city was a magnet attracting the bankrupt, the troubled, and the needy, all those that could cost the city much and offer little in return.

Though Chicago, Pittsburgh, Cleveland, Milwaukee, and Los Angeles may not have formed the most advantageous unions, at least they were still gaining territory. They were growing at a reduced rate, but they were growing. Central cities such as Boston and Saint Louis failed to expand at all, and during the 1920s these aging urban centers sought desperately to force some municipal marriages. In the minds of urban boosters in the city club and chamber of commerce a higher rank in the census figures meant more business, increased business meant growth, and growth meant prosperity. Boston and Saint Louis, which did not conform to this model, seemed in danger of slipping behind their sister cities. Thus, city leaders in both Boston and Saint Louis appealed to their state legislatures for a means to consolidate the metropolis, but in neither case were expansionists to achieve their ends.

After its 1912 merger with suburban Hyde Park, Boston failed to annex any new territory. Fearing a humiliating decline in population rank in the upcoming federal census, Boston's Mayor Andrew Peters in 1919 sent the first of a series of petitions to the Massachusetts legislature asking for the annexation of surrounding cities and towns and the creation of a "Greater Boston."[112] Mayor James Curley continued Peters's efforts in the 1920s, petitioning "for the consolidation into one municipality of all cities and towns lying wholly or partly within ten miles of the State House." Petition followed petition, with Curley asking for merger legislation in 1923, 1924, 1925, and 1926.[113] But Massachusetts lawmakers failed to respond to the requests, and Curley's reputation as a seamy political boss did not aid the cause of consolidation.

In Missouri, Saint Louis expansionists were more successful in winning the cooperation of the state. Missouri's constitution of 1875 had granted the city of Saint Louis extensive home rule powers, but it had made no provision for annexation to home-rule cities. Consequently, the alteration of the municipality's boundaries required a constitutional amendment. The Missouri Constitutional Convention of 1922 drafted an amendment that would allow annexation of sections of suburban Saint Louis County, but voters defeated the proposal in a statewide referendum. Another annexation amendment appeared on the state ballot in November 1924, and this time Missouri's electorate approved a procedure for adjusting the boundaries of Saint Louis City and adjoining Saint Louis County. Under this scheme, a board of freeholders composed of nine members from the city and nine from the county would propose a plan for altering the boundaries and submit the plan to the voters of city and county for approval by both.

In 1926, after a period of deadlock, the board submitted a scheme for the consolidation of the city and the entire county into one giant municipality of 553 square miles. The suburban Saint Louis County Chamber of Commerce quickly attacked "the centralization of municipal authority over tremendous areas," arguing that "local self government has always been the keystone of American institutions."[114] The *St. Louis County Leader,* published in suburban Clayton, warned of increased taxes and claimed that central-city politicians "are grasping at the straw of 'County and City Consolidation' to save them from drowning in the gaping gulf of ever increasing annual deficits in their city budget."[115] In the suburb of Maplewood the local newspaper called the plan "so preposterous ... that we cannot see how any fair-minded citizen could conscientiously support it."[116] And in Webster Groves the local editor concluded that the suburb "would stand to gain absolutely nothing from such a plan" but only suffer through the invasion of immoral influences dedicated to establishing "saloons, soft drink parlors, pool rooms, dance halls and this type of undesirable so-called amusements."[117] Saint Louis County officials reinforced this editorial assault, and Probate Judge Sam Hodgdon conducted a long campaign to arouse suburbanites to the threat facing them. During the constitutional amendment battle of 1924 he had asked: "If you were willing ... to sacrifice the flower of young American manhood to preserve the sovereignty of Belgium and France, will you not do as much for your own people in St. Louis County?"[118] In 1926 he repeated this theme, evoking memories of the Kaiser as he recalled "we sacrificed our men and money to preserve local self-government for Belgium and France."[119] Big-city Huns were preparing to violate the frontier between city and county, and the county chamber of commerce, the suburban newspapers, and Hodgdon were all issuing calls to arms.

In the ensuing election battle, the city suffered serious defeat. County voters chose by a margin of two to one to reject the plan. The proposal carried only 30 of the 126 precincts in the county, suffering the worst defeat in the outlying farm areas. The rural Kassebaum precinct voted 274 to 1 against the scheme, and the farm precinct of Melrose cast 202 ballots against the plan and 1 for it.[120] County farmers had no desire to pay for the sewers and streets of the expanding metropolis, and thus they would not approve the creation of an imperial Saint Louis.

Urban leaders faced similar problems in the western city of Portland, Oregon, where the annexation of outlying territory had almost ceased after 1915. In 1925 Oregon's legislature authorized creation of a commission to study unification of governments in the Portland area, and two years later the commission recommended a constitutional amendment allowing consolidation of Portland and Multnomah County. The legislature approved such an amendment, but as in Missouri, the state's voters had to ratify any addition to the constitution. The reform-minded Portland City Club failed to raise sufficient funds to pay for a statewide publicity campaign, and the proposed amendment lost by a vote of 57,613 to 41,309. The next legislature refused to reconsider the question, and Portland was not to absorb another inch of territory until 1948.[121] Elsewhere similarly ambitious schemes for a "Greater Atlanta" or a "Greater Newark" failed as the prospects for central-city expansion dimmed.

Yet in many cities those concerned with the problems of metropolitan rule were not willing to abandon hopes for government unification. The traditional procedures of annexation and consolidation had failed, but such procedures were products of the nineteenth century and suited to a nineteenth-century world. By the 1920s voters were no longer sanctioning consolidation schemes as readily as in earlier decades, for the central cities no longer enjoyed such an advantage in municipal services. Special districts and counties were providing services formerly reserved to major cities, and the suburban municipality had expanded its range of responsibilities and raised its level of performance. Those suburban municipalities that still proved incompetent were the ones that succumbed to central-city ambitions. But these limited acquisitions did not satisfy central-city boosters. Fearful of stagnation, chamber of commerce leaders demanded growth no matter the consequences. Growth, however, seemed increasingly difficult. If the central city was to continue expanding, a new solution to the problem of boundary adjustment would be needed. During the 1920s and 1930s it took the form of fresh efforts by suburban leaders to cement the metropolitan fragments.

6

THE FEDERATIVE
METROPOLIS

Nineteenth-century annexation procedures had failed to unite the metropolis, and by the 1920s American urban leaders were searching for an alternative. In a nation dedicated to popular consent, lawmakers could not readily discard the firmly established principle of local self-determination and reimpose a system of forcible annexation. Yet Oak Park, Wauwatosa, Webster Groves, and Beverly Hills firmly refused to sacrifice their independence for the sake of urban unity. How, then, could Americans achieve metropolitan cooperation? How could Cleveland improve its census rank and eliminate the waste of overlapping areas of authority while satisfying separatists in Lakewood, East Cleveland, and every other suburb? How could Americans reconcile the conflicting desires for central-city expansion and local self-rule? Americans of the 1920s idolized bigness and growth, and they conceived of stagnation as a sin. But they also revered the supposed intimacy of small-town or suburban neighborhood government. They were devotees of particularism in their segregated society, but they were also worshipers of size. They had imperial dreams and parochial desires. The problem was to fashion a new form of government that both satisfied these grandiose ambitions and allayed fears of amalgamation.

To discover a solution to this dilemma, metropolitan leaders turned to the British experience. The British long had struggled with the problem of fragmentation in the great London metropolis, but in 1888 they created the London County Council and adopted a scheme that encompassed both metropolitan cooperation and neighborhood self-government. The 117-square-mile county of London contained twenty-eight boroughs, each of which exercised authority over a wide range of subjects including local street improvements, street lighting, garbage collection, public libraries, local parks, and the registration of vital statistics. Superimposed on this collection of separate municipalities was the London County Council, a body authorized to deal with those metropolitan problems that the boroughs could not handle individually. For example, the council was responsible for the metropolitan sewage system, for drainage within the metropolitan area, and for public health care. A dual-level, federative system thus existed with power shared between the neighborhood units and an overarching metropolitan agency. The borough of Kensington and the city of Westminster each had their own mayors and aldermen with all the ceremonial trappings so characteristic of the British municipality. But both were within the domain of the London County Council and participated in the cooperative federation that governed Britain's greatest city.[1]

Such a scheme appealed to many of the twentieth-century Americans who sought a reconciliation between city and suburb. This federative or borough plan imposed some unity on the metropolis without compromising the integrity of suburban governments. Lakewood could survive, but Cleveland could expand; Wilkinsburg could remain Wilkinsburg, but Pittsburgh could rise from eighth place in population to fourth. Suburban neighborhoods would not abdicate all governmental authority and merge into the vast and politically undifferentiated mass of the central city. But the central city would not choke in a noose of suburban municipalities. The plan would allow diversity within union, and would satisfy the American passion for bigness and the equally American devotion to government that remained close to the people. It would perpetuate the segregated pattern of American society and government while imposing some degree of integration.

As early as the 1890s Massachusetts lawmakers were investigating and debating the merits of dual-level metropolitan rule. Between 1889 and 1895 the Massachusetts legislature established three state agencies to handle metropolitan problems: one to govern sewage disposal in the Boston metropolitan area, another for the supply of water to the district, and a third to supervise the development of a metropolitan park system. This makeshift response did not appeal to some who favored home rule and the unification of local authorities rather than state interference and a proliferation of agencies. Consequently, the legislature appointed a special metropolitan commission to investigate the possibility of restructuring the government of the Boston area. In 1896 this commission recommended the creation of a county council for the Boston region similar to London's County Council. Metropolitan area voters would elect this Greater Boston Council, which was to assume responsibility for water, sewage, and the metropolitan park system. Moreover, the commissioners expected the metropolitan county eventually to maintain major traffic arteries and to provide public transportation for the metropolis. Services of a purely local nature, those which did not demand uniform regulations, were to remain the responsibility of the twenty-nine municipalities constituting the metropolitan county.[2] The Massachusetts commissioners sought some means for uniting a badly fragmented urban area, and they believed that London's county council scheme provided the answer.

Leaders in suburban Boston differed in their responses to the plan. Most seemed hostile, and according to the *Boston Herald*, politicians viewed the metropolitan county plan "as something so foreign to current methods and habits of thought as to be out of the question." The mayor of Lynn considered the scheme a giant annexation plot and announced that he believed "in Lynn remaining Lynn." Nahant's chairman of the board of selectmen labeled it "an outrage," while a "well known gentleman" in Dedham "regarded the plan as Utopian" and said that there "will be time enough to talk about creating a metropolitan county twenty-five years hence." Leaders in Arlington, Brookline, Newton, and Wakefield could perceive few advantages to this plan, but in Chelsea, Malden, Melrose, and Waltham officials backed the proposal. Waltham's mayor claimed that "the formation of such a county would be for the better management of the water, sewer and park departments," and a Melrose leader believed that the plan would result in "a more perfect highway system, and all metropolitan systems could be worked out more advantageously with a great saving in cost to all cities and towns interested."[3] Yet the majority of the suburban politicos seemed to fear the scheme even though the *Boston Herald* assured them that "they would carry on their local governments under their city and town names precisely as they have . . . in the past, except that in county matters they would act in common with those municipalities where their interests are nearest allied."[4]

State lawmakers were also less than enthusiastic about this innovative and imaginative scheme. Consequently, year after year the legislature's Committee on Metropolitan Affairs postponed any decision concerning the recommendation, until in 1906 the Massachusetts House of Representatives finally defeated a bill creating a Metropolitan Boston Council. In 1919 the state's legislators did, however, consolidate the metropolitan park, sewage, and water commissions to form the Metropolitan District Commission, a body of five commissioners appointed by the governor for five-year terms. But this metropolitan agency was in fact a state agency, not a new form of local government or a new model of municipal rule. It was an example of the central authorities intervening and assuming responsibility for metropolitan problems in the absence of any local agency capable of performing the task.

Elsewhere, Americans continued to search for a solution that did not entail state intervention and control. The Greater New York Charter of 1897 created the five boroughs of the Bronx, Manhattan, Brooklyn, Richmond, and Queens, but borough officials had only minimal power and this was not a federative plan like that of London or the one proposed for Boston. Each borough elected a borough president who had the right to a seat on the city's board of public improvement and could vote on matters before the board that solely affected his particular borough. The borough president also presided over the borough's local improvement boards, although these boards could only recommend that the city make certain improvements on the streets or other public works. The actual initiation of such projects was the responsibility of the central city government. Each borough did retain a separate board of education, and these boards were the only borough agencies capable of formulating and implementing policy. In areas other than education, borough government was at best advisory and at worst nonexistent. In fact, the boroughs exercised almost no power under the charter of 1897, for this feigned decentralization was merely a mild concession to local sentiment.

Some felt true decentralization was necessary in the newly consolidated metropolis and urged changes in the charter. The editors of the *Outlook* claimed that "consolidation tends to weaken the sense of public responsibility on the part of the individual citizen, and tends to lessen his knowledge of and interest in public affairs." They argued that "for these reasons, the largest possible borough independence ought to be guarded as carefully as the largest possible independence for cities and commonwealths."[5] The Charter Revision Commission, appointed by Governor Theodore Roosevelt in 1900, also felt a need for some redistribution of responsibility. The counsel to the commission observed that the boroughs were "faring badly under the centralized local government" and were "sadly in need of local improvements and couldn't get them."[6]

Responding to these complaints, in 1901 the state legislature approved charter amendments that revised the powers of borough officers. The powers of some borough officers were enhanced; others were diminished. Still the result in no way resembled a federative scheme of rule. Under the revised charter, the borough presidents became submayors who supervised building inspection and all work on streets, sewers, and public buildings within their particular boroughs. Moreover, the local improvement boards could initiate all street and sewer schemes financed by local assessments. Each of the borough presidents was also a member of the most powerful policymaking body in the city, the Board of Estimate and Apportionment, and each could vote on all issues before that board and not simply on those issues that dealt exclusively with his own boroughs. Yet the revisions of 1901 abolished the borough boards of education, placing complete control of schooling instead under a central board appointed by the mayor. As Mayor Robert Van Wyck of New York City observed, the charter revisions of 1901 created borough presidents who "are in every sense of the word commissioners of public works" while the city superintendent of schools "is made an autocrat."[7]

The amendments of 1901, then, provided some administrative decentralization with some borough supervision of street and sewer construction. But there was no division of responsibility as there would have been under a federal system. Under such a system the local unit would enjoy complete authority over certain local services while a metropolitan government would administer a limited number of functions best handled on a regional scale. Boroughs did exist in Greater New York, but they were not semiautonomous units of local government united in a metropolitan federation. There was no Brooklyn city council or Bronx borough council comparable to the surviving Westminster city council or Kensington borough council in metropolitan London. In 1930, metropolitan reformers concluded of the New York plan that "centralization was carried so far and borough autonomy allowed so restricted a sphere as to make the scheme inconsistent with true principles of federalism."[8] Thus, New York City's scheme of partial dispersion of administrative responsibility was no solution to the split between city and suburb, for this type of sop to localism could not satisfy suburbs jealous of their independent authority. The borough schemes of 1897 and 1901 were neither innovative nor imaginative enough to serve as models for metropolitan reform.

A federative system may not have existed in New York City, but other expanding cities of the early twentieth century continued to consider means for dividing power within the metropolis. For example, in 1909, when Los Angeles attempted to consolidate with the harbor cities of Wilmington and San Pedro, the city amended its charter to permit the creation of borough governments in "territory hereafter annexed."[9] Supposedly separatists in Wilmington and San Pedro would be able to take advantage of this provision, thus retaining some degree of self-government under the suzerainty of the city of Los Angeles. Each borough would elect five trustees who were to constitute the government of the borough. This arrangement was seemingly validated in 1911 by an amendment to the California state constitution. The amendment stipulated that a city charter might "provide for the division of the city . . . into boroughs or districts, and . . . provide that each such borough or district may exercise . . . general or special municipal powers."[10] Seemingly, then, cities in the state of California could embark on programs of decentralization that might result in federative rule such as existed in London.

In fact, when residents in the Wilmington district of Los Angeles petitioned for borough status, they confronted unexpected difficulties. When the City Council of Los Angeles would not authorize an election on the borough question in the Wilmington district, Wilmington residents appealed to the judiciary. In 1917, however, the Supreme Court of California ruled against the Wilmington residents, claiming that "the Constitution is undoubtedly opposed to a system extending the right of borough government to a part of the territory of the city and denying it to another portion." If borough government was to exist, the entire city would have to be divided into boroughs. According to the California Supreme Court, the state constitution "provides that borough government when established shall extend over all." Thus the court invalidated the Los Angeles charter provision that would have allowed Wilmington to enjoy borough rule while maintaining centralized government in the remainder of the city.[11]

Massachusetts, New York, and California had failed to implement any truly federative scheme. Nowhere, prior to 1920, had Americans approximated the federative plan of London by creating a broad-purpose metropolitan municipality that combined cooperation and local autonomy. Both city leaders and state legislators in New York and Massachusetts had regarded the London model as too unorthodox, too alien to the American tradition of unitary urban rule. Consequently, they had rejected notions of federative government. Suburbanites, on the other hand, increasingly were rejecting the idea of unitary consolidation, and coerced union was no longer possible under the American system of law. Faced with this dilemma, many retained an interest in a new format for metropolitan rule, although prior to 1920 the traditional structure of government prevailed.

By the 1920s, however, enthusiasm for a federative plan was mounting, and few seized upon this scheme more quickly than did the growing congregation of municipal management experts who worshiped regularly before the altar of efficiency. The cult of efficiency had grown rapidly during the early twentieth century as business leaders, reform politicians, and political scientists realized that one could apply the modern, efficient, rational methods of a smooth-running business to the municipality. Those who admired the assembly-line world of Henry Ford and believed economy to be the highest virtue shuddered when confronted with the overlapping authorities, duplication of efforts, and makeshift, haphazard organization of the metropolis. They spoke not of the right to local self-determination but of economies of scale. They viewed municipal government not as an instrument to satisfy the whims of the local populace, but as a provider of necessary services. The municipality sold water just as the A&P sold groceries, and it built sewers and streets just as the real estate developer built houses and skyscrapers. Why, then, should not the city operate as efficiently and with as much business acumen as the chain store or the builder? Government was a business, and the essence of a successful business was economy and efficiency.

This dedication to economy and efficiency dated from the last decades of the nineteenth century, and it gained momentum rapidly during the years prior to World War I. As early as 1882, the young Theodore Roosevelt organized a reform club in New York City dedicated to electing men "who will administer their offices on business principles."[12] Two years later Roosevelt would write of the need to conduct "the business of the city according to the rules of common honesty and efficiency."[13] Meanwhile, the mayor of Brooklyn, Seth Low, was attempting to achieve this business-like efficiency in urban administration, and he collected the laurels of reform-minded advocates of good government throughout the nation.

Municipal efficiency assumed the status of a science in the early twentieth century as businessmen sought to apply Frederick W. Taylor's theories of scientific management not only to the factory but also to the city hall. Efficiency experts introduced uniform accounting procedures, time sheets and efficiency records for personnel, centralized purchasing, standardization of salaries, and all the other accouterments of rational business administration. But perhaps the most notable product of the efficiency crusade was the city manager plan, a plan whereby a professional administrator would manage the city and its public services instead of elected amateurs. During the 1920s, the city manager crusade rose to a peak of fervor as such major cities as Cleveland, Kansas City, and Cincinnati chose to adopt city manager plans and citizens in Minneapolis, Saint Paul, and Seattle voted on manager schemes. In the business-oriented 1920s, efficiency and professionalism assumed a sacred aura as urban leaders sought to apply business know-how to the municipal corporation.

This crusade for efficiency appealed most strongly to the nation's business leaders and to the upper-middle class of America's cities who wanted better services and lower taxes. As early as 1894, a group of leading businessmen in New York City, including Cornelius Vanderbilt and J. P. Morgan, urged the election of a municipal government that would act "solely in the interests of efficiency and economy."[14] Railroad magnate E. H. Harriman was a staunch financial backer of research on the question of municipal efficiency, and his wife endowed the first school to train professional public administrators. The founder of the city manager movement was Richard Childs, son of the millionaire manufacturer of Bon Ami Cleanser. John H. Patterson, head of the National Cash Register Company, was responsible for the adoption of city manager government in Dayton, Ohio, the first major American city to attempt the scheme. By the 1920s the Mellon family was willing to sponsor any good-government reform in the Pittsburgh area that did not threaten the position of their beloved Republican party. George Eastman, the plutocratic founder of Eastman Kodak, provided the impetus for city manager reform in Rochester, New York.

Moreover, the well-to-do, white-collar neighborhoods housing the professionals and business leaders voted most strongly in support of city manager plans and other efficiency reforms. In the 1920s the middle-class south side of Kansas City ardently supported a city manager plan.[15] In the Seattle referendum of 1925, the middle-class districts of Madrona, University, Ravenna, North Broadway, and Montlake led the city in support of city manager government.[16] Likewise, the following year in Minneapolis, the white-collar, middle-class wards were bastions of support for the city manager plan.[17] Throughout the 1920s it was the middle-class, white-collar wards in Cleveland that provided the votes in favor of city manager rule.[18] Efficiency reform became a fetish of members of the white-collar middle-class who abhorred the traditional corruption and supposed waste of city government and who long had tinkered with the municipal mechanism in the hope of creating a smooth-running operation. The middle class admired order, rationality, and economy, and the fragmentation of the metropolis offended their sense of order just as much as the chicanery and favoritism of the political machine did. If these members of the middle class lived in the suburbs, a sentimental devotion to their hometown, the economic consideration of lower taxes, and a fondness for exclusionary zoning ordinances might temper their enthusiasm for a rational scheme of metropolitan consolidation. But their orderly, rational minds would have to admit that the haphazard, helter-skelter pattern of suburban rule was unsatisfactory, and that something needed to be done.

Throughout the nation the public-spirited, white-collar citizenry sponsored organizations that sought to achieve the twin ideals of economy and efficiency. In 1897 Cleveland residents formed the Citizens League to lead the struggle for honest, orderly, and thrifty government. To the north, the Detroit Bureau of Government Research confronted the nightmarish tangle of governmental authorities in Michigan's largest metropolis. The Chicago Bureau of Public Efficiency fought the battle for cheaper but better government in Cook County, and in 1917 it published a study of the area's political fragmentation.[19] Californians devoted considerable effort to the subject as well, with the Tax Payer's Association of California seeking some reorganization of the Los Angeles metropolis as early as 1917.[20] Moreover, by the 1920s the Tax Association of Alameda County had initiated a campaign to merge Oakland, Berkeley, Alameda, and a scattering of lesser municipalities into one efficient whole. In almost every major city the local chamber of commerce turned its attention to the happy prospect of businesslike public administration. Prominent business leaders organized the Civic Club of Allegheny County to aid in the reform of Pittsburgh, the United Taxpayers League in Milwaukee, and the Commonwealth Club of California to promote enlightened, economical rule in San Francisco. During the 1920s America's greatest success appeared to be in the realm of business, and city government seemed its greatest failure. The solution was, then, to apply business know-how to the sick cities, thereby eradicating the debilitating effects of the fragmented metropolis.

Consolidation of the metropolis under one government seemed the best means to achieve economy and efficiency, and devotees of efficient government strongly backed efforts to achieve city-county consolidation in Saint Louis, Milwaukee, Portland, and elsewhere. Faced with suburban obstinacy, however, those favoring metropolitan reorganization soon realized that compromise was necessary. Consolidation proposals repeatedly faced defeat as suburbanites clung devotedly to their small municipal units, dreading the day that Oak Park, Whitefish Bay, or Beverly Hills would lose its separate identity and sink into oblivion. If it was to win the favor of suburban voters, the new metropolitan scheme needed to preserve the identities of the suburbs and to allow them to exercise some governmental authority. The dual-level system of metropolitan rule thus seemed the most viable alternative, for it satisfied both the traditional sentiments of localism and separatism and the twentieth-century demands for efficient administration.

No one recognized the merits of the federal structure more clearly than did the leading metropolitan reformer of the 1920s, Thomas H. Reed. Reed had impeccable credentials as a good-government reformer. He was the member of an old Boston family, a graduate of Harvard, former attorney for the New York State Anti-Saloon League, executive secretary to California's progressive Governor Hiram Johnson, past city manager of San Jose, California, and then professor of municipal government first at the University of California and later at University of Michigan. He was a man of strong moral convictions, a Congregationalist, Progressive Republican, anti-saloon leaguer, and a man devoted to efficient, economical government. In pursuit of this goal, he dedicated forty years of his life to service as the traveling salesman of metropolitan government. In 1921-22, he led the effort to establish a dual-level borough structure in Oakland's Alameda County. Later in the 1920s, he was director of research and resident expert for the Pennsylvania Commission to Study Municipal Consolidation in Allegheny County, and immediately following the failure of this Pittsburgh effort he rushed to assume a similar post with the City and County Metropolitan Development Committee in Saint Louis. In 1930 he assisted in drafting a plan for unification of the governments of metropolitan Boston, and eight years later he headed a project that recommended reorganization of the government of Atlanta and its suburbs. From Massachusetts to California, Reed crusaded for a new form of urban rule to unify and coordinate public services in the metropolitan areas.

Year after year Reed preached the gospel of metropolitan reform before dentists, druggists, and housewives in the suburbs of San Francisco, Saint Louis, or Pittsburgh, repeating his arguments in the pages of professional journals read by political science professors, city managers, and urban planners. Time after time he told his listeners and readers of the need "to conceive of local government in terms of larger units." Yet he reminded them that they "must not forget that there is in metropolitan regions ... a great diversity of conditions which makes the centralization of all the local government powers in one authority ... financially and administratively unfortunate." Reed admitted that dual-level structures "retain too much governmental overhead" but "they do ... provide recognition for the rights and interests of existing population groups and have been considered more feasible from the point of view of placating the spirit of local patriotism."[21] Each political fragment within the metropolis had its particular interests that needed to be recognized. Consolidated rule may have been cheaper, but it did not take into account the diverse interests of the various fragments. Federative rule, on the other hand, did. The federal plan was not a perfect medicine to heal the shattered metropolis, but at least it was sugar-coated with the spirit of particularism and possibly acceptable to the American palate.

Political science professors, professional civic reformers, efficiency experts, and the faithful followers of the good-government cause all, then, turned to the federative scheme as a means of approaching their goal of maximum quality services at minimum cost. They had worked together for the adoption of city manager rule, and the London County Council plan now pointed the way to a still more perfect government. Reformers had been modeling and remodeling municipal charters for decades as their dedication to economy and efficiency mounted. Now they sought to apply their ideas on a metropolitan scale.

This innovative compromise between localism and unification also appealed to another vital segment of the metropolitan population, the suburban commuter. Businessmen living in posh Mount Lebanon and working in downtown Pittsburgh, lawyers with homes in University City and offices in Saint Louis, and industralists having mansions in Shaker Heights and plants in Cleveland all suffered from metropolitan schizophrenia. They regarded themselves as hailing from Pittsburgh, Saint Louis, or Cleveland and were proud boosters of these cities. They belonged to the local city club and chamber of commerce, and they abhorred the idea that their city might drop from the seventh largest in the nation to the eighth or from eighth to ninth. They were devotees of civic reform in the central city and were members of central-city clubs that sought to achieve economy and efficiency in government. Since they worked, shopped, and spent the better part of their lives in the central city, they could not ignore its problems. During the 1930s approximately 80 percent of the employed residents of East Cleveland, Lakewood, and Shaker Heights worked in the central city of Cleveland, while only 11 percent of the gainfully employed citizens of University City worked in that Saint Louis suburb. The average resident of the Cleveland suburbs shopped at a downtown department store once a week, and seventy percent maintained their bank accounts at central-city banks rather than suburban institutions.[22] Earning, spending, and saving were all functions the suburbanite performed in the central city, and this urban core dominated a segment of his or her varied life.

Yet the suburbanite's home, church, and schools were in the outlying municipality, and this community commanded loyalties too. Commuters were fond of their well-governed, well-planned dormitory towns and not eager to witness the invasion of big-city bootleggers, tax collectors, or greedy developers dedicated to lowering the status of their communities through construction of cheap dwellings. Commuters were loyal to the central city but protective of the suburb. They believed that merger implied efficiency and were dedicated to this modern idol. Yet they also remained attached to the local fragment. These suburbanites sought the best of both worlds, and the dual-level federal scheme seemed an admirable solution to the schizoid dilemma.

America's leading expert on suburbia during the 1920s, Harlan Douglass, emphasized this dual loyalty in his classic study, *The Suburban Trend*. Douglass was himself a devoted suburbanite living in Upper Montclair, New Jersey, and he knew from experience the "excessively bifocal type of civilization" of suburb and city. According to Douglass, suburban commuters suffered from split personalities because their "social loyalties are divided, and run in opposite directions." "Man works in the city with half of his will and loves it with half his heart" but "the other half he reserves for the suburbs."[23] The central-city business leader who lived in the suburbs wanted the central city to grow, but did not want to abandon suburban autonomy. The central city would stagnate and decline if there were no expansion, yet destruction of the suburb with its excellent schools and immaculate planning was a dire prospect. Given these divided loyalties, the white-collar commuter needed some means of social reintegration. And federative metropolitan rule provided this means without destroying the protected status of the suburb. It would preserve the particularism cherished by so many suburbanites yet satisfy the white-collar commuter's central-city boosterism.

Suburban residents, moreover, realized that cooperative metropolitan efforts might well upgrade the quality of life in the suburbs. Many suburbs still suffered problems with sewage, water, or fire protection, and the creation of metropolitan parks, transit systems, and highways was beyond the capacity of any single suburb. Recreation and roads were increasingly vital to the affluent suburban automobile owner, who hoped the local government would provide wooded preserves and well-paved parkways for leisure time enjoyment. Likewise, real estate developers urged the extension of municipal services to unincorporated tracts so that they could proceed with the development and sale of these lands. The 1920s were a boom era, and considerable money might be made if government could be lured into servicing remote speculative subdivisions. In metropolitan areas throughout the nation, most suburbanites believed that their governments performed adequately. They certainly did not want to replace them with boss rule by the central cities. But the suburban governments had not yet attained perfection, and some believed that federative metropolitan rule might offer advantages that traditional units could not supply.

This was especially true in areas where special-purpose metropolitan authorities did not yet exist to deal with the individual problems of servicing the metropolis and where county governments were relatively limited in function. For example, in 1930 the states of Pennsylvania and Missouri had not yet created any metropolitan authorities in their major urban areas; in both the Pittsburgh and Saint Louis areas suburbanites relied on the traditional municipal and township governments for services. Moreover, neither Allegheny County, Pennsylvania, nor Saint Louis County, Missouri, were among the vanguard of counties that were assuming municipal functions at a rapid rate. Suburban Saint Louis suffered serious sewage problems, and the disposal of waste in the streams of Saint Louis County was an issue that involved every one of the multitude of political units lying along those streams. Similarly, suburban Pittsburgh needed a system of highways to link city and suburb, but the needed metropolitan highways would cut across city and township lines and involve municipalities throughout the metropolis. Suburbanites needed action, and in those areas where special-purpose metropolitan districts were not yet a reality and county government was old-fashioned, a federative plan seemed especially desirable. The federative scheme would permit the central city to aid the suburbs in achieving better highways and sewers, yet the central city would not interfere with those services that were superior in the suburbs or with those laws that reinforced social segregation. The central city would not intervene in the government of the admirable suburban schools or compromise the local zoning ordinances of exclusive suburbia, but it would provide help where help was needed. Federation thus offered the advantages but not the disadvantages of consolidation.

Consequently, in metropolitan areas across the country, white-collar suburbanites initiated the struggle to achieve dual-level government, and they remained the strongest supporters of the plan. Before men such as Thomas Reed were even called into the fray, business leaders and professionals from the suburbs were campaigning for metropolitan rule of the type existing in London. Among the strongest supporters of federation were many suburbanites who had fought bitterly the earlier attempts to annex the suburbs to the central city. Although they had opposed consolidation with a unitary municipal mammoth, federation seemed appealing, for federation would preserve the suburb as a separate governmental entity while not depriving the city of its just census rank or the metropolitan population of better services at a lower cost. Federation would maintain many of the defenses of particularism but achieve many of the rewards of imperialism. Many suburbanites, including some who long had jousted with the central city, now turned to federation as an attractive alternative to either consolidation or chaos.

In Pittsburgh, for example, a long-time opponent of central-city annexation schemes, Joseph T. Miller, assumed leadership of the crusade for federative metropolitan rule. Miller was the model businessman in the age of Babbitt. He was a Republican, a Presbyterian, a resident of fashionable Edgewood, a member of the Edgewood Club, and in 1921 he attained the summit of fraternal glory, serving as national president of Sigma Chi. He retired each evening to a neat neocolonial home on an emerald green plot on tree-lined Maple Avenue. But during the day he was an executive with the Mellon-owned Pennsylvania Water Company, a company that sold water primarily to Pittsburgh's suburban municipalities. Thus, his prosperity depended on the continued existence of the suburbs, and in 1911 he was one of the organizers of the League of Boroughs, Townships and Cities of the Third Class of Allegheny County, a group dedicated to defending suburbia from the expansionist policies of the city of Pittsburgh. He served first as assistant secretary of the league, later as secretary, and finally as president, winning a reputation as the suburb's most valiant defender.[24]

However, Joseph Miller was not simply a nay-sayer, a man devoted to preventing change. In 1923 the governor of Pennsylvania appointed him to a commission dedicated to studying metropolitan consolidation in Pittsburgh's Allegheny County. This appointment launched his career as the architect of Pittsburgh's borough plan for decentralized municipal rule. For the next fifteen years, until his death in 1938, he was the unquestioned leader of the struggle for metropolitan reform. Following his premature retirement in 1929 from the Pennsylvania Water Company, metropolitan reorganization became his primary focus of endeavor. He wrote on the subject for the *National Municipal Review* and the *American Political Science Review*, attempting to explain how "the vast problems of the greater community may be rightly solved" while "the essential needs of the individual communities are protected."[25] Miller believed that the metropolitan voter need not choose simply between separatism and consolidation. Instead, there was a middle way that preserved the parts while benefiting the whole.

Miller's colleagues on the metropolitan government commission were primarily suburbanites of a similar persuasion. Only five of the twenty-four commission members resided in Pittsburgh, and fifteen of the members were active in Miller's League of Boroughs and Townships. Like Miller, they had long fought centralized, consolidated rule. Now, in the 1920s, they presented a new alternative for governing the Pittsburgh metropolis.

In the Cleveland area, suburban residents also led the campaign for dual-level metropolitan rule. Their number included some who, like Miller, had fought previous annexation attempts. For example, in 1922 a real estate agent named William Greenlund helped draft the Lakewood Chamber of Commerce's lengthy report attacking merger with Cleveland.[26] By 1930, however, this Lakewood resident had assumed chairmanship of the Fact Finding Committee of the Regional Government Committee of 400 and was arguing the case for federative metropolitan rule in the pages of the *National Municipal Review*. The following year he served in the Ohio Senate, where he introduced a measure that would permit the dual-level scheme of government in Cuyahoga County. According to Greenlund, he and likeminded citizens sought to "grant certain outstanding metropolitan functions to a central county government" while allowing "the municipalities, large and small, to retain local functions and powers."[27]

Suburban residents also dominated the Citizens League of Cleveland and led its campaign for the adoption of dual-level metropolitan government. During the period from 1930 to 1932, when the League campaigned most vigorously for the creation of a federative metropolis, thirty-six of the forty-nine persons serving on the league's executive board were residents of suburban municipalities. As is shown in table 7, the city of Cleveland Heights dominated the board, while only thirteen members were residents of the central city of Cleveland. Two of the four presidents of the league during these years were from Cleveland Heights

TABLE 7.   Residence of Members of Citizens League Executive Board, 1930–32

Cleveland Heights	23
Cleveland	13
Shaker Heights	9
Lakewood	2
Bratenahl	2

SOURCES: Cleveland City Directories for 1930 and 1932

and two were from Cleveland.[28] The Citizens League, like so many good-government groups, expressed the attitudes of concerned citizens living in fashionable suburbs like Cleveland Heights and Shaker Heights. It spoke for the suburban elite rather than for the central-city electorate, and during the 1920s and 1930s this suburban elite was dedicated to dual-level metropolitan rule as a means for unifying the metropolis and achieving economical, efficient government.

No one opposed fragmented metropolitan rule more vehemently than the League's director, Mayo Fesler, a resident of the city of Shaker Heights. Fesler was a dour, stiff-collared, bespectacled gentleman from a small town in Indiana. He had attended a small Methodist college in his native state and had pursued graduate studies at the University of Chicago. After a short stint at teaching, he accepted a position as secretary of the Cleveland Citizens League, and he devoted the remainder of his life to the cause of good government.[29] He despised waste and corruption, and worked tirelessly for "relief from the duplicating and overlapping political subdivisions in the county which now elect a total of 899 officials every four years."[30] From his Cleveland Citizens League office he waged war on suburban officialdom, but each evening he returned to his home in suburban Shaker Heights.

Meanwhile, in the Saint Louis region, suburbanites also were in the forefront of the campaign for a federative metropolis. In early 1926, when the Board of Freeholders was debating whether Saint Louis County should unite with the city of Saint Louis, two county members on the board introduced federal schemes of metropolitan union. Webster Grove's city attorney, Robert A. Roessel, suggested "the creation of a metropolitan area ... with a super-governing body over the entire area, vested with supreme authority in those problems which affect the welfare of the whole area," and county representative Clarence Shotwell proposed a similar plan.[31] But the city faction insisted on a consolidation scheme that would perpetuate the traditional centralized municipality. When the consolidation scheme appeared on the ballot in the autumn of 1926, Roessel and like-minded backers of the federal scheme bitterly opposed such a single-level municipal giant. Before an audience in suburban Kirkwood, Roessel claimed that, "it is a recognized fact in municipal government ... that as our cities grow in size their administration becomes less economical, less efficient and less honest." In support of his argument he pointed to "the very recent and shocking scandals that have besmirched many of our large American cities." According to Roessel, "the overgrowth and overdevelopment of our cities is the sorest spot in American government," and he and a majority of the other suburban voters refused to further this evil through the creation of a bloated municipality of more than five hundred square miles.[32]

Two of Roessel's staunchest allies in the attack on consolidated rule were Joseph Matthews of suburban Kirkwood and George W. Stephens of Webster Groves. Matthews was president of the Corno Mills Company, makers of "Three Minute Oat Flakes," "Three Minute Wheat Flakes," and "Three Minute Hominy Grits Flaked." He also served as director of Saint Louis's largest bank and was generally representative of the metropolitan business elite. Stephens, on the other hand, was a native of Wapello, Iowa. He had earned a doctoral degree from the University of Wisconsin and, since 1919, had served as professor of economics at Washington University in suburban Clayton. In 1926, as vice president of the Committee Opposed to Annexation, Matthews campaigned vigorously against "this plan of merger which is bad and unfair for both city and county."[33] Professor Stephens, the brains behind the antiannexation effort, blasted the merger scheme because "it seeks to bring under a common jurisdiction communities and groups whose interests and needs are by no means identical."[34] Roessel, Matthews, and Stephens all agreed that the giant consolidated municipality was a grotesque product of greedy imaginations in the central city. This municipal gargantuan would strip suburbanites of governmental authority, leave them politically impotent, then violate their interests and ignore their needs.

Once the consolidation scheme had suffered defeat, however, these suburbanites rallied in support of a borough plan of metropolitan rule. The Saint Louis County Chamber of Commerce had attacked the 1926 merger scheme sharply, but it went onto sponsor the committee that drafted the dual-level federative scheme in 1929 and 1930. The chairman of this committee was Robert Roessel, and he, together with Thomas Reed, was primarily responsible for authoring the innovative plan. Professor Stephens served as vice chairman of the campaign committee for adoption of the federal proposal, while Joseph Matthews acted as the committee's treasurer. Like Joseph Miller and William Greenlund, Roessel, Stephens, and Matthews were not simply obstructionists dedicated to preserving suburban particularism at the expense of the central city. Instead, they were metropolitan reformers who sought to create a new form of urban rule that allowed neighborhood rule within a structure of regional cooperation. They were innovators, not isolationists. The old tradition of urban rule seemed to be failing, and the alternative they proposed might satisfy the suburban electorate as well as voters in the central city.

In Milwaukee too, suburbanites proposed adoption of a federative plan, but central-city officials discarded their suggestions. The village attorney of fashionable Shorewood, Charles Hammersley, spoke publicly against consolidation with Milwaukee, advocating instead a dual-level scheme that guaranteed "absolute autonomy to the separate municipal units on local questions."[35] Yet the supervisor of annexation for the city of Milwaukee recommended "that the citizens of Milwaukee County oppose any plan providing for the establishment of the borough plan ... as being a makeshift method of partial unification." Under such a scheme, he argued, "the large number of needless officials in control of our suburban governments would retain their jobs," and the ills of fragmentation would remain.[36] Recognizing this, Milwaukee city officials advocated nothing less than total consolidation, and the Shorewood solicitor's comments resulted in no action.

Along the Pacific coast, however, business leaders from the suburbs were more successful in drawing support for a borough plan of metropolitan rule. In 1923 the Three Cities Chamber of Commerce representing the fashionable suburbs of Burlingame, Hillsborough, and San Mateo first proposed the amalgamation of San Francisco and San Mateo Counties under a borough plan of government. According to the chamber president, "San Francisco must have added area" while development of San Mateo County could benefit from "the larger finances of a larger city."[37] The chamber believed "that something must be done to improve our local system of government if we are to progress as we should," and they looked forward to the development of a deep water harbor at San Mateo and to the growth of local industry once San Francisco applied its public monies to the county's problems.[38] In suburban Redwood City, the local newspaper also called for cooperative union with the central city, and the Menlo Park Chamber of Commerce added its voice to the growing chorus praising the virtues of mutual endeavor for city and suburb.[39] According to these San Mateo County boosters, both central city and suburbs would profit from the scheme, with one acquiring room for growth and an opportunity for a higher census rank and the other obtaining city funds for the development of transportation facilities, a water supply, and other vital public services.

The Three Cities Chamber of Commerce realized, however, "that a great many people in San Mateo county are opposed to annexation," and thus it refused to accept a system of centralized, consolidated municipal rule. Instead, the chamber promised that it "will insist that the local communities affected by the annexation move be allowed to maintain their independence, and for that reason we have directed the committee to work out a borough system of government."[40] Some were not satisfied with such assurances, and the mayor of Burlingame asserted that "unless I become convinced that the borough system will not take from us our rights and privileges, I am opposed to the annexation."[41] If San Francisco and San Mateo were to unite, the unification scheme would have to ensure true local autonomy for the suburban regions. Otherwise Burlingame's mayor and like-minded individuals would mobilize their forces in opposition to the proposal.

San Mateo's campaign for federative rule proceeded at an irregular pace for the next nine years until finally it sputtered to a halt in 1932, before the issue could be presented to county voters.[42] In the Pittsburgh, Cleveland, and Saint Louis areas, however, men like Thomas Reed, Joseph Miller, William Greenlund, Mayo Fesler, Robert Roessel, and Joseph Matthews persisted in their efforts to reorder urban government. There the suburban electorate would have an opportunity to express its judgment. But frequently these good-government reformers and metropolitan-minded suburbanites faced opposition from suburban officials fearful of losing their jobs. Thus civil war broke out in the suburbs, with political scientists, waterworks executives, real estate agents, and cereal manufacturers banding together in the cause of metropolitan reform.

During the ensuing struggle, suburbia would prove not to be a bastion of myopic middle-class commuters opposed to change or to any link with the central city. Mount Lebanon, Cleveland Heights, and University City were not stuck in a mire of complacent apathy. Instead, these suburbs and their white-collar residents led the forces of change, the forces dedicated to remodeling America's urban governments. Suburbanites sought a compromise between the fragmentation of the suburban ring and the unitary rule of the central city. They wanted to integrate the segregated metropolis through federation, not to mongrelize American life through the miscegenation of consolidated rule. They opposed both annexation and total amalgamation because each threatened the advantages derived from suburban independence. But they welcomed central-city growth and believed that the much-vaunted goal of efficiency would result from unification. Faced with this dilemma, suburban reformers turned to London's experience as a middle way that would satisfy both the central-city boosterism of commuters and the persistent suburban desire for a neighborhood autonomy. Throughout the nation, many of those who previously had fought annexation schemes began trying to create a new tradition of metropolitan government, and during the 1920s and early 1930s the Pittsburgh, Cleveland, and Saint Louis areas would become the scenes of their greatest efforts.

7

METROPOLITAN REFORM AND THE STATE

In November 1928, voters along Philadelphia's Main Line, in the coal towns of the Lehigh Valley, and from the farms of Lancaster County all entered their polling booths and voted on a scheme of metropolitan government for Pittsburgh. Two years later Missourians from the Ozarks, Kansas City, and Saint Joseph determined the future of metropolitan rule in Saint Louis. And in 1933 Ohioans from Cincinnati to Toledo and from Youngstown to Dayton cast ballots on the question of creating a dual-level federative structure in Cleveland's Cuyahoga County. In Pennsylvania, Missouri, and Ohio men like Joseph T. Miller, Robert Roessel, William Greenlund, and Mayo Fesler were striving to reorder the traditional pattern of urban rule. In doing so, each had had to battle complex procedural webs, for in each state a new mode of urban government required a state constitutional amendment. This in turn meant a long contest in the legislature, a costly referendum contest, and approval by state voters who were hundreds of miles from the metropolitan region, ignorant of urban problems, and intolerant of anything that smelled of big-city politics. The battle for metropolitan reconciliation had to be fought not only in Allegheny, Saint Louis, and Cuyahoga counties but throughout the states of Pennsylvania, Missouri, and Ohio. And voters in Slippery Rock, Bald Knob, and Pee Pee Township might well decide the fates of Greater Pittsburgh, Greater Saint Louis, and Greater Cleveland.

Metropolitan reformers began their battles for statewide sanction with skirmishes in the legislatures. The sovereign states were responsible for the legal structure of the local governments, and state lawmakers played a major role in any attempt to reform metropolitan rule. In the capitol chambers of Harrisburg and Columbus, reformers first presented their innovative schemes for union, and in the assembly halls they first faced the challenges of their foes.

The legislative battle for a federative scheme in the Pittsburgh region began in 1919, when State Senator W. W. Mearkle of Pittsburgh introduced a bill to create a "municipal division board" for Allegheny County. Mearkle's measure called for the establishment of a weak metropolitan board that would be denied powers of taxation but was to be dedicated to achieving "harmonious relations between the different municipal corporations" within Allegheny County and promoting "the establishment of a uniform system of municipal improvement" throughout the county.[1] It was a toothless proposal; the board was to rely on persuasion and voluntary cooperation in its efforts to promote metropolitan unity. Backers of the bill assured suburbanites that the creation of the municipal division board would not "affect in any form or manner the political governments of the different municipalities," but the suspicious spokesman of the League of Boroughs and Townships believed creation of the board would mean the "gobbling up by Pittsburgh of all the other municipalities and townships in Allegheny."[2] Joseph Miller and his colleagues at this point were unwilling to consider any plan that proposed a redistribution of power within the metropolitan area, especially when the scheme emanated from representatives of the expansionist city of Pittsburgh. The Pennsylvania Senate shared the league's doubts, and the measure suffered a quick and easy defeat.

This, however, was just the beginning, for Pittsburgh's urban boosters were dedicated to improving the city's census rank through annexation of the entire county. In 1919 the Pittsburgh Chamber of Commerce established a special committee on city and borough relations aimed at achieving "the cultivation of a spirit of civic unity between the city proper and the citizens of suburban communities in Allegheny county."[3] Pittsburgh's population would more than double if the city absorbed the entire county, and chamber members recognized that Cleveland, Detroit, and even Los Angeles were about to outpace Pittsburgh in the upcoming census. Something had to be done. By the summer of 1920 the Chamber of Commerce urged that "there must be some detailed plan evolved without delay so that it can be ready for presentation to the Legislature next January."[4]

The reform-minded Civic Club of Allegheny County was also eager to achieve some form of metropolitan union. In 1920 club president Alexander Dunbar drafted his own plan of federative rule, a plan that included a metropolitan government responsible for regional planning, major thoroughfares, and the public health and safety of the metropolis. The individual boroughs, cities, and townships would continue to exercise all other functions of local government, and big-city expansionists would not violate suburban autonomy. Again the scheme was unacceptable to the League of Boroughs and Townships, and league president Joseph Miller spearheaded a publicity campaign against the Dunbar proposal.[5]

But the wave of enthusiasm for reform was rising, and prospects of Pittsburgh becoming the fourth largest city in the nation stirred the passions of local boosters. Consequently, the metropolitan question reappeared before the state legislature in 1923, amid demands for action. Faced with new proposals for the creation of a metropolitan district, Miller and his suburban league introduced their own substitute measure calling upon the governor "to appoint a commission of twenty-four persons, sixteen of whom shall be residents of boroughs and townships . . . to study the subject of consolidation of the various municipalities."[6] Mayor William Magee of Pittsburgh agreed to back this compromise stance, and it easily passed the legislature and received the governor's signature.

Due to the bill's apportionment of members among cities, boroughs, and townships, suburban borough and township leaders dominated the newly created investigating commission. Consequently, the suburban members were able to elect Joseph Miller chairman, and the commission's report largely would reflect the views of this staunch suburbanite. In 1925 the commission recommended passage of a constitutional amendment that would permit the creation of a single municipality encompassing all of Allegheny County. Within this county-wide municipality, the existing cities, boroughs, and townships "would still control their local affairs," for the suburban-dominated commission believed that in small municipalities "there is less tendency to mass inertia," for citizens are "not stupified into inaction by the mere immensity of organization."[7] Pennsylvania's constitution required that any constitutional amendment receive the approval of two consecutive legislatures and then the sanction of the state's voters. It was a lengthy process, but with luck Greater Pittsburgh would exist in time to achieve fourth place in the 1930 census.

Miller's scheme suffered a setback, however, when in 1925 the commission's proposed amendment died in committee. But Miller was not willing to abandon his efforts; he now turned for aid and advice to Professor Thomas Reed of the University of Michigan, a man who spurred the suburban leader's zeal for metropolitan reform. Consequently, Miller was prepared to act quickly when Pennsylvania's governor called a special session of the legislature in 1926. He arranged for a Pittsburgh senator to introduce the proposed amendment once again, and he lobbied vigorously for its passage, collaring every lawmaker bound for Harrisburg.

Miller's proposed amendment of 1926 was more detailed than that of the previous year. The amendment authorized the legislature to draft a charter uniting the governmental units within Allegheny County and creating a new municipal corporation known as the City of Pittsburgh. This giant municipality would exercise the powers and duties that belonged traditionally to the county and to the local poor districts; it would also exercise other powers as specified by the legislature. A popularly elected board of commissioners would govern the municipality, and it would enjoy the authority to create special districts within the county for the construction or maintenance of public improvements benefiting more than one of the constituent boroughs, cities, or townships. To forestall burdensome taxation of unimproved and rural lands in sprawling Allegheny County, Miller's amendment also authorized the classification of real estate as urban, suburban, and rural, with a separate system of assessment for each. The traditional municipalities would continue to exercise all powers not specifically delegated to the metropolitan unit and would retain their separate governmental identities.[8] It was, then, a dual-level plan designed to appeal to the schizoid loyalties of suburbanites like Miller.

While attempting to win legislative endorsement of this plan, Miller first jousted with his chief adversary in the metropolitan dispute, Senator William Mansfield from Pittsburgh's industrial suburb of McKeesport. Mansfield was the editor and publisher of the *McKeesport Daily News* and a loyal and devoted resident of the largest working-class suburb along the Monongahela River. McKeesport claimed a population of fifty-two thousand, 40 percent of whom were immigrant Slavs and Italians; the suburb also enjoyed the title "Tinplate Capital of the World." It was the type of sooty, grimy town that was giving the Pittsburgh area a bad reputation throughout the nation. Yet Mansfield was dedicated to preserving its autonomy and to thwarting the dangerous reforms sponsored by Pittsburgh business leaders and by residents in the more attractive residential suburbs such as Miller's Edgewood.

Mansfield was a member of the Senate Judiciary Committee, the committee assigned to examine the proposed constitutional amendment. While the measure was in committee, Mansfield insisted on amending the provision that provided for voter approval of the metropolitan charter. Miller's proposal had required that a majority of voters in a majority of the governmental units of Allegheny County approve the charter of the new metropolitan municipality. Now Mansfield succeeded in changing this requirement to a majority of voters in two-thirds of the county's cities, boroughs, and townships. Mansfield felt that it was too late to scuttle the constitutional amendment, but he was dedicated to making the task of metropolitan reform as difficult as possible.

There followed an unfortunate mix-up that further raised the barriers to change. Through either an error by the state printer, or chicanery by

Senator Mansfield, or confusion among the reformers, the phrase "two-thirds" was inserted in the proposed amendment so that it read "a two-thirds majority ... in each of at least a majority of all the cities, boroughs, and townships" rather than "a majority in each of at least two-thirds" of the governmental units.[9] Thus, when the amendment finally passed the state senate and house of representatives, it required a two-to-one vote in favor of the new metropolitan scheme in each of a majority of the 123 units within Allegheny County. Only through a landslide victory among suburban voters would metropolitan reorganization succeed.

But Miller and his colleagues were willing to accept the challenge posed by the revised amendment, and they continued to rally support for federative metropolitan rule. In the spring of 1926 Miller struck at the heart of the enemy forces by mailing post cards lauding the scheme to forty-five hundred confirmed opponents of county-wide unification. Moreover, he began an ambitious speaking campaign throughout Allegheny County, addressing women's luncheons, Rotary Club meetings, fraternal lodges, the prestigious Pittsburgh Chamber of Commerce, and the less distinguished Board of Trade in the puny suburb of Etna. Miller's metropolitan commission distributed five thousand copies of a pamphlet describing its recommendations, and Pittsburgh newspapers spread the metropolitan gospel as preached by Joseph Miller. In 1927, the Pennsylvania legislature quickly approved the proposed amendment for the second time, as required by the constitution. Now Miller and the metropolitan scheme faced a statewide referendum.

While Miller was hustling his plan through the legislative chambers of Harrisburg, reformers in Cleveland were fighting much the same battle in Ohio's state house. As early as 1917, Cleveland's reform-minded Citizens League submitted to the Ohio legislature a constitutional amendment "permitting the consolidation of city and county governments in counties of more than 100,000 population." The proposal would have allowed the creation of unitary county-wide municipalities, but it included no provision for a dual-level system.[10]

Ohio's lawmakers showed little interest in the Citizens League's scheme, but at each succeeding biennial session Cleveland's reformers badgered representatives in Columbus with further plans for metropolitan amalgamation. In 1919 the Citizens League submitted a new amendment proposal that again authorized city-county consolidation yet provided that the unified cities and counties might establish "boroughs or assessment districts as may be most convenient and equitable."[11] Then, in 1921, this same group submitted a more detailed amendment proposing a borough scheme of government.[12] And in 1923, 1925, and 1927 still other plans for metropolitan government appeared before Ohio's lawmakers.[13] Each of these reform measures, however, faced defeat either in legislative committees or on the floor of the general assembly.

The Citizens League's legislative battle of 1927 was representative of its futile efforts in Columbus. During that session, the Special Committee on Taxation, headed by Chester Bolton from Cleveland's suburb of Lyndhurst and John Dempsey of suburban Bratenahl, reported to the general assembly on the waste in Ohio's scheme of local government and recommended consolidation of units in metropolitan areas. Representative John A. Hadden of suburban Cleveland Heights responded to this suggestion by introducing the Citizens League amendment that provided for a borough plan of federative metropolitan rule.[14] Since the proposal required a reorganization of Cuyahoga County government, it was referred to the rural-dominated house committee on county affairs. Present at the committee-hearings was a full array of reform foes, including the law director, engineer, and mayor of suburban Lakewood; the city manager and solicitor of Cleveland Heights; a representative of the East Cleveland Kiwanis Club; and the mayor of the Cincinnati suburb of Norwood. These enemies of amalgamation claimed that the federal scheme was simply "sugar-coated annexation" and "that the good old American System of county government, so sage and sane for years, is still good enough." Committee members attacked the amendment proposal because "the Citizens League didn't consult farm organizations," "the people of Ohio hadn't asked for this," and "it would cost too much to print the [referendum] ballots."[15] After a three-hour argument in which Lakewood's law director and a Citizens League attorney "hurled irony at each other," the County Affairs Committee voted to pigeonhole the proposal. Five farmer-legislators combined with two small-town representatives and two lawmakers from Toledo and Cincinnati to block the reorganization of metropolitan Ohio.[16]

Faced with massive resistance from suburban officials and rural Ohioans, the metropolitan reformers recognized the need for a fresh strategy. Consequently, they sought an alliance with the state's chief farm organizations, the Ohio State Grange and the Ohio Farm Bureau Federation, and with the state's leading business association, the Ohio Chamber of Commerce. Though the Citizens League, the Grange, the Farm Bureau, and the Chamber of Commerce represented widely varying interests, they shared a common belief in efficient and economical government. Grange leaders were dedicated to lowering rural taxes, while the Chamber of Commerce yearned for reduced tax rates in the city, and the Citizens League's constant goal was clean, streamlined government that would be functional, efficient, and without waste or excessive expenditure. Duplication of governmental efforts and the overlap of government agencies were horrors to each of these groups, and they joined efforts to form a committee to study the reform of local government in Ohio.

The Grange and the Farm Bureau, however, would not conspire to destroy the right of local self-government, nor would they tolerate any schemes for the creation of monolithic municipal giants. Grange leaders argued that "if this is to remain a government of, for and by the people, then government must be kept reasonably close to the people."[17] Thus the Grange representative who chaired the statewide committee insisted "that the proposed constitutional amendment provide that no township or municipality give up any of its powers of local government until its electorate votes to do so at an election."[18] If the fragmented units in Cuyahoga County or any other populous Ohio county were to merge, then they must do so only with the consent of the voters in outlying regions. Farmers along the rural periphery of Cuyahoga County were not to become city folks unless they chose to be.

Consequently, the committee recommended a complex procedure for achieving a dual-level federative government, a procedure that would in large measure protect the interests of metropolitan minorities. According to the proposed scheme, any county, whether large or small, could revise its structure of government simply by drafting and adopting a county charter. General laws governing county organization would not apply to these charter counties, and this proposal would thus allow a diversity of government arrangements and creation of local structures tailored to local conditions. Moreover, any county having at least one million inhabitants could organize as a municipal corporation, with the county charter specifying what municipal powers were to be exercised by the county-wide municipality. Cuyahoga County could then create a metropolitan government similar to the London County Council, preserving existing units while facilitating cooperation and regional coordination. But Cuyahoga County could only establish itself as a municipality if the metropolitan charter won the approval of voters in Cleveland, voters in the county outside Cleveland, voters in the county at large, and voters in "a majority of the combined total of municipalities and townships" within the county boundaries. To achieve metropolitan rule, reformers would have to jump four electoral hurdles, winning the support of the entire county, the central city, the suburbs as a whole, and a majority of the fifty-nine cities, villages, and townships. It was an awesome challenge, but such a system of concurrent majorities momentarily allayed Grange and Farm Bureau fears of forcible amalgamation.[19]

With the powerful backing of the state's leading civic, commercial, and farm organizations, reformers submitted this proposed amendment to the Ohio legislature during the session of 1931. Leading the legislative struggle in favor of the reform were two state senators from the suburbs,

William Greenlund of Lakewood and Robert Taft from Cincinnati's suburb of Indian Hill. Throughout the 1920s, Taft had been the leading legislative spokesman for Ohio's cities, having served as chairman of the House Committee on Cities. His younger brother Charles Taft II assumed leadership of the statewide publicity campaign for local government reorganization, and his wife was a trustee and active leader of the Ohio League of Women Voters, a group that would rally enthusiastically behind the cause of metropolitan reform. Metropolitan reorganization was thus becoming a family project of Ohio's most distinguished political dynasty.

Foes of reform, however, were not willing to defer to such political thoroughbreds as the Tafts, and they quickly massed their forces in Columbus. Leading the opposition was the Association of Township Trustees, a group dedicated to preserving township government and township officialdom. The association warned in its literature that Greenlund's measure "will set up a one-man control in county government . . . and will take away from us our great American heritage of local self-government."[20] Allied with the township trustees were the state's gravel dealers, who profited from the construction and maintenance of gravel township roads. According to the statehouse correspondent for the *Cincinnati Enquirer*, "Less stringent regulation for purchase and less intimate knowledge of the market on the part of the township officials are said to provide advantage to the gravel interests in that they ofttimes . . . can sell at a higher price than obtainable in cities where prices and agreements are subjected to more searching scrutiny."[21] And uniting with the gravel dealers and township leaders were those resolute opponents of change, the suburban officials. The Local Self Government League of Cuyahoga County, an organization representing officials in forty-nine suburban political units, formally denounced the borough plan, claiming that "this proposed amendment originated in a small group of theoretical uplifters in the city of Cleveland" who were attempting "to force upon citizens of Cuyahoga County some untried and impractical form" of government "which would result in the loss of self-identity and local self-government . . . in suburban towns and cities."[22] Suburban mayors, like rural trustees, had not assumed office in order to preside over the dissolution of their domains. Thus they did not intend to compromise the autonomy of their municipalities by entering into suspect alliances with the rapacious central city.

Among the most outspoken critics to appear before the Senate committee considering metropolitan reform were Robert Roehm, solicitor for the Cleveland suburbs of Solon, University Heights, Chagrin Falls, Maple Heights, and Bentleyville; and Mayor Harry Baker of suburban Norwood. Roehm sarcastically attacked big-city government and referred to a recent scandal that resulted in the sentencing of three Cleveland councilmen to the Ohio penitentiary in Columbus. Amid "a roar of laughter," Roehm shouted, "We don't want a glorified city government; we had three City Councilmen who qualified before a grand jury for entry into one of your large institutions here."[23] Baker seconded Roehm's statements and insisted that "the seat of government should be kept where the people walk." Moreover, Baker insulted Senator Taft when he turned his back on Taft while the senator was questioning him, and "it was several minutes before Taft, flushed in face, composed himself or made effort to redirect his inquiry."[24] Suburban officials were defiant, and the Republican Mayor Baker was even willing to enrage a major Republican leader from his own county.

Many appeared before the senate committee to counteract the propaganda of Baker and Roehm. Charles Taft II "discoursed for nearly a half hour on the subject, voicing firm faith in the bill and its ability to coordinate powers and functions of local government."[25] Among the other supporters present were representatives of the Ohio Chamber of Commerce and the Ohio League of Women Voters as well as Mayo Fesler and the chairman of the Citizens League's committee on regional government, Isidor Grossman of Shaker Heights. Together with the Tafts, these champions of reform sought to sell the idea of local government reorganization by speaking of the effectiveness of "business in government" and of the need to apply business efficiency to county rule.[26]

The Tafts and Greenlund won senate approval of the amendment, but the measure still faced a contest in the house. Again the contestants met for battle at a legislative hearing. Robert Roehm appealed to the house County Affairs Committee to protect Cuyahoga County farmers and to "keep them from being swallowed up by the city slickers."[27] The solicitor of Cleveland Heights argued that "there is no need for this amendment to the constitution," for "if it is true the sentiment in the suburbs is for annexation, all they have to do is to circulate petitions."[28] And the solicitor of Euclid and Cuyahoga Heights presented a similar position.[29] The Chamber of Commerce and the Citizens League countered, and William Greenlund attempted to assure the anxious suburban officials that "you are not going to lose your jobs; don't worry about that."[30] Greenlund's rhetoric, however, had little impact, and the house committee voted nine to one to shelve the proposed amendment. All the rural members and the antireform representatives of Cincinnati's Republican machine voted against the proposal; only Representative Schumacher of Cleveland voted for it.

Though the Grange, the Chamber of Commerce, the Tafts, the League of Women Voters, the Citizens League, and a score of other economy-minded good-government groups supported the proposed amendment, the legislature had again refused to act positively. It had responded instead to the arguments of rural and suburban officialdom, of Cincinnati machine hacks, and of the gravel interests. Repeatedly the state's lawmakers had failed to respond to the pleas of metropolitan reformers; the rural-dominated general assembly even failed to accept a proposal fashioned in large measure by the grand master of the Ohio State Grange and by the legislative agent of the Ohio Farm Bureau. The scheme was new and untested and was still associated with suspect big-city interests and impractical good-government dreamers. Consequently, it was not yet palatable to the unimaginative Columbus solons.

Frustrated with the legislature, reformers now adopted an alternate plan of action. In Ohio a proposed amendment could win a place on the ballot without legislative approval if at least ten percent of the state's voters signed a petition asking for submission of the amendment to the general electorate. Thus, in 1932, a committee that included former Secretary of War Newton Baker of Cleveland, Charles Taft II, and former president of Ohio State University, William Oxley Thompson, began circulating a petition asking that the county reorganization scheme presented to the 1931 legislature appear on the ballot. Ohio's League of Women Voters and the Ohio Business and Professional Women's Clubs solicited signatures for the proposal as did a variety of civic groups in Cleveland and throughout the state. The League of Women Voters organized a Special Committee on County Government, and, according to the League president, "every local League was asked to appoint a member to this Committee, and in addition there were four district chairmen appointed so that throughout the campaign there might be a very close organization." The special committee's chairwoman, Mrs. Walter Schaeffer of Dayton, "spent long hours at home preparing instructions to guide the campaign and before the end of August had visited practically every League in the State to lend them the inspiration of her own enthusiasm and advise with them." Those local chapters that did not share Mrs. Schaeffer's enthusiasm suffered retribution, and in June 1932 the board of directors of the state League voted "that action be taken toward withdrawal of recognition of the Akron League" because its members "were not willing to cooperate" in the amendment campaign.[31]

While Ohio's women were collecting signatures, Grange leaders were shying away from the reform measure which seemed so beneficial to Cleveland and to the state's other urban areas. In June 1932 the Grange's chief lobbyist in Columbus stated that "it was not probable that state officials of the farm organizations will take either affirmative or negative action as to the proposed amendment." Yet within the next month, the Grange Executive Committee "unanimously voted to disapprove the amendment in its present form," arguing that the measure "would deprive certain local units of power without their consent."[32]

Despite the collapse of the shaky alliance with agriculture, the reformers were finally to win a victory as they gathered sufficient signatures to ensure a vote on the issue in November 1933. After sixteen years of study, debate, and campaigning, Ohio's electorate was to decide the future of the fragmented metropolis. Civic reformers successfully had bypassed obstructionists in the state legislature, and now they faced a major referendum battle.

Meanwhile, in Missouri, reformers were struggling with the same issues and problems as their brethren in Ohio and Pennsylvania. In 1926, during the campaign to establish a single unitary government for the city and county of Saint Louis, suburban leaders had proposed dual-level federative schemes. Following the defeat of the consolidation plan, leaders in both the city and the suburbs were eager to consider a borough structure. At the meeting of the National Municipal League in Saint Louis in November 1926, Professor Thomas Reed enhanced local interest in the London County Council model by reading a paper on "Dual Government for Metropolitan Regions."[33] And the Chambers of Commerce in both city and county soon agreed to establish a City and County Metropolitan Development Committee headed by Webster Groves's solicitor, Robert Roessel, and aided by the ever-present Professor Reed who had just completed his duties as research director for the Pittsburgh metropolitan commission. The Industrial Club of Saint Louis appropriated $30,000 for an investigation of the metropolitan problem, and Roessel and Reed embarked on their campaign to refashion the government of Saint Louis.

The Metropolitan Development Committee drafted a lengthy constitutional amendment that authorized Saint Louis City and Saint Louis County to draft a municipal charter for the creation of the "City of Greater Saint Louis." This proposed amendment, however, guaranteed that the existing municipalities would retain their separate identities and that each would be known as a municipal district of Greater Saint Louis. Moreover, the municipal districts would continue to exercise all those functions that the metropolitan charter did not grant to the enlarged city. The amendment did not specify the duties of the metropolitan government, but Roessel told suburban audiences that the greater city government would probably "take over the parks and playgrounds ..., take over all sewer problems," and "assume the health work, taking over all hospitals and the sanitarium."[34] Whatever its duties, it would never be able to extinguish the governments of Webster Groves, University City, and Clayton nor would it deprive the suburbanite of his grass-roots democracy.

Roessel and his colleagues now had to place this scheme on the state-wide ballot, and they wisely chose to do so through the petition procedure as employed in Ohio. The Saint Louis reformers sought to avoid a prolonged battle in the legislature, and in 1928 they organized the Citizens Committee of 1,000 that would circulate the necessary petitions, place the proposal on the ballot, and then seek the support of the state's voters. Heading this vital Citizen's Committee was Eugene Ruth, president of the Saint Louis County Chamber of Commerce and mayor of University City.

Ruth and his workers were able to collect a sufficient number of signatures for the proposal to be placed before the electorate in November 1930. Now the alliterative trio of Reed, Ruth, and Roessel had to convince voters from the Arkansas border to Iowa and from the Mississippi River westward to Kansas that the innovative scheme of dual-level government would benefit Saint Louis and do no harm to the remainder of Missouri. In Missouri, as in Ohio and Pennsylvania, it would be an awesome task, but statewide popular sanction was a prerequisite for local reform.

In each of the three states, then, metropolitan reformers had succeeded in leaping the first barrier to creation of an innovative federative scheme of urban government. In Pennsylvania and Ohio they had faced opposition from suburban politicos like Mansfield and Roehm, and in both states they had compromised in order to reach the referendum stage. Vested interests such as the gravel dealers and the township officials had proved obstacles, and the farm groups had been at best troublesome allies and at worst fervent foes. But in each of the states reformers had succeeded in placing the issue on the state ballot, and if the voters would approve, then reform leaders would have the authority to proceed with their plans for restructuring urban rule. Victory at the polls, however, was to prove a difficult task, as metropolitan reformers confronted both rural prejudice and voter indifference.

The late 1920s and early 1930s were particularly inopportune times for city dwellers to turn to their rural cousins for aid. A rift between urban and rural interests had been developing throughout the early twentieth century, and by 1930 in some areas it was unbridgeable. For the most part, urban residents and rural dwellers disagreed on the issue of alcohol prohibition, with the rural districts supporting the "dry" position and the cities favoring the "wets." In the Ohio referendum of 1933, the wet-dry split may have influenced especially rural votes on metropolitan rule, because on the same ballot as the metropolitan question was a proposal for the repeal of prohibition. In some states, such as Ohio, the issue of reapportioning the legislature was also a source of spirited conflict between urban and rural areas, and throughout the 1920s lawmakers from Ohio's cities attempted to enact reapportionment measures that would grant urban areas a larger share of the legislative seats. In Ohio, Missouri, and Pennsylvania farmers and small-town residents felt embattled by the forces of the big city. The farmer did not share in the great prosperity of the 1920s, and the census of 1920 had reported that for the first time in American history rural Americans were in the minority. The power and influence of rural America was receding, and in Pennsylvania, Ohio, and Missouri the attitudes of rural and small-town residents toward big-city reform ranged from indifference to hostility. During the 1920s and 1930s, rural Americans could not feel any enthusiasm for the increased authority and might of a Greater Pittsburgh, a Greater Cleveland, or a Greater Saint Louis.

In Pennsylvania, rural areas and small towns actually showed little interest in big-city schemes of metropolitan rule. Pennsylvania's leading farm organization, the State Grange, took no stand on the proposed amendment, and the small-town newspapers were equally indifferent to what was happening in Pittsburgh. The *Potter Enterprise* failed to comment on the merits of the amendment, stating simply that it was "not of general interest," and the *Wellsboro Gazette* repeated this opinion.[35] The *Bedford Gazette* recommended voting against all fourteen of the amendments on the ballot, claiming that the large number of proposals was due to the chicanery of "the bosses." But the *Gazette*'s editor expressed no specific criticisms of the metropolitan plan, and neither did his colleagues in small towns throughout the state.[36]

Rural and small-town Ohioans were more outspoken in their views on government reorganization. The State Grange continued its opposition, arguing that "there is a possibility that local powers might be taken away without the consent of some of the local subdivisions."[37] In northeastern Ohio, the *Cadiz Republican* claimed that the amendment authorized "a scheme by which the big cities may unload a portion of their excessive costs . . . into neighboring communities, and it would increase their power and political influence in County and State Affairs."[38] The *Paulding County Republican* in northwestern Ohio insisted that the amendment "was instigated and begotten in the interest of the large cities" so that "the cities could work their will on the stubborn taxpayers of adjacent territory and take them in whether they liked it or not."[39] In the state's least populous county, the McArthur *Republican Tribune* reprinted the argument distributed by the township trustees association and predicted that the amendment "would allow the creation of huge, unwieldly municipalities which could NOT be operated effectively" and "would permit the expansion of corrupt politics dominating most of the big cities, into suburban and rural areas now well governed."[40] And in the crossroads village of Camden, the local newspaper referred to the amendment as "dangerous" and stated that "it is difficult to conceive of a proposal which could cause . . . greater confusion and difficulties."[41]

Missouri residents outside the Saint Louis area seemed confused and unsure about the federative plan proposed in that state. A newspaper editor in Troy, Missouri, expressed the attitude of many when he admitted that he was "in doubt on this proposal" and consequently "a No vote is safer than Yes."[42] In rural Gasconade County, the local editor admitted that "we are at a loss as to what is right and what is wrong" with regard to the amendment, but since the proposal seemed "objectionable to almost the whole of Saint Louis County," the editor believed "the rest of the State should not impose it upon them."[43] The *Jefferson County Republican* of DeSoto, Missouri, presented "no recommendation" on the proposal, whereas the *Warrenton Banner* offered tepid support, observing that "we see no harm in giving the two commonwealths" of city and county "the right to determine by vote" whether they want a metropolitan charter.[44] Missouri's Farm Bureau, however, was definite in its opposition to the scheme, arguing that "it is unfair to the farmers of Saint Louis county that their farms should become a part of the city of Saint Louis with the consequent increase in taxes."[45] Rural residents could not understand the problems and proposals of the metropolis, and the president of the state bar association observed that "the outstate voter is in a quandary, due to his unfamiliarity with the situation in Saint Louis City and Saint Louis County."[46] But in both Ohio and Missouri the leading farm organization had taken a definite stance against metropolitan reform.

In the suburbs less confusion prevailed, but in each of the three metropolitan areas suburbanites were sharply divided on the issue. Some suburban leaders favored the plan as a means of saving tax dollars and providing a happy mean between the two extremes of unitary, consolidated central-city government and wasteful metropolitan fragmentation. Others believed the dual-level scheme was simply the first step on the path to suburban oblivion and warned their brethren along the urban fringe to avoid the temptation of these fanciful schemes before it was too late.

Many Pittsburgh suburban officials expressed enthusiasm for the amendment and joined in Joseph Miller's crusade. Homestead's local newspaper interviewed nineteen prominent officeholders in the suburbs along the south bank of the Monongahela River and sixteen of them endorsed the proposed amendment, one expressed some doubts, and two remained undecided. The officials generally favored the amendment because it would eliminate the threat of forcible annexation to Pittsburgh and maintain local control over local questions while it would also result in improved services at a lower cost. One Munhall councilman noted that "the boroughs and townships lose no prestige" under the plan, "and it will give public improvement." The president of the Mifflin

Township Board of Commissioners reiterated the fact that the suburbs would maintain their autonomy, and argued that the plan "is the one way the individual municipalities can save themselves from being forcibly annexed." Others mentioned the economic benefits derived from being a part of the fourth largest city in the nation. A councilman from Homestead argued that "the Allegheny county district has been losing a lot of industries during the past couple of years" and hoped that metropolitan government would result in "the location of small industries here." Another Homestead councilman claimed that "with this district known as the fourth largest city ... it will mean that this honor will attract diversified industries to the county."[47] Miller's scheme seemed the panacea for many of the region's ills, and many suburban officials were ready to board the bandwagon.

A few local officeholders, however, were immune to the metropolitan lure, and they expressed their misgivings. The center of discontent was McKeesport, where Senator Mansfield, aided by McKeesport's city solicitor, continued his campaign to halt the expansion of Pittsburgh. Likewise, the city officials of Duquesne voted to withdraw from Miller's League of Boroughs and Townships after that organization endorsed the metropolitan scheme.[48] In McKeesport and Duquesne, leaders spoke and wrote against the proposal but their voices were lost amid the euphoria created by the Miller forces. Suburbanites envisioned a harmonious union of autonomous boroughs, townships, and cities and a greater Pittsburgh that no longer would need to trail Cleveland, Detroit, or Los Angeles. This seemed the best of all possible worlds to most Allegheny County residents, and Mansfield and his cronies could do little to tarnish the vision.

Some suburban newspapers did side with Mansfield and attack the proposal, but others endorsed the metropolitan scheme enthusiastically. In the working-class suburb of Duquesne, the local editor claimed that "you may call it 'metropolitan', ... 'greater city' or any name you will, but the scent of annexation clings to it still."[49] Moreover, he noted that several Pittsburgh city councilmen had dubbed the metropolitan amendment "a nightmare of vagaries," and several attorneys held "to the belief that its passage would throw the country into fifty years of litigation."[50] Wilkinsburg's suburban weekly assumed a different stance and assured its readers that the amendment would forestall Pittsburgh's efforts to annex the suburbs. According to the *Wilkinsburg Progress*, "it all narrows to the question of nailing down our present borough government so that it will stay put while at the same time helping ourselves to a population rating exceeded only by New York, Chicago, and Philadelphia." The amendment contained "ironclad safeguards that give absolute protection to every minority interest," and it would bolster the prosperity of the region.[51] Consequently, Wilkinsburg's editor could perceive no reason to oppose the scheme.

In Ohio, suburban officeholders and editors failed to recognize any advantages to be derived from metropolitan reform. As early as 1931 Mayor Frank Cain of Cleveland Heights had formed the Self-Government League of Cuyahoga County to protect suburban municipalities from the aggressions of the central city. And in the amendment campaign of 1933 the Cleveland Heights mayor continued his struggle to preserve the status quo. While Cain's opponent for the office of mayor endorsed the amendment "as a means towards governmental economy," Cain himself bluntly announced that "I am opposed to any changes," and he wondered "why Cleveland Heights can't be let alone."[52] The Cleveland Heights mayor argued that "it is a known fact the weakest governments in America are those of the large cities" and predicted that the borough scheme would lead to higher taxes and corrupt rule. Moreover, Cain's suburb would receive no benefits from a change in government because it could already boast of "the best garbage and rubbish collections, the cleanest streets, the soundest policy on extension of improvements," and it suffered no crime or vice.[53]

Frank Cain's suburban colleagues also mobilized in opposition to the proposed reform. Mayor Amos Kauffman of Lakewood argued that the amendment "is a plan for the forcible annexation of suburbs to larger cities."[54] Berea's city solicitor warned "that Berea will be submerged in a county-wide political subdivision with Cleveland holding the reins of legislative power" if the amendment passed.[55] And Lakewood's city law director also worked to defeat the proposal.[56] County officials likewise attacked the amendment that authorized a restructuring of county rule and thus threatened their jobs.

Suburban editors were equally outspoken, as they repeated warnings that federative metropolitan rule meant absorption by the city of Cleveland. The *Lakewood Post and West Shore Post* argued that the proposed amendment was "nothing more than a subtle annexation plan" and claimed that "this is no time to fool with further ideas of reformers."[57] Meanwhile the *Suburban News and Herald* also warned that "the amendment is designed to make possible the taking away of all civil authority from townships, villages and cities within the county, and to centralize such civic authority into one single unit."[58] And the *Berea Enterprise* reprinted the allegations made by the Ohio Home Rule League, that passage of the amendment would result in consolidation, corruption, and monster municipalities.[59]

Residents of Saint Louis County heard and read many of these same charges from their suburban leaders. The mayor of suburban Florissant argued that the proposed amendment "is grossly unfair to the people of St. Louis County, provides ... for a substantial increase in taxes and paves the way for untold extravagance in the cost of government."[60] Maplewood's City Council believed the proposition "would be detrimental to the citizens and taxpayers of our City" and passed a formal resolution urging Maplewood residents to vote against metropolitan reform.[61] Likewise, the Richmond Heights Board of Aldermen argued that the amendment was "vague and fraudulent in its design, creating powers that have never before been recognized," and believed that it would produce "a supermunicipal organization interfering with the rights of our citizens without conferring any benefits."[62] Moreover, the Pattonville Improvement Association called "upon each of our members to write a letter to every relative, friend and acquaintance residing in the state outside St. Louis county requesting their aid in saving our county from utter ruin and final extinction."[63]

County officials were especially vehement in their attacks on the scheme, for they did not relish the probable elimination of their jobs. Judge Sam Hodgdon spoke of the central city's desire "to prey upon its weaker neighbor" and compared it to the Kaiser's territorial designs in the World War. Hodgdon believed that "the County should be permitted to continue its wonderful growth with its own local self-government" and county residents should be allowed to "avoid [the] tax burden and other things they so dislike in large city government."[64] The four Saint Louis County Circuit Court judges issued a joint statement attacking the proposed federal plan as "a dangerous experiment in municipal government having no counterpart in operation anywhere." According to the judges, the amendment "confers power to deprive our people of the last vestige of local government, ... authorizes an increase in taxes in St. Louis County ... of at least 100 percent," and "instead of simplifying municipal government complicates it by attempting to provide a super-government."[65] Moreover, Judge Arthur Lashley observed that "the larger the city, the more graft and waste" and that "the ideal municipal government is a small community ... where the people know their officials, and where the officials know the people and their problems."[66] In the opinion of Lashley, Hodgdon, and their colleagues, small government was good government, and suburban residents were fools to accept the corruption and taxes of the big city.

Leaders of county farm organizations, the suburban bar, and both political parties in Saint Louis County agreed with the judges and joined the attack upon metropolitan reform. The secretary of the Saint Louis County Farm Bureau reminded voters that "there are nearly 300,000 acres of farm land in our county." This land, he claimed, would be assessed as city property and the resulting "tax burden would be so

great that you would be forced to give up your farm."[67] Likewise, the
Fenton Farmers' Club unanimously condemned the amendment "as
unwise, unnecessary and extravagant" and declared "that farm lands
fifteen and twenty miles from St. Louis is [sic] not necessary for urban
development."[68] While farmers feared increased taxation of agricultural
lands, the president of the county bar association warned of "untold
litigation" that would arise from the metropolitan scheme. Moreover,
the bar resolved that the amendment "threatens the County of St. Louis
with destruction and its people . . . with ruinous taxation."[69] Republicans
and Democrats were united in opposition to the metropolitan plan, and
the Saint Louis county central committees of both parties condemned it,
with the Republicans calling upon voters to "preserve our County from
destruction."[70]

Similar warnings of impending oblivion filled the pages of the suburban weeklies in Saint Louis County. Clayton's *Watchman Advocate*
claimed that the whole metropolitan "movement from its inception has
been characterized by trickery and deceit," and this same newspaper
predicted that passage of the amendment would mean "a governmental
and political slavery, the consequences of which will be felt in every
home in this county."[71] The *St. Louis Countian*, published in suburban
Kirkwood, lauded the government of Saint Louis County, warned of the
threat from the central city, and ominously advised voters that "the
time to kill a snake is when it first shows its ugly head and not after it
has bitten your children."[72] Kirkwood's *Monitor* warned that the proposal was just one more step in the big city's campaign to extend its
power and control not only throughout the metropolitan region but over
the entire state.[73] On the other hand, the Webster Groves weekly thought
the central city could contribute nothing to the government of the suburbs and described the incompetent police protection of Saint Louis city
where "gangsters run wild, murderers go uncaught, [and] banks are
robbed without any arrests."[74] According to suburban editors, the city
offered only sin, corruption, waste, and extravagance, and any union
with the aggressive but inept city of Saint Louis would only end in higher
taxes and tarnished public morals.

Despite this outcry against metropolitan reform, many suburban
leaders continued to support the amendment and to campaign for its
acceptance. Among its active supporters were the mayors of University
City, Huntleigh Village, Richmond Heights, Bridgeton, Glendale, and
Valley Park as well as the candidate for mayor of Kirkwood and the
University City solicitor.[75] Moreover, the University City Board of Aldermen formally endorsed the proposed amendment and issued a statement
explaining its action. According to the University City aldermen, metropolitan growth had created "problems within our territory that are

beyond the power of any single municipality or of the county as now constituted to deal with." The statement claimed that Saint Louis County required better sewers, an extensive park system, and improved health care, and that the "greater city" would be able to provide these services and facilities without destroying "the existence and the rights of self-government of the municipalities." Moreover, University City's leaders predicted optimistically that metropolitan rule "will enable us to cut our tax rate by 16 or 18 cents as well as to secure lower rates on water, which may mean a reduction equivalent to as much as a 40-cent tax rate."[76] Suburban advocates of the plan thus spoke of lower taxes and improved services while their opponents warned of higher taxes and central-city dictatorship.

In the central city itself, leaders also differed on the merits of the metropolitan scheme. Generally business leaders and the metropolitan newspapers supported the amendments enthusiastically, whereas some central-city political figures expressed doubt. Business leaders were the traditional bulwarks of the movement for efficiency and economy in government, and this applied as much to the metropolitan reform cause as to the city manager plan. To these people, the merger of overlapping, inefficient units seemed a logical, up-to-date, businesslike idea. Likewise, newspaper editors long had been self-appointed Jeremiahs of the urban scene, specializing in attacks on corruption and waste. Metropolitan fragmentation seemed to encourage such waste, and both business leaders and editors believed that federation would raise the city's census rank, enhance its economic prestige, and attract further business to the community. But among politicians, the disruption of the existing political structure aroused some misgivings. Change would inevitably limit the political power of some and compromise the prerogatives of certain officeholders. Consequently, political leaders were destined to be more skeptical of metropolitan schemes; but even many party moguls, mayors, and council members rallied around the banner of federation.

Pittsburgh's commercial interests had long backed the metropolitan plan, and the Chamber of Commerce and Allied Boards of Trade continued their active support. The members of the powerful Mellon family stood solidly behind their employee Joseph Miller, and they used their considerable influence in support of Miller's scheme. The president of the Westinghouse Air Brake Corporation, A. L. Humphrey, lived only a block from Miller in suburban Edgewood, and he too joined in the growing enthusiasm for his neighbor's proposal. Humphrey spoke of the "commercial, financial, and industrial prestige" derived from being the fourth largest city, and observed in a speech before the Chamber of Commerce that "the new rank which will be conferred upon our city by the metropolitan legislation will benefit us far more in a material way than anything else that has happened for more than two generations."[77] Pittsburgh's metropolitan dailies expressed similar hopes for the future, hopes exhilarating to the central-city banker and industrialist.

Originally, leaders of the Pittsburgh city government and the Civic Club of Allegheny County had felt less enthusiasm for the scheme. When he first considered Miller's plan in 1927, Mayor William Magee argued that it would place too heavy a burden on the populated urban districts. Every expanding suburban area would demand street lights and paving, and since these areas would be part of the greater city, the metropolitan rulers would have to comply with the demands. Pittsburgh was not even able to meet the need for street paving within its existing boundaries, let alone assume responsibility for the eight hundred square miles of Allegheny County. Moreover, Magee criticized the graded tax system whereby densely populated urban land would be taxed at a higher rate than developing suburban properties or undeveloped rural tracts.[78] H. Marie Dermitt, erstwhile secretary of the Civic Club, likewise claimed that "the boroughs are certainly going to benefit at the expense of the taxpayers of the city of Pittsburgh." According to Miss Dermitt, Miller was a "politician" and thus could not be trusted, his scheme was unworkable, and "Pittsburgh will be immensely burdened under the complicated machinery."[79] Pittsburgh's Civic Club did, however, endorse the amendment, and both Miss Dermitt and Mayor Magee were to join Miller's crusade prior to the referendum in November 1928.[80]

In Cleveland too, central-city leaders rallied behind the proposal for metropolitan county rule, though a few did express doubts. The *Cleveland Press* urged its readers to "vote for real economy" and "cut out a whole wasteful chain of vermiform appendices and other vestigial remnants" cluttering the governmental structure of Cuyahoga County.[81] The *Cleveland News* endorsed the proposed amendment with less verbosity, noting that the existing constitution did not allow the "elimination of unnecessary offices, regional control of inter-city functions, centralization of authority," or any of the other structural reforms so necessary for efficient, modern rule.[82] The *Cleveland Plain Dealer* claimed that "it is absurd to believe that a county largely devoted to industry can be adequately served in these Twentieth Century days of fast transportation and instantaneous communication by a form of government written into the Constitution more than 80 years ago." According to the *Plain Dealer*, passage of the amendment "will herald a new day in the larger counties of the state now afflicted with a form of government which invites waste, extravagance, bad management and irresponsible political control."[83]

One of the few prominent Clevelanders to attack the reform amendment was Saul Danaceau, a leading political figure in the city and chief architect of Cleveland's city charter of 1931. Danaceau argued that the amendment "will bring no advantage to Cleveland and will open the door to many disadvantages." According to Danaceau, "the ultimate aim of the amendment is the establishment of some borough plan," but that would only "burden ... the city with the heavy debts of some outlying districts, run up wastefully for the installation of services for which there has never been a demand and will not be for many years, if ever." Under the federative scheme, "Cleveland would lose control over its lakefront, its system of transportation, its water and sewer facilities, and would get exactly nothing in return." Danaceau said that he was "interested in the welfare of the city first," and the borough plan seemed to threaten that welfare. [84]

In contrast, Saint Louis business leaders felt no qualms about the metropolitan plan. One of the leading backers of the proposal was Morton May, president of the Famous & Barr Department Store. May told reporters that the metropolitan scheme "will add greatly to the prestige of St. Louis" and "means a great deal to the future commercial, industrial, and civic growth of St. Louis."[85] Sidney R. Baer, secretary-treasurer of May's chief competitor, the Stix, Baer & Fuller Company, agreed with his rival and argued that the amendment "affords St. Louis and St. Louis County an opportunity to go forward with renewed impetus."[86] A local industrialist echoed Baer's words and predicted that passage of the amendment "will speed the progress of this entire community."[87] But Robert L. Lund, general manager of the giant Lambert Pharmacal Company, summed up the attitude of many when he said of the scheme, "I believe it is good business."[88]

Political leaders in Saint Louis felt, however, that it was not good politics. To the dismay of Roessel, Ruth, and Reed, the three chief officials of the city of Saint Louis publicly denounced the scheme and urged voters to defeat the proposal in November. The mayor, the president of the Board of Aldermen, and the comptroller jointly stated, "that the disadvantages to the city and the obligations imposed upon its taxpayers" by the metropolitan plan "outweigh any possible advantage that may inure to the city or its inhabitants." According to these officials, "the municipal functions of the city of St. Louis can be administered more economically by the city alone than through a division of these functions between it and the Greater City."[89] Walter Neun, president of the Board of Aldermen, explained that the officials' "objection ... was ... on financial grounds principally," but their opponents thought otherwise.[90] Professor Reed charged that "politicians of St. Louis and St. Louis County are opposed to this measure because it interferes with their vested powers."[91] The Citizens Committee headed by Mayor Ruth of University City agreed with Reed and argued that the officials apparently wanted "out-and-out annexation of the cream of the county, with consequent augmented patronage and no disturbance of the political picture."[92] Robert Roessel claimed bitterly that Neun and his colleagues opposed metropolitan government because they feared it would deprive them of free municipal opera passes.[93] Whatever their motives, the city fathers dealt a serious blow to the reform effort and bolstered the forces of those eager to preserve the status quo.

In each of the metropolitan areas, then, politicians had misgivings about the expense of the reform schemes and the dangers they posed to their political power, whereas leaders in business and the press had rosy visions of a future municipal federation. Mayor Magee of Pittsburgh doubted the merits of the scheme as did the mayor of Saint Louis, Saul Danaceau in Cleveland, and numerous suburban officials such as Frank Cain. Yet Morton May, Sidney Baer, the Mellons, A. L. Humphrey, and the owners and editors of the metropolitan dailies all believed that reform was good business. It supposedly would streamline and modernize local government, and it would boost the census rating of the city, drawing industry and commerce to the enlarged municipality. Metropolitan government was in large part the product of chambers of commerce in Pittsburgh, Cleveland, and Saint Louis, and it seemed much more a businessman's reform than a politician's.

The Mays and Mellons, however, would not decide the issue. Instead, the electorate would do so, and in both Pennsylvania and Ohio the state's voters sided with the reform party. Only in Missouri did the proposed amendment suffer defeat. In each of the states, the metropolitan plan received its strongest support in the big cities and suburbs but failed to win acceptance among rural and small-town voters. The metropolitan areas seemed willing to restructure their own governments, but feed clerks and farmers were suspicious.

This is evident from the election returns in the referendum contests. In Pennsylvania, the metropolitan amendment carried both of the two largest counties in the state, Philadelphia County and Allegheny County, as well as two suburban counties in the Philadelphia area, Delaware County and Bucks County. Of the sixty remaining counties, the amendment won a majority in only three. Likewise, in Ohio, the amendment won a majority in each of the eight most populous counties in the state, including both Cuyahoga and Hamilton Counties, but it carried only thirteen of the eighty smaller counties. And in Missouri the amendment won only in the city of Saint Louis, though in Jackson County, the site of Kansas City, the proposal lost by only a small margin. As is shown in table 8, in each state a majority of voters in counties with populations of 250,000 or more approved the amendment proposal,

TABLE 8. Voters Favoring the Metropolitan Proposals in Counties of Various Sizes

Population	Pennsylvania	Ohio	Missouri
Counties of 250,000 or more	65.2%	62.9%	50.9%
Counties of 50,000–249,999	37.6%	51.9%	43.0%
Counties below 50,000	31.1%	39.8%	26.5%

SOURCES: Election data from the *Pennsylvania Manual 1929* (Harrisburg, 1929), p. 506; *Official Manual of the State of Missouri, 1931–1932* (Jefferson City, Mo., 1931), pp. 269–70; *Ohio Election Statistics 1934* (Berea, Ohio, 1935), pp. 257–59.

but in counties with populations of less than 50,000, the amendment won a favorable reception from only 31.1 percent in Pennsylvania, 39.8 percent in Ohio, and 26.5 percent in Missouri.[94] Rural and small-town voters in each of the three states failed to accept the proposed big-city reform. Instead, they followed the advice of the Grange and the Farm Bureau, casting their ballots against the metropolitan schemes.

But in Pennsylvania and Ohio the huge majorities garnered in the cities of Pittsburgh and Cleveland more than compensated for the losses in rural regions. Seventy-nine percent of Pittsburgh's voters backed the amendment, and almost 70 percent of Cleveland's electorate cast ballots in favor of the reform measure. The Ohio amendment carried all thirty-three wards of the city of Cleveland by landslide margins, winning the approval of at least 60 percent of the voters in each. The story was much the same in Pittsburgh. In both cities the reform schemes won support in every neighborhood and from every element of the population.

Suburbanites in the Pittsburgh and Cleveland areas also lined up loyally behind the forces of metropolitan reorganization. In the Allegheny County area outside Pittsburgh, 61 percent of the electorate voted for the metropolitan amendment, while in the suburban region of Cuyahoga County 59 percent backed the reform proposal. Yet support for the amendments varied widely among the suburban municipalities. As is shown in Table 9 in both Allegheny and Cuyahoga Counties, the suburban units of higher economic status were more likely to favor reform than were the units inhabited by a lower economic class; there is a significant correlation in both counties between support for the amendments and the median rents charged for residences. In both Pennsylvania and Ohio the amendment won its greatest electoral triumphs in the posh suburbs, polling larger percentages of positive votes in these communities than in the central city itself. Pennsylvania's metropolitan amendment garnered 85 percent of the votes in elite Rosslyn Farms and equally prestigious Thornburg, 84 percent in elegant Osborne, and 80 percent in both the golden township of Mount Lebanon and in Miller's and

TABLE 9. Support for Metropolitan Amendments on the Basis of Median Monthly Rentals—Allegheny County 1928 and Cuyahoga County 1933

Distribution of suburban units—Allegheny County 1928

Median value of monthly rentals	Support for metropolitan reform					
	80%+	*60%-79%*	*40%-59%*	*20%-39%*	*0%-19%*	*Median*
$40+	6	1	1	0	0	81.5%
$30-39.99	6	8	1	0	0	79%
$20-$29.99	5	17	11	1	0	68%
$ 0-$19.99	1	19	23	15	5	52%

Distribution of suburban units—Cuyahoga County 1933

Median value of monthly rentals	Support for metropolitan reform				
	60%+	*45%-59%*	*30%-44%*	*0%-29%*	*Median*
$50+	9	2	1	0	61%
$40-$49.99	5	5	2	2	55%
$30-$39.99	2	7	7	4	43%
$ 0-$29.99	0	2	6	2	39.5%

Correlations among support for metropolitan amendments, monthly rentals, and distance from central-city business district

Metropolitan area	Value of rentals	Distance
Pittsburgh	+.63	−.56
Cleveland	+.54	−.39
Saint Louis	−	−.56

SOURCES: Computed on basis of data from Abstract of Elections 1933, Cuyahoga County Board of Elections, Cleveland, Ohio; Civic Club of Allegheny County Records, Archives of Industrial Society, University of Pittsburgh Library, Pittsburgh, Pennsylvania; Gow, "Metropolitics in Pittsburgh," pp. 304-6. Economic data derived from *Real Property Inventory of Allegheny County* (data collected in February 1934); Green, *Population Characteristics Cleveland 1930;* Green, *Supplement to Population Characteristics Cleveland 1930; Population and Housing, Statistics for Census Tracts—Cleveland, Ohio and Adjacent Area, 1940* (Washington, D.C., 1942), pp. 130-38. Correlations were derived using procedures described in Richard Jensen and Charles Dollar, *Historian's Guide to Statistics* (New York, 1971), chap. 3. One small unit in Cuyahoga County, Warrensville Township, is excluded from the economic computations because of insufficient economic data and another, Chagrin Falls Township, is excluded from all calculations because of its tiny size (no more than five voters) and lack of economic data. North Randall is also excluded from the tables and computations because no separate voting returns were reported for that minuscule village. Two boroughs that are only partially within Allegheny County (McDonald and Trafford) are excluded from the Allegheny County figures, and little Sewickley Heights Township is excluded from the rental computations because of insufficient economic data. The Cuyahoga County rental figures are an average of Howard Whipple Green's equivalent monthly rental figures for 1930 and the census bureau's median contracted or estimated monthly rent figures for 1940. Both figures are estimates for all housing units, both tenant-occupied and owner-occupied. The Allegheny County numbers are based solely on actual rental units. Since

Humphrey's hometown of Edgewood. Seventy-two percent of the voters in wealthy Shaker Heights endorsed Ohio's amendment proposal as did an equal percentage of the electorate in exclusive Gates Mills, an outlying community of country estates. Moreover, in Cleveland Heights, that stronghold of Citizens League chieftains, 61 percent of the suburbanites favored the amendment that would authorize the creation of a federative metropolitan government.[95] Mayor Frank Cain's isolationism was not representative of opinion in Cleveland Heights. Instead, the metropolitanism of the Citizens League was of prevailing influence in this elite suburb.

Suburban regions at the bottom of the economic ladder, on the other hand, opposed metropolitan schemes in both Pennsylvania and Ohio. Only 11 percent of the voters in working-class Elizabeth favored the Pennsylvania amendment, while only 12 percent did so in Senator Mansfield's sooty suburb of McKeesport. The proposal also won the support of only 12 percent of the voters in the neighboring working-class borough of Versailles. In Cuyahoga County's poor, semirural villages of Valley View, West View, and Glenwillow, the Ohio amendment won the approval of only 22 percent, 27 percent, and 37 percent of the voters, respectively. Moreover, only 42 percent of the voters in the industrial pocket of Cuyahoga Heights favored the proposal. In working-class Independence, where the Wisnieskis and the Kubiceks dominated municipal government, only 34 percent of the electorate endorsed metropolitan reform, and in the village of Orange, where Mayor Podojil and Councilmen Stovicek and Votava ruled, only 20 percent cast their ballots in favor of the scheme. Residents in those working-class suburbs that suffered from grossly incompetent municipal rule, among them the soon-to-be-annexed borough of Hays, did vote heavily in favor of the federative amendments. But in those blue-collar communities that were capable of surviving as independent units, smaller percentages of voters sided with proamendment forces. In blue-collar suburbia, imaginative programs of metropolitan rule won less favor than they did in Mount Lebanon or Shaker Heights. Instead, these less affluent areas generally voted for the status quo and against reform.

In both Allegheny and Cuyahoga Counties, the rural areas and small towns farthest from the central city were strongholds of opposition to metropolitan rule. In fact, there is a significant negative correlation between distance from Pittsburgh and percentage of support for Pennsylvania's metropolitan amendment (see table 9). In Cuyahoga County

the rental data are based on estimates by data collectors or statisticians, the correlation figures should only be regarded as rough indicators of strength of association between economic status and support for metropolitan federation.

too, the bulk of the municipalities at the edge of the county opposed the county reform proposal, the notable exceptions being such villages as Gates Mills and Moreland Hills where wealthy Clevelanders maintained country homes. In Forward Township, located fifteen miles from the heart of Pittsburgh, only 13 percent of the electorate voted for the metropolitan amendment; and in East Deer Township, located fourteen miles from the city center, only 20 percent of the voters supported the measure. The suburb of Mount Oliver, in contrast, was surrounded by Pittsburgh and lay only two miles from the city center, and in that community 82 percent of the citizenry favored metropolitan rule. Four other suburban units lay within a three-mile radius of the city center, and in each the amendment won approval among a large portion of the populace. In Millvale 83 percent of the voters favored the proposal, in Greentree 78 percent, in Reserve Township 73 percent, and in Crafton 69 percent.

Cleveland's nearest neighbors were also among those most eager for reform, whereas the county's outlying districts opposed the idea of change. In those eastern suburbs that lay closest to the city center, Bratenahl and East Cleveland, two-thirds of the voters cast their ballots in favor of the amendment. Sixty percent of the voters in the western suburb of Lakewood supported county reform as did 58 percent of the electorate in the southern suburb of Newburgh Heights. At the distant southern edge of Cuyahoga County, however, 28 percent of Strongsville's citizenry favored metropolitan rule, and in equally remote Olmstead Township voters defeated the proposal by a margin of better than two to one. Truck farmers and the other semirural denizens of exurbia showed little enthusiasm for a metropolitan confederacy. They lived miles from the urban core, and they felt no more concern for Cleveland and Pittsburgh than they did for Akron or Altoona. Reform would just mean higher taxes for them, and the resulting metropolitan services would prove of little benefit to these outlanders who lived beyond the periphery of urban settlement. The farmer would not gain from improved suburban sewer service, new commuter thoroughfares, or county parks. But he would have to pay for them.

Despite opposition from working-class and rural districts, metropolitan reform generally received an endorsement from suburban voters in Allegheny and Cuyahoga Counties. Yet in Saint Louis County the story was different. Missouri's voters defeated the proposed amendment decisively, and in suburban Saint Louis County the plan won approval from only 40 percent of the voters. Though the outcome was different in Missouri than in Ohio or Pennsylvania, the general pattern of support was similar. The Missouri amendment won its strongest support in the wealthy areas nearest the city and polled the fewest favorable votes along the relatively poor rural fringes of the county. As in Pennsylvania and Ohio, there was a wide divergence of opinion on metropolitan government within the suburban region, corresponding to the heterogeneity of suburban interests.

Detailed economic data are not available for all the precincts in Saint Louis County in 1930, but it does seem that the heart of metropolitan support was in the white-collar, upper-middle-class communities. Fifty-nine percent of the electorate in wealthy University City supported the scheme and 60 percent of the voters in affluent Glendale approved metropolitan rule. The upper-middle-class haven of Richmond Heights also favored the amendment, as did four of the six precincts in elite Clayton. In lower-middle-class Maplewood, however, only 35 percent of the voters endorsed the reform measure, and in the predominantly black, working-class precincts of Dunbar, South Dunbar, and South Kinloch the amendment won a favorable response among only 36 percent of the electorate. Likewise, in the lower-income area immediately beyond the southern city limits of Saint Louis, only 38 percent of the voters marked the ballot in favor of metropolitan reform. [96]

Even more significant, perhaps, was the sharp split between the inner ring of densely populated suburbs and the outer rim of farms and woodlands. Tables 9 and 10 illustrate this point clearly. As in Allegheny County, there was a significant negative correlation between support for the metropolitan amendment and distance from the heart of the central city. In the seven precincts of southeastern University City that lay nearest to downtown Saint Louis, 70 percent of those voting approved the amendment. In the three Clayton precincts immediately beyond the Saint Louis corporation line, 64 percent of the electorate cast ballots in support of the scheme. These University City and Clayton precincts all lay within a six-mile radius of the center of Saint Louis. In contrast, the Saint Louis County village of Grover was twenty-three miles from the city and the village of Allenton lay twenty-six miles from the hub of the metropolitan area. The residents of these communities had more in common with the dirt farmer in the Ozarks than with the lawyers and bank presidents of University City, and they absolutely opposed a shotgun marriage with the city of Saint Louis. Grover's citizens rejected the metropolitan amendment by a vote of 278 to 5, and Allenton's returns were equally lopsided, with 8 votes in favor of the amendment and 98 opposed.

In Pennsylvania, Ohio, and Missouri central-city voters and residents of the inner ring of upper-middle-class suburbs had sanctioned the work of Joseph Miller, the Citizens League, Robert Roessel, and Eugene Ruth. The metropolitan schemes had been largely the handiwork of the suburban elite from Edgewood, Cleveland Heights, and University City, and

TABLE 10. Support for Metropolitan Amendments on the Basis of Distance from City Center—Allegheny County 1928, Saint Louis County 1930, and Cuyahoga County 1933

Distribution of suburban units—Allegheny County 1928

Distance from city center (miles)	Support for metropolitan reform					
	80%+	60%-79%	40%-59%	20%-39%	0%-19%	Median
2-6	14	19	6	0	0	77%
7-10	3	19	15	5	1	61%
11-19	1	8	15	11	4	48%

Distribution of suburban units—Saint Louis County 1930

Distance from city center (miles)	Support for metropolitan reform				
	60%+	40%-59%	20%-39%	0%-19%	Median
6	24	16	9	1	58.5%
7-9	6	27	14	7	45%
10-14	1	4	9	15	19.5%
15-30	0	0	2	7	8%

Distribution of suburban units—Cuyahoga County 1933

Distance from city center (miles)	Support for metropolitan reform				
	60%+	45%-59%	30%-44%	0%-29%	Median
4-7	7	3	2	0	61.5%
8-11	6	8	5	3	48%
12-15	3	6	9	5	40%

SOURCES: Abstract of Elections 1933, Cuyahoga County Board of Elections, Cleveland, Ohio; Civic Club of Allegheny County Records, Archives of Industrial Society, University of Pittsburgh Library, Pittsburgh, Pennsylvania; Gow, "Metropolitics in Pittsburgh," pp. 304-6; *St. Louis County Leader* (Clayton, Mo.), 7 Nov. 1930, p. 1. The units in Allegheny and Cuyahoga Counties are townships and municipalities. The units in Saint Louis County are precincts.

the voters in these suburbs and in others like them did not shirk from expressing approval for the work of their neighbors. These white-collar suburbanites were neither myopic in their vision of metropolitan problems nor parochial in their loyalties. Joseph Matthews lived in Kirkwood, owned mills in East Saint Louis, and attended directors' meetings in the heart of the city. Joseph Miller's home was in Edgewood, his office was in Wilkinsburg, and he was director of a savings and loan company in East Pittsburgh. Morton May and Sidney Baer lived in Clayton, owned department stores in downtown Saint Louis, and speculated in real estate throughout the metropolis. And A. L. Humphrey was a member of the Athletic and Duquesne Clubs in downtown Pittsburgh, his home was in Edgewood, but his company's factories were in Swissvale and Wilmerding. The daily activities of such men—their work, their social life, their acquaintances—extended throughout the metropolis, regardless of municipal boundaries. They were not citizens of the north side, south side, east side or west, but citizens of the metropolis with interests and ties throughout the sprawling urban area. They had no fears of losing their voice in government if their residential suburbs joined in a metropolitan federation. Area-wide cooperation posed no threat to them, for they were metropolitan figures.

Moreover, they were the traditional devotees of structural reform in the city. It was the white-collar, upper-middle-class business leader and professional who had for decades tinkered with municipal charters and sponsored the new and different schemes for governing the urban area. These individuals had rallied behind the city manager plan, the short ballot, home rule, and the other panaceas for corruption and waste. They were battle-worn veterans in the army of good-government reform, and civic betterment was their hobby. The groups that they trusted— the city clubs, the city and county chambers of commerce, the reform leagues—all supported metropolitan federation, and the political science professors who had taught the younger members of the upper middle class preached metropolitan federation as holy writ in their classrooms. Their schools, their clubs, and even their churches were mouthpieces for civic reform, and they were immersed in the good-government, economy-efficiency tradition.

But the territory beyond the central-city limits was not a homogeneous region of gray-flanneled, white-collar commuters. Instead, it was a mixed area of working and middle-class residents as well as vestigial farmers and small-town isolationists not ready to accept union with the big city. McKeesport's metal workers had no metropolitan vision, for they worked in McKeesport, lived in McKeesport, shopped in McKeesport, and played euchre at McKeesport's Sons of Italy Hall. Residents of the industrial suburbs did not belong to downtown clubs where they might share good times with men having interests throughout the metropolis. Their life encompassed a narrower geographical range, and their activities were more parochial. Moreover, the blue-collar worker and the immigrant were not so immersed in the efficiency reform tradition as was the white-collar native. They might occasionally have sided with structural reforms such as home rule, and the working class in the central city does not seem to have opposed metropolitan federation ardently. But structural reform was not second nature to them, and they did not respond automatically with enthusiasm when the words *economy* and *efficiency* were spoken.

Likewise, the truck farmer in Middleburg Heights or the dirt farmer in Grover shared no dreams of a "Greater Saint Louis" or a "Greater Cleveland." They had no link with the heart of the metropolis, they resented urban residents, and they feared big-city power. Their social contacts did not extend beyond the local Grange Hall and the nearest Methodist church, and they felt no more kinship for the men of University City, Shaker Heights, Saint Louis, or Cleveland, than they did for Chicagoans or San Franciscans hundreds of miles away. Federation could well result in new tax burdens, and yet they would reap few benefits from the change. Moreover, they did not leap automatically aboard the good-government bandwagon. Like their blue-collar brethren they were not knee-jerk devotees of urban structural reform. Urban reformers favored reapportionment of state legislatures and a reduction of rural power. Thus the urban reformer was not necessarily to be trusted.

These exurban separatists, together with rural voters throughout the state, had defeated Missouri's proposed amendment. But in Ohio and Pennsylvania reformers had triumphed in the first round of their battle. Now they faced an even more difficult contest, for a metropolitan charter in Allegheny County required approval by two-thirds of the voters in a majority of outlying units, and a Cuyahoga County charter needed to top the four hurdles. The suburban reformers had won two out of three on the state level, triumphing in Pennsylvania and Ohio but losing in Missouri. Now they laid plans for a final victory.

8

"THE MOST MAGNIFICENT OPPORTUNITY"

Early in December 1928 Joseph Miller wrote H. Marie Dermitt that "there is the most magnificent opportunity" for drafting a "great constructive" metropolitan charter.[1] And in November 1933 the *Cleveland Plain Dealer* summed up the attitude of Cuyahoga County reformers in the wake of victory when its editorials blared "Let Cuyahoga Lead" and urged "the importance of taking early steps to secure for Cuyahoga a sounder, more economical plan of government."[2] Following the passage of the metropolitan amendments, hopes of grand reform and constructive renovation ran high among men such as Miller, groups such as the Citizens League, and newspapers such as the *Plain Dealer*. They had fought for years to achieve their ends and now actual reform appeared within their grasp. Pittsburgh was on the verge of becoming a great federated municipality and the fourth largest city in the nation, whereas Cleveland seemed about to emulate London by yielding governmental powers to a metropolitan county council. The struggle to break free from the legal traditions of unitary municipal government and expansion through annexation appeared to be approaching a successful conclusion. But the barriers to legal reform were massive, and both Miller and the Citizens League would soon find tradition an impregnable foe.

The first task confronting reformers in both Pittsburgh and Cleveland was to sketch more detailed plans for the dual-level structure they had envisioned. Moreover, they had to distribute the powers and duties of government among the elements of this new metropolitan polity. Allocating power, however, is a delicate task that is bound to arouse conflict and debate. And in both Pittsburgh and Cleveland the job of determining the responsibilities of the traditional municipal units and the new metropolitan government proved fraught with difficulties.

Pennsylvania's constitutional amendment authorized the state legislature to draft Allegheny County's metropolitan charter, but Joseph
Miller was not willing to surrender control over Pittsburgh's destiny to a
group of Harrisburg lawmakers. Consequently, following the amendment victory in November 1928, he reconvened his Metropolitan Plan
Commission which set to work on a charter that they hoped would
receive rubber-stamp approval by the state legislature. Throughout the
early months of 1929, Miller, his advisor Thomas Reed, and the other
commission members endeavored to fashion a document that balanced
suburban fears of amalgamation with demands for centralization. At
one point a representative from suburban Mount Lebanon objected to
the excessive centralization that would result from the charter provision
on recreation, whereas Marie Dermitt, the erstwhile defender of central-
city interests, attacked the same provision on the grounds that it allowed
too great a dispersion of authority.[3] Such conflicts were typical, and
Miller and Reed assumed the task of balancing the charter so that the
scales of authority would not tip too far on the side of the central administration nor dip too deeply in the suburbs' favor.

The product of this balancing act was submitted to the legislature in
March 1929. The proposed scheme provided for a board of seven commissioners elected by wards. This board would serve as the chief governing body of the metropolis and would have an administrative chief,
known as the president of the board, to be elected at large. This president would, with the consent of the commission, appoint the heads of
the departments of finance, health, planning, safety, public works, law,
regional transit, parks and recreation, public art, personnel, research
and information, and welfare. As indicated by these departmental titles,
the metropolitan board was to assume a wide range of powers and
responsibilities. It would enjoy the power to levy taxes and impose
special assessments, to make and enforce health regulations, to formu-
late a master plan and to approve subdivision plats, to create zoning
districts, to maintain a metropolitan police force that would supplement
local police departments, to regulate and maintain through streets, to
recommend standards for local fire departments and appropriate funds
to aid these departments, and to regulate the emission of smoke, a vital
power in a metropolis known derisively as "Smoke City." Moreover, the
proposed board would have the authority to acquire waterworks, to
regulate transportation franchises, to aid in the development of parks
and recreation facilities, to control the placement of monuments and
other public art, and it would assume those duties with regard to the
poor and mentally ill that the city of Pittsburgh and the Allegheny
County directors of the poor traditionally had exercised.[4]

Miller and his suburban-dominated Metropolitan Plan Commission had allocated a handsome array of duties to the proposed metropolitan overlords. However, the existing boroughs, cities, and townships would retain their names and identities, their fire and police departments, their garbage services, their control over local streets and street lighting, their public libraries, and their local parks. The proposed scheme did abolish the municipal mayor's court and the aldermen's courts; and it deprived the justices of the peace of their judicial authority. A significant reserve of local power remained, however, to balance the central authority of the metropolis.[5] The metropolitan board would serve metropolitan needs, and the local municipalities would serve local needs. Thus Miller and his colleagues had struck a compromise between the demands of an interdependent metropolis and the desire for continued local self-government. The choice was no longer between the twin poles of annexation and fragmentation. Instead, the metropolis would unite, and the suburbs would survive.

This may have satisfied city and suburbs, but it did not appeal to politicians in Harrisburg. In their opinion, the Miller plan was too visionary, it eliminated too many local offices, and it threatened the traditional political structure of which they were prominent beneficiaries. Earlier the Metropolitan Plan Commission had rejected the idea of creating a city manager for the new metropolis because of objections by the powerful Republican state chairman. Now legislators would force more changes in the proposed scheme.

The chief legislative figure responsible for remodeling the charter was State Senator M. G. Leslie of Pittsburgh. Leslie delayed introduction of the charter in the senate in order to seek the advice of leading Republican officials from Allegheny County. He also consulted with a group of lawyers, who advised that "government is a matter of growth and development and therefore a revolutionary change of existing institutions should cause one to pause." According to Leslie's legal analysts, "a much safer method of developing this charter would be to begin with a framework closely resembling the county government."[6] Leaders in Harrisburg did not want to gamble on untried, untested forms of government, and they felt that the least reform was the best reform.

Moreover, Allegheny County politicians opposed charter provisions that seemed to reduce their authority. Mayor Kline of Pittsburgh, who wanted to retain his power to appoint magistrates to preside over the mayor's court, denounced the proposed charter for depriving him of this right.[7] Pittsburgh city councilmen "viewed with dismay" the loss of a portion of their traditional authority over city streets and over the awarding of construction and repair contracts.[8] And the city of Pittsburgh joined with the newly created antimetropolitan Allegheny League of Municipalities to attack Miller's charter before the Senate Judiciary Committee.[9] Other political leaders refused to endorse any proposal that abolished the offices of directors of the poor. Still others looked askance at the creation of an efficient, non-political personnel department, for offices in Allegheny County had never been distributed under a civil service system and a personnel bureaucracy appeared to threaten the traditional patronage system.

Thus lawmakers would have to refashion the innovative document of Joseph Miller and his colleagues if it were to win the approval of political leaders in Pittsburgh and Harrisburg. From March to May 1929, legislative committees overhauled the proposed charter, reducing the powers of the metropolitan board and restoring the perquisites endangered by the commission scheme. Under the revised charter the mayors, aldermen, and justices of the peace were to retain their judicial powers; the directors of the poor would continue to govern welfare agencies within the county; and there would be no departments of safety, planning, parks and recreation, public art, or personnel. The metropolitan board would, however, enjoy authority over the construction and maintenance of through streets and the regulation of traffic on these arteries, and it would possess broad powers with regard to sewage and water supply. Moreover, it would control public transit within the metropolitan zone, and it could maintain a police force to supplant the county sheriff's office.[10] Lawmakers in Harrisburg were willing to accept the federal principle of dual-level government, but they opposed innovation that would disrupt the political status quo radically.

Reaction to the legislative butchering of Miller's charter was mixed. The academic efficiency experts generally had viewed politics as an unfortunate obstacle to good government, and they despised this dismembering of a model blueprint. Professor Martin Faust of the University of Pittsburgh labeled the revised document a "politicians' charter" and claimed that "the charter was completely emasculated to conform to the desires of the politicians."[11] Thomas Reed's colleague at the University of Michigan, Rowland Egger, congratulated Reed and the commission for "their outstanding contribution to the science of politics" but noted darkly that "the reform features of the charter which threatened the control of the 'organization' were excised."[12] That master of metropolitan conciliation, Joseph Miller, was again willing to compromise. Refusing to adopt the bitter stance of Professor Faust, Miller referred to Senator Leslie as "an outstanding Republican organization leader" and claimed that the legislative revisions "were made by men of the highest legal ability and were adopted in order to reconcile conflicting opinions and influences." Moreover, the suburban leader argued that "certainly 100 percent of the real fundamental survived" the legislative process, and he believed "the charter as amended by the Legislature to be a tremendous forward step over existing conditions."[13]

Thus, Miller and the Metropolitan Plan Commission endorsed the revised charter and prepared themselves for the vital ratification election in June 1929. Despite their supposedly magnificent opportunities, lawmakers and reformers in Pennsylvania had modeled a less than magnificent metropolitan charter. During the early months of 1929 reformers had acceded to political realities and conformed to the wishes of elected officials. Miller and his colleagues had been compelled to operate in the real world of Pennsylvania politics, and the resultant charter reflected the need to compromise with party leaders whose interests all too often were self-interests. The Pennsylvania plan was not what Miller and his commission had hoped, but it did offer an alternative to fragmentation and disunity. Professor Egger even predicted that Pittsburgh would serve as an example for "future solutions to the problems of metropolitan government in the United States."[14]

In Cleveland the procedure for drafting a metropolitan charter was more complex and time consuming. Under the Ohio amendment, an elected commission of local residents would draft the charter, and the state legislature would play no role in the process. But Cuyahoga County voters were not to elect this charter commission until the next general election in November 1934, one year following the adoption of the constitutional amendment. Moreover, at this general election county voters would have to approve the drafting of a charter. In other words, the task of constructing a metropolitan charter would not begin until after the voters had again sanctioned the idea of county reform and had chosen a commission. Then the charter itself would have to win the approval of a majority of voters in the county, a majority of voters in the central city, a majority of voters outside the central city, and a majority of voters in a majority of the county's political units. Reformers thus faced two more vital referenda in Cuyahoga County and the awesome challenge of the notorious four hurdles.

In 1934 as in the amendment contest of 1933, the metropolitan battle continued to be a three-way struggle. On one side was Mayor Frank Cain of Cleveland Heights, who advertised himself as the staunch defender of suburban interests, and at the other extreme were Saul Danaceau and his friends at the so-called Soviet table of the Cleveland City Club, who sought to defend the central city. Somewhere in between were Mayo Fesler and his Citizens League, a reform group dominated by central-city business leaders who lived in the fashionable suburbs.

These three factions were to battle for control of the county charter commission, and each presented a slate of candidates in the commission election of November 1934.

The slate sponsored by Cain's Self-Government League included the former mayor of Lakewood, the city law director of that suburb, the former solicitor of Bedford, another lawyer who served as solicitor for a number of small suburbs, a Cleveland Heights councilman, and the mayor of Warrensville Heights. Only two of the fifteen candidates on the Cain slate resided in the city of Cleveland, and Cain and his followers readily admitted that their suburban ticket was dedicated to blocking the aggressions of the central city. The candidate from Berea opposed a county charter if it "means that the individuality of Berea is to be swallowed up," and he observed that "there is some goodness outside of mere bigness."[15] Cain himself reiterated his oft-stated belief "that Cleveland Heights is better off under its present government than it would be under any changes in the county government." According to the Cleveland Heights mayor, "the suburbs have been pictured as having horns," but "we merely want to keep control over those things which we believe we can do better than anyone else."[16] And in Cain's opinion the suburbs could do almost anything better than anyone else.

A number of suburban newspapers rallied behind the Self-Government League slate. The *Garfield Heights Record* endorsed Cain's ticket and warned every suburbanite to "acquaint himself with the dangers which threaten the suburbs, should they be left without friendly representation on the commission."[17] Likewise, the *East Cleveland Signal* backed those self-avowed defenders of suburbia because it "will mean a furthering of the present clean government which the suburbs have enjoyed" and continued freedom from the "vicious phases of government."[18] Lakewood's *Suburban News and Herald* claimed "that too much intrusion into a well managed government such as Lakewood has might be costly to the taxpayers" and urged voters to support Cain's candidates, "who will fight for just governmental rights."[19]

Saul Danaceau, on the other hand, feared that suburban ideas of just governmental rights might cost Cleveland a fortune, thus threatening the welfare of the central city. According to Danaceau, "there is a real danger that the suburbs might want to get all the benefits that Cleveland has to offer without assuming the responsibility shouldered by Cleveland taxpayers." If elected to the commission, this central-city leader agreed "to give a lot of attention to the ... surrender of any of Cleveland's rights to the suburbs."[20]

Running on the Danaceau slate were a total of nine candidates, most of whom were local Democrats associated with the Soviet table of the Men's City Club. The Soviet table was an informal gathering of like-minded Cleveland leaders who, according to the *Plain Dealer,* "diag-nosed, dissected, and denounced" the various "acts of municipal, state, national and international officialdom."[21] Five of the Soviet table slate were residents of Cleveland, two were from Cleveland Heights, one from Lakewood, and one from East Cleveland. Six were lawyers with offices in the heart of Cleveland, and they represented what suburban officials referred to as "downtown interests." They had experience as a counter-reform group and were primarily responsible for abolishing the office of city manager in Cleveland. Because of this, that intolerant reformer, Mayo Fesler, despised them, and they in turn reveled in the abuse heaped upon them by the Citizens League. The league's bulletin attacked Danaceau and his colleagues as "that small group of political mal-contents ... whose chief function ... seems to be to arouse suspicion, stir up opposition to reforms which do not originate with them, and to vent their personal spleen in unbridled and totally unwarranted attacks on individuals and organizations which are sincerely trying to bring about constructive improvements."[22] When confronted with this charge, one of the leading Soviets laughed and said, "Why, that sounds like a pretty good description of the table."[23]

Finally, the third ticket of commission candidates represented the mainstream of metropolitan reform. A special nominating committee headed by the elder statesman Newton Baker had selected this third slate, and it enjoyed the endorsement of the Citizens League, the Cham-ber of Commerce, the League of Women Voters, and those other groups that had pushed long and loyally for unification of the metropolis. Included among the fifteen candidates on the reform slate were the mayors of suburban Brecksville and South Euclid, the city solicitor of Parma, the president of the Cleveland Chamber of Commerce (who resided in Lakewood), the president of the Cuyahoga County League of Women Voters (also from Lakewood), and the head of the political science department at Western Reserve University. Ten of the candi-dates were suburban residents and only five lived in the central city. But they represented all the varied elements of the metropolitan reform tradition, including business, academia, and the carpet-bag good-government forces that lived in the suburbs but sought to uplift the quality of life in the central city.

This reform ticket received support from a variety of distinguished sources. Both the mayor and the city solicitor of Shaker Heights backed the reform slate. The mayor told reporters that he would favor a dual-level metropolitan scheme in which the metropolitan government "had jurisdiction over all utilities, sewage disposal, health and police detective work."[24] Cleveland's metropolitan dailies likewise endorsed the re-formers, agreeing with the Shaker Heights mayor on the need for cooperative government action. The *Cleveland Press* complained of the "waste, duplication of functions, [and] decentralized control" that characterized Cuyahoga County government and argued that the reform candidates were "people of high capacity" who were "eager to take positive action for efficiency and economy."[25] The *Cleveland Plain Dealer* claimed that the reform slate "includes none but those thoroughly conversant with the need for modernizing the antiquated form of government."[26] In both central city and suburb, then, some leaders desired an overhaul of local government machinery, and the ticket endorsed by Mayo Fesler and the Citizens League seemed ready to make the needed repairs and adjustments.

The election returns in November 1934 demonstrated the strength of reform sentiment. None of the Cain slate won a seat on the commission, and only two of the Danaceau candidates were successful. The Citizens League ticket won the other thirteen commission seats, and sixty percent of the electors voted in favor of creating a county charter commission.

As is indicated by table 11, the pattern of voting in 1934 closely resembled that of 1933. Again, in the inner ring of elite suburbs, overwhelming majorities voted in favor of a county charter commission, with more than seventy percent of the electorate in Cleveland Heights and Shaker Heights supporting reform. In fact, there was an even stronger correlation between economic status and support for metropolitan reform in 1934 than there had been in 1933. Poorer, working-class suburbs were less enthusiastic for change in 1934 than they had been a year earlier. Among the predominantly blue-collar residents of Newburgh Heights, support for county reorganization plunged from 58 percent in 1933 to 23 percent in 1934. Moreover, the poor, semirural districts on the fringe of Cuyahoga County remained adamantly opposed to the creation of a charter commission, with less than 20 percent of the voters in West View and Glenwillow backing the proposal.[27]

Likewise, the Citizens League slate swept the major white-collar commuter suburbs, far outpolling those supposed suburban advocates who ran on Frank Cain's slate. Cain's candidates ran no better in Cleveland Heights or Shaker Heights than did Danaceau's, and their chief source of support was not in the suburbs but in that rural zone more than eleven miles from Cleveland's core. The boondocks rallied around the Cain ticket, whereas the Soviet table ran strongest in the central city, and the metropolitan reformers sponsored by the Citizens League reaped handsome majorities in both city and suburb. In 1934, as in 1933, voters in Cleveland Heights and Cleveland shared similar views on metropolitan rule. No difference of opinion divided the city and elite suburb. Instead, in both 1933 and 1934, they were united behind the banner of federated government.

TABLE 11. Support for Metropolitan Charter Commission on the Basis of Median Value of Monthly Rentals and Distance from City Center—Cuyahoga County 1934

Distribution of suburban units

Median value of monthly rentals	Support for county charter commission				
	60%+	*40%–59%*	*20%–39%*	*0%–19%*	*Median*
$50+	10	2	0	0	66%
$40–$49.99	3	8	3	0	55.5%
$30–$39.99	2	10	8	0	45%
$0–$29.99	0	3	4	3	28%

Distribution of suburban units

Distance from city center (miles)	Support for county charter commission				
	60%+	*40%–59%*	*20%–39%*	*0%–19%*	*Median*
4–7	6	4	2	0	58%
8–11	6	12	3	1	56.5%
12–15	4	7	10	2	39%

Correlations among support for county charter commission, monthly rentals, and distance from central-city business district

	Value of rentals	Distance
Cuyahoga County	+.63	−.26

SOURCES: Computed on basis of data from Abstract of Elections 1934, Cuyahoga County Board of Elections, Cleveland, Ohio. Economic data derived from Green, *Population Characteristics Cleveland 1930*; Green *Supplement to Population Characteristics Cleveland 1930*; *Population and Housing, Statistics for Census Tracts—Cleveland, Ohio and Adjacent Area, 1940* (Washington, D.C., 1942), pp. 130–38. Rental figures averaged from the 1930 and 1940 data. Again, there are no election data for North Randall, and Warrensville Township is not considered in the rental tables or correlations, while Chagrin Falls Township is excluded from all calculations.

The great rift was not between the city and the elite commuter suburb, but between Cleveland Heights and Newburgh Heights, between Shaker Heights and West View. City and elite suburb shared a common boosterism, for residents in both favored a greater and more prosperous Cleveland. Likewise, they shared a common belief in efficiency reform. But West View's semirural outlanders were not among the ranks of metropolitan boosters; and Newburgh Heights factory workers no longer felt the lure of middle-class reform. The split in the metropolis was not a simple split between central city and suburbs, a neat conflict between the urban core and the outer rings of urban population. Instead, the forces of the central city and the elite suburbs were allied against the semirural and blue-collar suburbs. In 1934 as in 1933, the central-city resident and white-collar suburbanite had beaten this rural-blue-collar coalition, and now the charter commission could proceed with its duties and attempt to cope with the problems of a fractured and fragmented metropolis.

The charter commission, however, was far from united in its views on metropolitan rule. On one side was the faction dedicated to creating a strong metropolitan authority and to restricting sharply the powers of the member municipalities. Unswerving in their loyalty to this stance were the two chieftains of the League of Women Voters who served on the commission, Helen Hellman of Cleveland Heights and Maude McQuate of Lakewood. Among the other members who generally allied themselves with these women was a labor leader who lived in Shaker Heights, and three or four members from the central city, including one member of the Soviet table. The Citizens League supported these advocates of thorough metropolitan reorganization strongly, urging that the county unite in a single dual-level municipal corporation.

Opposing this group was the faction that favored a more moderate scheme whereby the county council would assume a limited number of municipal duties that the constituent governmental units could not handle adequately by themselves. This moderate faction included one former and one future mayor of Cleveland, the mayors of Brecksville and South Euclid, the president of the Cleveland Chamber of Commerce, and the commission member from the village of Chagrin Falls at the eastern edge of Cuyahoga County. The *Plain Dealer* expressed the attitude of these commission members when it stated "a preference for a charter which accomplishes something and will pass at the polls, rather than a charter of ideals which would be practically certain of defeat."[28] Maude McQuate, Helen Hellman, and Mayo Fesler and his Citizens League represented the suburban reform idealists, and their opponents included the political realists who feared an adverse suburban vote in November.

During the early months of 1935, the idealists seemed to have the upper hand, and the commission initiated plans for a county-wide federative municipality. Under the proposed scheme for a strong metropolitan government, the new municipality of Greater Cleveland would have the authority to plan, maintain, and construct main highways, sewage systems, parks, and other major public works and would enjoy the power to grant public franchises. It would also assume control of public hospitals and welfare institutions, govern public relief within the county, and assume responsibility for public health inspections and regulations. Moreover, the metropolis would maintain its own police department with authority throughout the county. The boroughs or municipal subdivisions would retain the rights to determine local tax rates and budgets; to construct and maintain local streets, sidewalks, parks, and playgrounds; to provide local street lighting and cleaning; to maintain fire and police forces; to own and operate public utilities under metropolitan supervision; and to enact minor local regulations that would not conflict with the metropolitan ordinances.[29] This scheme resembled that framed by the Metropolitan Plan Commission in Pittsburgh, but, like the charter drafted by Miller and Reed, it would face insuperable opposition.

Various commission members attacked the plan sharply. The mayor of Brecksville, who was also a professor of law at Western Reserve University, was outspoken in his criticism of such an innovative and untested scheme. He told the commission that "I regard this as a dishonest thing to try to put over on the people" because "you're telling them they are still municipal corporations, bless their hearts, when in fact they are something never seen before."[30] A commission member from Cleveland admitted that "if I were a dictator, I would create at once a municipal corporation covering the whole county," but he realized the mood of voters from outlying areas and argued that "it would be fatal to try to do that now."[31] And the commission representative from Chagrin Falls explained that she "wouldn't dare go home" if she backed a plan that seriously threatened the autonomy of her village.[32]

Troubled by the threat of a strong metropolitan authority, suburban foes also began to mobilize their forces. In January 1935 municipal officials in the western half of Cuyahoga County banded together to form the Suburban Charter League, an organization dedicated to blocking the success of metropolitan schemes. Among those attending the first meeting were the mayors of Lakewood, Rocky River, Berea, Brook Park, Strongsville, North Royalton, Linndale, Parma Heights, and Independence. Also present was Edward Blythin, a future mayor of Cleveland who at that time was solicitor of Strongsville, Middleburg Heights, and North Royalton, and who was, according to the *Berea Enterprise*, "the best informed man on the suburbs' side in the charter controversy."[33] Mayor Kauffman of Lakewood told the gathered suburbanites that "the charter commission is just feeding us annexation in a mild form," and he asked plaintively, "why do we have to continue to be hounded into something we do not want."[34] Mayor Carl Stein of Rocky River spoke of the ethnic division between city and suburb when he observed that "our people in Rocky River are 90% Americans; they in Cleveland are 80% foreigners."[35] Such arguments, however, failed to appeal to Mayor Wisnieski of Independence, Mayor Uhinck of Parma Heights, Mayor Lakawitz of Linndale, or P. J. Kowallik from Broadview Heights. The Welsh-born Blythin avoided any ethnic references, noting simply and persuasively that "I haven't heard one iota of any scheme that would cut down the cost of government."[36]

In rural Strongsville, fourteen miles from the urban core, Mayor Leonard Bean resorted to drastic tactics to ensure the autonomy of his community. Mayor Bean was a "good-natured, heavy-set, man-of-all-trades" who served as local school bus driver and had earned the affectionate nickname of "Beanie" from Strongsville's school children.[37] But now this genial, mild-mannered bus driver donned the garb of a Jefferson Davis and campaigned for the secession of Strongsville from Cuyahoga County. Bean planned to ask the legislature to redraw county boundaries so that Strongsville would fall within adjacent Medina County. To demonstrate local sentiment, community leaders circulated petitions calling for secession, and about ninety-eight percent of Strongsville's voters signed. According to the village council president, only ten local renegades refused to sign the separatist manifesto.[38] Residents of rural North Royalton and Brecksville also talked of secession, whereas the village of Chagrin Falls considered separation from Cuyahoga County and union with adjoining Geauga County.[39] Leonard Bean was not prepared to sacrifice the decent government of Strongsville and suffer under big-city suzerainty, and neither were others on the outskirts of the metropolis.

Amid this uproar, the more moderate faction of political realists assumed control of Cuyahoga County's charter commission. On 31 May 1935 the commission finally and decisively rejected the idea of a federative, county-wide municipality.[40] Only four of the thirteen members present voted in favor of such a scheme, the four being the two women from Cleveland Heights and Lakewood, the Shaker Heights labor leader, and one Clevelander. The others recognized the political impossibility of imposing such a plan on men such as Leonard Bean, Edward Blythin, and Amos Kauffman. In Cleveland the commission members bowed to political realities just as Joseph Miller had yielded to the political organization in Allegheny County and Harrisburg.

Cuyahoga County's commission members bowed so low, in fact, that they finally refused to create a metropolitan charter. Rather than divest the suburbs of any municipal functions and face the dreaded four hurdles, the commission decided simply to reorganize county government. Under the constitutional amendment of 1933, such a reform required approval by only a simple majority of the county voters. Cuyahoga County's commission members had preferred a minor reform victory to a major defeat.

The charter that the commission presented to county voters abolished all existing county offices, established a county board with legislative authority and a single county executive, and allocated the former tasks of county sheriff, treasurer, auditor, prosecuting attorney, and coroner to a set of departments headed by appointees of the county executive. This scheme centralized authority, reduced the number of elected officials, and supposedly would result in more efficient and more responsible county rule. Though the charter divested the suburbs of none of their municipal duties, it did vest in the reorganized county certain powers usually associated in Ohio with municipal rather than with county governments. For example, it authorized the county board to enact ordinances, a power in the past exercised only by municipalities. Moreover, it created a county police department with authority to enforce both county and municipal ordinances, whereas county sheriffs traditionally had not enforced city and village ordinances. Further, the charter authorized the use of the initiative and referendum procedure and the establishment of a civil service commission, again marked departures from the past practices of county governments. Thus, the Cuyahoga County charter was not even a watered-down metropolitan scheme like the Greater Pittsburgh charter, although it did grant to the county certain powers usually associated with municipalities. The result was growing doubt about whether the charter would, in fact, have to pass the four hurdles.

Though the Pittsburgh and Cuyahoga charters provided for little or no centralized metropolitan authority, the ratification campaigns in both areas again centered on the issue of central-city aggression. Suburban foes of reform viewed even these modest changes as the first steps in an assault upon local self-government. Consequently, suburban leaders dusted off the familiar rhetoric of past campaigns and again presented it to the voting public.

In the Pittsburgh area many suburban leaders backed the proposed charter, and it won the endorsements of the Allegheny County Association of Township Commissioners and of Miller's League of Boroughs and Townships. The *Wilkinsburg Progress* continued its support for reform, observing that "none of the municipalities of Allegheny county are self-sufficient. The progress of each is bound up in the progress of the others," the Wilkinsburg editor argued, and "greater growth is possible only by greater cooperation." The president of the Penn Township board of education echoed the newspaper's sentiments, urging county residents to "build our community in one day from a large number of small towns to the fourth city of the United States by voting 'Yes' on the Metropolitan Charter."[41]

But the traditional opposition persisted. The Business Men's Association of working-class Duquesne denounced the charter, refusing "to be buncoed by ... ultra-liberal promises," and the *Duquesne Times* argued that the "men behind the scheme are planning annexation of

Allegheny county's prosperous industrial units to the city of Pittsburgh."
According to the *Times*, the grasping sponsors of the proposed charter
only "want to know ... where these municipalities keep the money bags
and how much they have on hand." Consequently, the Duquesne editor
urged his readers to "protect the integrity and future of your city by
voting against the scheme."[42] Senator Mansfield continued his opposition to metropolitan rule, speaking before local groups on the dangers of
amalgamation. Before an open forum in suburban Homestead, he
argued that "it would not be long until the local fire and police departments would be done away with," and he explained how the political
machine would manipulate metropolitan board elections. Moreover, he
believed that boroughs and townships that did not approve the charter
should not be included within the metropolitan district. Even though a
majority of the units had endorsed the charter by two-to-one margins, a
renegade, antimetropolitan community such as McKeesport should not
suffer the yoke of metropolitan rule, he felt.[43]

   In Cuyahoga County, local officials and suburban newspapers echoed
Mansfield's sentiments. Mayor Amos Kauffman of Lakewood continued
his attacks on county reform, noting "the ease with which a [charter]
amendment ... could be adopted to force the suburbs to become a part
of the county-city government." According to Kauffman, "the tendency
is to take from the suburbs the right to determine the important question
of annexation," and the county charter somehow seemed part of this
trend. Moreover, this charter supposedly would enhance the influence of
Clevelanders over county government so that "the suburbs would be at
the mercy of the voters of ... Cleveland," and it would increase taxes
while generally contributing nothing to the people of Lakewood.[44] The
Lakewood Post and West Shore Post agreed with Kauffman, stating
that "we are as little satisfied with the charter to be presented as we
were with the idea of virtual annexation which actuated pioneers of the
county idea." According to the *Post*, the county charter was "an opening wedge," and the charter commission intended "that further 'reforms' ... be inaugurated at some later date." This opening wedge, the
paper argued, "represents a definite danger to the welfare of this community," for it would aid the forces of consolidation and "only through
maintaining definite political identity can Lakewood enjoy to the full,
the advantages that are its birthright."[45] Though the *Berea Enterprise*
did not "feel the new charter would ... swallow up or violate suburban
municipalities, as scareheads are proclaiming," still it urged the electorate to "vote no and be safe."[46]

   Reform groups, on the other hand, endorsed the Cuyahoga charter
but regretted the absence of a federative metropolitan plan. The Citizens
League recommended adoption but insisted that the commission should

have created a county-wide municipality, or "at least should have trans-
ferred to the county those functions which were metropolitan in character."[47] Cuyahoga County's League of Women Voters believed "that
the charter is an improvement over the present system," but noted sadly
that it "does not meet the difficult problems of our metropolitan area
with its 116 taxing units and their multiplicity of ... local officials."[48]
The Cleveland newspapers had fewer doubts, and the *Plain Dealer*
boldly defended the charter from those who insisted it "threatens the
isolation of Cleveland's municipal neighbors."[49]

Pittsburgh's charter also received a long list of endorsements. The
embittered Professor Faust described the Allegheny County charter
campaign as "a glorious love feast" with the Chamber of Commerce,
Boards of Trade, League of Women Voters, and the Democratic and
Republican machines working together to achieve adoption.[50] The *Pittsburgh Post-Gazette* observed that "no proposition ever went to the
people with greater unanimity of indorsement" but argued that "it is
inevitable that there should be zeal for the Metropolitan project" among
those "who view it in an unprejudiced manner."[51] Westinghouse president A. L. Humphrey continued his active support, proclaiming publicly
that the metropolitan plan means expansion and prosperity." Most city
leaders seemed to agree with Humphrey that the charter offered "added
achievement and added glory for the workshop of the World."[52]

Despite the ballyhoo and boosterism, neither charter succeeded at the
polls. Pittsburgh's charter received a favorable vote from sixty-eight
percent of the county's electorate, but won the necessary two-thirds
majority in only 48 of the 122 governmental units, 14 short of the required number. Cuyahoga County's charter also won a county-wide
majority, with 53 percent of the voters expressing approval. But in 1936
the Ohio Supreme Court ruled that the charter had in fact vested the
county with municipal functions and that it thus had to pass the four
hurdles.[53] This it had failed to do, having won the support of only 49.8
percent of the county voters outside of Cleveland and having captured a
majority of the votes in only 12 of Cuyahoga County's 59 cities, villages,
and townships. In Pittsburgh and Cleveland, the majority did not rule,
for minority safeguards had prevented the realization of change.

Metropolitan reformers failed to win as impressive majorities in these
charter elections as they had in the earlier amendment contests. Yet the
white-collar suburbanite remained loyal to the cause, and again voters
in Edgewood and Mount Lebanon backed the reform proposal by
margins of better than two to one. Residents of elegant Thornburg voted
eighty-seven to two in favor of Pittsburgh's metropolitan charter, and in
equally prestigious Rosslyn Farms the vote was fifty-nine for and twelve
against. Citizens in the less affluent areas and outlying districts of

Allegheny County were more erratic in their voting behavior, and in some of these boroughs and townships the returns in June 1929 differed radically from those of November 1928. Fifty-three percent of those casting ballots in Homestead opposed the amendment in 1928, whereas only 13 percent opposed the charter of 1929. In contrast, only 40 percent of the Harrison Township electorate opposed the amendment of 1928, but 79 percent expressed disfavor toward the metropolitan charter of 1929. The working-class and outlying areas of Allegheny County were, then, less consistent in their vote on the metropolitan issue. As is shown in tables 12 and 13 in 1929 as in 1928 there was a definite tendency for the wealthy commuter suburbs to favor reform and the outlying mill towns and rural areas to oppose it.[54]

In Cuyahoga County this same tendency was again evident (see tables 12 and 13). As in the two previous elections, voters in swank Shaker Heights, Cleveland Heights, and Bratenahl rallied behind the forces of reform and supported the proposed charter by a two-to-one margin. The industrial suburbs along the Cuyahoga River Valley proved less enthusiastic about county reorganization, and their blue-collar residents voted against the proposed charter by better than two to one. Along the rural fringe, the truck farmers marched to the polls and for the third time expressed their bitter opposition to any change in county rule.[55]

In both Pennsylvania and Ohio blue-collar workers in outlying factory towns and working-class dormitories repeatedly had expressed their antagonism toward any measure that might compromise the independence of their municipalities. They did not dream of efficiency, economy, or metropolitan grandeur. These were the fantasies that delighted the business and professional communities, the people who sought to boost the fortunes of the metropolis, improve the services in the suburbs, and perpetuate the existence of the outlying units. The residents of Shaker Heights and Mount Lebanon believed in the metropolitan community and sought to establish a political structure for this community. The citizenry in Newburgh Heights and McKeesport did not.

Likewise, the outlying farmer and rural resident felt no kinship with the citizenry of Pittsburgh and Edgewood or Cleveland and Cleveland Heights. They did not want to pay higher taxes to support metropolitan services that would benefit the commuter and city dweller. These citizens along the edges of the metropolis favored their existing, inexpensive governments, untainted by big-city influences and well adapted to the needs of rural America.

Though these exurbanites and their allies in the blue-collar suburbs were a minority within the metropolis, they could block reform because

TABLE 12. Support for Proposed Charters on the Basis of Median Value of Monthly Rentals—Allegheny County 1929 and Cuyahoga County 1935

Distribution of suburban units—Allegheny County 1929

Median value of monthly rentals	Support for metropolitan charter					
	80%+	*60%-79%*	*40%-59%*	*20%-39%*	*0%-19%*	*Median*
$40+	3	4	1	0	0	75%
$30-$39.99	1	12	2	0	0	71%
$20-$29.99	5	11	13	4	1	59%
$0-$19.99	7	19	10	15	12	52%

Distribution of suburban units—Cuyahoga County 1935

Median value of monthly rentals	Support for county charter				
	60%+	*40%-59%*	*20%-39%*	*0%-19%*	*Median*
$50+	3	8	1	0	52%
$40-$49.99	2	7	5	0	46%
$30-$39.99	0	4	13	3	33%
$0-$29.99	0	1	4	5	18.5%

Correlations among support for proposed charters, monthly rentals and distance from central-city business district

Metropolitan area	Value of rentals	Distance
Pittsburgh	+.42	−.58
Cleveland	+.69	−.33

SOURCES: Computed on basis of data from Abstract of Elections 1935, Cuyahoga County Board of Elections, Cleveland, Ohio; Civic Club of Allegheny County Records, Archives of Industrial Society, University of Pittsburgh Library, Pittsburgh, Pennsylvania; *Pittsburgh Post-Gazette*, 27 June 1929, p. 2; Gow, "Metropolitics in Pittsburgh," pp. 304-6. Economic data derived from *Real Property Inventory of Allegheny County* (data collected in February 1934); Green, *Population Characteristics Cleveland 1930*; Green, *Supplement to Population Characteristics Cleveland 1930*; *Population and Housing, Statistics for Census Tracts—Cleveland, Ohio and Adjacent Area, 1940* (Washington, D.C., 1942), pp. 130-38. Rental figures averaged from the 1930 and 1940 data. Again, North Randall, Warrensville Township, Chagrin Falls Township, Trafford, and Sewickley Heights Township are excluded from consideration because of insufficient data.

of Ohio's rigorous four hurdles and Pennsylvania's awesome two-thirds requirement. As one Pittsburgh reformer noted, "it would be difficult to elect the twelve Apostles if one had to get a two-thirds vote from all the boroughs and townships in Allegheny county."[56] Safeguards protected the minority from majority rule, and these safeguards proved insurmountable. For reformers, the challenge was too great, the barriers were too high, and the opposition was too determined.

TABLE 13. Support for Proposed Charters on the Basis of Distance from City Center—
Allegheny County 1929 and Cuyahoga County 1935

Distribution of suburban units—Allegheny County 1929

Distance from city center (miles)	Support for metropolitan charter				
	80%+	60%-79%	40%-59%	0%-39%	Median
2-6	10	21	6	1	72%
7-10	3	15	15	10	56%
11-19	3	11	7	19	46.5%

Distribution of suburban units—Cuyahoga County 1935

Distance from city center (miles)	Support for county charter				
	60%+	40%-59%	20%-39%	0%-19%	Median
4-7	4	4	3	1	46.5%
8-11	0	12	8	2	42.5%
12-15	1	4	13	5	31%

SOURCES: Abstract of Elections 1935, Cuyahoga County Board of Elections, Cleveland,
Ohio; Civic Club of Allegheny County Records, Archives of Industrial Society, University
of Pittsburgh Library, Pittsburgh, Pennsylvania; *Pittsburgh Post-Gazette*, 27 June 1929,
p. 2; Gow, "Metropolitics in Pittsburgh," pp. 304-6. Trafford, Chagrin Falls Township,
and North Randall are not included in the figures.

In both the Cleveland and the Pittsburgh campaigns, reform forces
were formidable but not formidable enough. Reformers accepted bland
metropolitan charters in order to placate politicians, suburban officeholders, and exurbia; yet even these tepid products of compromise failed
to win the requisite majorities. In both metropolitan areas the reform
parties had included the supposed wielders of power and wealth, but
these leaders could not overcome the opposition that had been evident in
the earlier constitutional amendment contests. The metropolitan power
elite had stood behind the reform cause; the business moguls, metropolitan dailies, political chieftains, and experts from the universities all
had rallied around the federative plans. In the end, however, the elite,
the most articulate, the most powerful, and the most learned in the city
lost to the farmers, the factory workers, and the xenophobic suburban
officials. Working-class and semi-rural suburbs had clashed with elegant, white-collar suburbs, and the working-class and exurban communities had triumphed. The Mellons, the Tafts, and the Morton Mays
were not to mold the future of metropolitan America. Instead, they lost
to the forces of "Beanie" Bean and William Mansfield.

9

THE CONTINUING CONFLICT

In December 1930 Joseph Miller embarked on his second campaign to achieve a federated metropolis, and throughout the few remaining years of his life he battled central-city leaders, Democratic politicians, and suburban obstructionists in a futile effort to realize the goal of a Greater Pittsburgh. Meanwhile, the Citizens League of Cleveland continued to sponsor county charter proposals that incorporated borough plans. And as late as 1961 eighty-year-old Thomas Reed submitted an advisory report to the United States House of Representatives on the merits of metropolitan reform.[1] The forces of Reed, Fesler, and Miller had suffered setbacks, but defeat did not stifle their enthusiasm for change. Attempts to reconcile the conflicting forces of separatism and consolidation would continue, and hopes for metropolitan federation would remain alive.

By the close of the 1930s the need for reform seemed increasingly apparent. Nightmares of central-city decline were becoming realities as the population of Cleveland dropped by almost 3 percent between 1930 and 1940, and the populations of Saint Louis and Boston each slipped by 1 percent. Pittsburgh's population inched slightly upward during the decade, but its age of vitality and growth had passed and an era of dotage and decay was approaching. By the 1950s, the number of major cities that were losing population had risen sharply, with fifteen of the cities that had ranked among the top twenty in 1940 dropping in population. During the 1960s, sixteen of these fell in total number of residents as the centrifugal flow of population continued. There was a successful revival of annexation activity in medium-sized cities after 1945, and some cities such as Jacksonville, Indianapolis, Kansas City, Oklahoma City, and San Diego absorbed vast tracts during the postwar decades. But the traditional urban giants suffered losses both of population and of industry and commerce, with a consequent weakening of the tax base.

Throughout these same decades suburban units flourished and proliferated. The number of municipalities in suburban Saint Louis County soared from twenty-one in 1930 to forty-one in 1940 and eighty-three in 1950. During the 1950s a new wave of municipal births added confusion to the already jumbled map of Los Angeles County, as the number of cities in that county increased from forty-five to sixty-eight. In 1959 Minnesota lawmakers placed a curb on the creation of new government units by making incorporations subject to the review of a state municipal commission; and in that same year Wisconsin's legislature vested similar power in the state director of regional planning. In the 1960s other states also toughened the requirements for incorporation, veering away from the hands-off policy of the late nineteenth century. Yet such measures only limited further fragmentation; they did not cement the fissures that already divided the metropolis.

Political fragmentation persisted and so did the patterns of social and economic segregation that underlay many of the governmental rifts. After immigration from southern and eastern Europe was restricted in the 1920s, the significance of the division between native and foreign-born diminished. But the influx of blacks into the northern cities from World War I onward increased the impact of racial particularism. Blacks flooded into the older neighborhoods of central cities. As a result, the proportion of Chicago's population that was black increased from 8 percent in 1940 to 33 percent in 1970; in Cleveland the figure rose from 10 percent to 38 percent; and in Saint Louis it rose from 13 percent to 41 percent. By the 1960s the typical American metropolis consisted of a black core and a surrounding white mass. There were some black specks in the white outer shell, but many of these were segregated black municipalities in the apartheid tradition of Brooklyn, Illinois. Thus, the Cincinnati suburb of Lincoln Heights, the Chicago suburb of Robbins, and the Saint Louis suburb of Kinloch were each all-black municipalities that, along with their white neighbors, perpetuated the American tradition of ethnic segregation. And this tradition of ethnic segregation continued to bolster the political fragmentation of the metropolis.

Likewise, partisan rifts reinforced the fragmentation of the past. During the 1920s the Republicans ruled both in the central city of Saint Louis and in Saint Louis County, both in Pittsburgh and in its suburbs, and in Cleveland and its surrounding communities. There were some differences in partisan loyalty from one section of the metropolis to another, but city and suburb were not sharply divided in partisan loyalties. In the 1930s the central cities and some of the suburbs headed into the Democratic column, whereas other suburbs remained staunchly Republican. By the 1960s most central cities were overwhelmingly Democratic. As such, they posed a sharp partisan contrast to the ring of Republican suburbs. In every election from 1896 through 1928 both the city of Chicago and the suburban remainder of Cook County voted for the same presidential candidate, an occurrence that was rare after the 1930s. In each election from 1916 through 1932 the city of Philadelphia and surrounding suburban Montgomery and Delaware counties cast a majority of votes for the same candidate for president. Yet from 1936 through 1960 a majority of Philadelphia voters regularly cast their ballots for the Democratic candidate while the citizenry of Delaware and Montgomery counties sided with the Republican presidential nominee in every race. And from 1916 through 1936 voters in the city of Saint Louis and in Saint Louis County supported the same presidential contender in every election but one, whereas from 1940 through 1960 voters in the city differed with voters in the county in their choices for president in all but one of the contests. Between 1932 and 1960 a partisan rift was widening between segments of the metropolis, and this added still another possible obstacle to metropolitan unity.

The metropolis thus remained fragmented. The fissures that had developed in the late nineteenth century had widened and deepened into crevasses, and the difficulty of bridging these gaps persisted. Metropolitan America was still a collection of insulated fragments, and unitary consolidation in Cleveland, Saint Louis, or Los Angeles seemed as remote a possibility as the restoration of the Bourbons to the throne of France. By the 1950s and 1960s the *ancien régime* of the imperial central city was only a memory.

Meanwhile, lawmakers continued to respond to fragmentation by creating special-purpose metropolitan districts and by encouraging inter-municipal cooperation. During the 1930s, 1940s, and 1950s the number of park boards, sewage districts, port authorities, and similar special-purpose units soared. Of the seventy-nine metropolitan special-purpose districts existing in 1956, fifty-one had been created since 1930.[2] Unification through nineteenth-century annexation procedures and twentieth-century borough plans had failed. Consequently, metropolitan citizens resorted to the special district.

In metropolitan areas throughout the nation, lawmakers created such makeshift authorities. Beginning in 1946 the sewage problems of metropolitan Pittsburgh came under the purview of the Allegheny County Sanitary Authority. As early as 1917 Ohio lawmakers had created the Cleveland Metropolitan Park District to plan and maintain parklands in Cuyahoga County. This agency was a model for the Hamilton County Park District, established in 1930, and for the Columbus and Franklin County Park District, which in 1947 assumed responsibility for parks in central Ohio. Unable to agree on either city-county consolidation or federative rule, Saint Louis area residents turned to the special district as an alternative. In 1949 their efforts resulted in the creation of the

Bi-State Development District to regulate port facilities and to promote economic development in both the Saint Louis and East Saint Louis areas. Moreover, in 1954 the Metropolitan Saint Louis Sewer District assumed supervision of sewage disposal in both the city and the county of Saint Louis. Farther west, the San Diego County Water Authority began providing water to the San Diego metropolitan area in 1944, and the Los Angeles County Air Pollution Control District assumed responsibility for that area's smog problems in 1948. Broad-purpose unified rule had seemed to threaten the vaunted self-government of local units in Pennsylvania, Ohio, Missouri, and throughout the nation. But single-function districts appeared less of a danger to state lawmakers in Columbus and Jefferson City, to semirural residents on the urban fringe, to suburban mayors protective of local autonomy, and to central-city politicians dedicated to the status quo.

The creation of such districts, however, did not reduce the number of governmental agencies but simply augmented the already awesome total. Metropolitan park and sewage authorities joined the legion of school districts, townships, and municipalities, thus adding to the confusion of the metropolis. Moreover, few citizens understood exactly who administered metropolitan parks and sewers, and where these faceless, unknown administrators derived their authority and funds. Citizens of Saint Louis or University City could blame their mayor and aldermen in an easily identified city hall for chuckholes in the streets and rusting equipment in their playgrounds, and they could vote them out of office at the next election. But how could one assault a metropolitan sewage commissioner when one did not know who appointed him and had no idea of where or in what manner to express his discontent? The maze of metropolitan rule was growing increasingly complex, and the voter in both suburb and central city was hopelessly lost.[3]

Adding to the confusion was the continued expansion of county government. By 1970 counties throughout the nation were supplementing and often supplanting the municipality as providers of public services. Of 150 major urban counties surveyed in 1972, 57 percent administered public libraries and 55 percent enforced zoning ordinances and maintained parks and recreation facilities. Thirty-three percent of the urban county governments were engaged in sewage disposal, 31 percent offered fire protection, and 21 percent provided garbage collection services and a water supply.[4] County home rule laws in seventeen states allowed counties to draft their own charters, frame their own structure of government, and determine for themselves the extent of their functions.[5] Legislators in state after state were maximizing the flexibility of county government and allowing the county to act in place of the municipality. By 1970 in some urban areas, neither incorporation nor annexation was necessary for the provision of traditional municipal services. The creation of metropolitan special districts and broad-purpose county governments had obviated the necessity of resorting to any form of municipal government.

Moreover, cooperation between suburban cities and county governments enhanced the quality of suburban services, further lessening the appeal of consolidation with the central city. In 1954 Los Angeles County contracted for the first time to provide all administrative services to an incorporated city, the city of Lakewood. A score of suburban cities in metropolitan Los Angeles soon adopted the Lakewood Plan. Through this arrangement, the county provides for everything from police to garbage collection and the city government serves primarily as a negotiating body to work out the terms of the contract with the county.[6] During the 1950s and 1960s some cities chose to contract for the complete range of services; others relied on the county for only certain functions or facilities. Thus a flexibility developed. Municipalities were able to select from the catalog of county services, buying some and reserving the power to provide others themselves according to their own particular needs and wishes. In California and elsewhere the simplicity of the nineteenth-century political structure had disappeared, and the functional line between city and county was becoming increasingly blurred.

Metropolitan special districts and the expansion of county government could not, however, satisfy the political reformer who continued to seek clear, orderly lines of authority; a reduction of wasteful, inefficient bureaucracy; and coordination of efforts among government agencies. The creation of special districts did not simplify metropolitan rule, and the expansion of county services, rather than clarifying local government structure, often confused it further. In the 1940s and 1950s political science professors and scholars in public administration were still teaching the dictates of Thomas Reed, and the need for efficiency and structural reform still fascinated reformers in the National Municipal League. White-collar leaders of the 1950s had been educated in this tradition, and they remained enthusiastic about the possibilities of reform. Moreover, central-city business leaders who were now witnessing population declines in Cleveland and Saint Louis again felt metropolitan reform might give a boost to the rapidly deteriorating urban core. There were, then, many crusaders for efficient, orderly rule who still hoped for realization of a federative scheme that would placate the suburban desire for self-government but achieve the great goal of union. And in the late 1950s a second generation of metropolitan reformers replayed the drama of the 1920s and 1930s in Cleveland, Saint Louis, and Miami.

The schemes of the 1950s were similar to those of the 1920s and 1930s. Cleveland's reformers again sought to create a new metropolitan county

government resembling the London County Council. Again they urged
that the county assume responsibility for sewage disposal, water supply,
major thoroughfares, public welfare and poor relief, public transit, port
facilities, metropolitan parks, regional planning, civil defense, and air
and water pollution. To achieve this goal reformers would have to fight
three election campaigns: one to amend the state constitution, one to
win approval for the election of a county charter commission, and one
for approval of the proposed metropolitan charter. As in the 1930s, reform forces won the first two contests, but in 1959 they lost the third.
During that same year Saint Louis reformers submitted to the electorate
a metropolitan district plan that provided for a metropolitan authority
that would govern public transit, traffic control, civil defense, assessment, land use planning, and sewage disposal throughout both Saint
Louis County and the city of Saint Louis. This plan also went down to
defeat. But in 1957 Miami area voters approved a metropolitan scheme
that permitted the county to exercise a wide range of functions, including
supervision of arterial traffic, public transit, water supply, sewage disposal, parks, hospitals, and public welfare.

In each of these cities the scenarios of the revived metropolitan campaigns were similar to those of previous productions. During the early
1930s Charles P. Taft II had led the Ohio cast of metropolitan reform
characters, and in the 1950s his son Seth Taft of suburban Chagrin
Falls played the starring role in Cleveland's metropolitan struggle. The
younger Taft had abandoned his family's traditional base in Cincinnati,
but he had not forsworn his father's principles. In the late 1940s he
joined a prestigious Cleveland law firm, and by 1952 he had already
become head of the Citizens League Committee on Metropolitan Government. In the mid-1950s he reached the pinnacle of reform gentility
when he was elected president of the Citizens League. Thus, in the
person of Seth Taft, those two great bulwarks of Ohio metropolitan
reform, the Taft family and the Citizens League, united in one effort to
achieve the thwarted dreams of Charles P. Taft II and Mayo Fesler.

Joining with the younger Taft in the renewed battle for metropolitan
federation was a group of men reminiscent of earlier reformers. An early
leader in the struggle of the 1950s was Bayless Manning, a resident of
suburban Euclid, who practiced law in the same firm as Taft and who
was, like Taft, a graduate of the Yale Law School. In this metropolitan
coalition Norton Long of suburban Cleveland Heights represented the
academic world, holding a position in the political science department
of Western Reserve University. And Mayo Fesler's successor as director
of the Citizens League, Estal Sparlin of suburban Cleveland Heights,
served as an admirable surrogate for the retired reformer.

In Saint Louis the cast of characters also bore a striking resemblance to those who had acted in the drama of 1930. Again the county and city chambers of commerce staunchly supported the plan as did those perennial good-government reformers, the League of Women Voters. Chancellor Shepley of Washington University led the academic contingent of metropolitan reformers, assuming the role played by George W. Stephens twenty-nine years earlier. Publishers of metropolitan dailies lined up loyally behind the scheme as did such major businesses as McDonnell Aircraft Company, Southwestern Bell, and each of the leading banks. The president of the Saint Louis Board of Aldermen, Al Cervantes, backed the federative proposal and thus represented one deviation from the standard pattern. Yet, true to form, no other major officeholders campaigned for metropolitan reform.

The opposition of public officials was noteworthy in both the Saint Louis and Cleveland metropolitan areas. In 1958 and 1959, as in 1930 and 1933, many central-city politicos and suburban potentates looked askance at any scheme that threatened to disrupt the status quo. They continued to guard their bastions of power and authority, and no high-toned reformers from Cleveland Heights or Clayton were going to rob them of their prerogatives.

Cleveland's central-city officials were staunchly opposed to the metropolitan charter of 1959. Mayor Anthony Celebreeze denounced the document publicly and warned that it would force Cleveland to share its services and assets with the suburbs. Celebreeze's utilities director argued that the people wanted "a simple county home rule charter, not a supergovernment which rips up the assets of our community."[7] Ralph Locher, the city's law director and a future mayor, observed that the public was "not ready to permit our city's assets to be liquidated."[8] The assistant city prosecutor and another future mayor, Carl Stokes, likewise followed Celebreeze's lead and earned a reputation as "an outspoken critic of the charter."[9] And Cleveland's former mayor and leading Democrat, Senator Frank Lausche, voted against the metropolitan plan.[10] The city's chief politicos wanted to protect Cleveland's interests, and this meant vetoing the innovative scheme of shared services and responsibilities.

Suburbanites joined Celebreeze and his clique in their fight against the charter and also warned of the dire consequences of metropolitan reform. Inheriting the mantle of Frank Cain, Mayor Wilson G. Stapleton of Shaker Heights was among the most outspoken opponents of federation. He told audiences that the "county under the charter could confiscate any city's valuables ... without so much as asking the owner 'by your leave.'"[11] In his speeches he took the same protective stance toward Shaker Heights that Winston Churchill took toward the British Empire, and he quoted the prime minister repeatedly, saying: "I did not become the queen's first minister to preside over the liquidation of Her Majesty's empire."[12] The members of the Mayors Association of Cuyahoga County were equally reluctant to surrender their domains, and they passed a resolution denouncing the proposed charter. Twenty-eight of the forty-four suburban executives voting on the resolution cast votes against metropolitan rule.[13] In the 1950s, as in the 1930s, suburban officials were dedicated to retaining their little realms of power.

In suburban Saint Louis County the response of officials was much the same. Mayor A. Ray Parker of suburban Brentwood, chairman of the antimetropolitan Citizens Committee for Self-Government, spoke of the "inherent dislike by our American voter of large, centralized government" and claimed that the voters feared "unnecessary increases in taxes and infringement of zoning and other powers now vested in local governments."[14] Saint Louis County Supervisor John McNary argued that metropolitan reorganization was no solution and observed that "voluntary cooperation among the city, the county, and county municipalities could go far toward meeting common problems."[15] The Richmond Heights City Council officially opposed the metropolitan scheme and "offered high taxes and control of zoning as reasons for opposing the plan."[16] And one suburban newspaper reprinted articles in which metropolitan reform groups were identified as "communist fronts."[17]

Leaders in the central city of Saint Louis likewise opposed the metropolitan plan of 1959, but their complaints differed from those of suburban officials and editors. Whereas county politicos attacked the scheme as imposing too much central authority, Saint Louis's mayor and aldermen criticized the plan as being too weak and as not achieving enough consolidation. Mayor Raymond Tucker consistently opposed federative schemes. On a television broadcast Tucker told viewers that "the plan itself is too weak and doubtful an instrument for carrying out the tasks assigned to it."[18] Moreover, according to Tucker, it did not reduce the number of governmental units and would not reduce taxes and expenditures. "As a result of the duplication of functions," Tucker noted, "the city would certainly not be able to reduce its tax rate by the amount of the new tax rate levied by the proposed Metropolitan District."[19] Saint Louis taxpayers supposedly would gain nothing from reform, and thus Tucker recommended defeat of the scheme.

While residents in greater Saint Louis and greater Cleveland were wrestling with metropolitan proposals, Miamians were engaged in their own battle for federative regional rule. Miami had not sought to achieve a federal or borough plan in the 1930s as had Cleveland, Saint Louis, and Pittsburgh. But even in Miami a pattern prevailed similar to that found in the earlier metropolitan contests. The contest for metropolitan reform in Miami during the late 1950s was, then, still another replay of the scenario so familiar to Reed, Fesler, and Miller.

In Miami as elsewhere business and academic reformers rallied behind the proposed federative charter. For example, the scheme enjoyed the backing of the *Miami Herald*, the *Miami News*, and the Miami-Dade Chamber of Commerce. The League of Women Voters in Miami, Miami Beach, Coral Gables, and Hialeah all supported the plan staunchly. In suburban Coral Gables the vice-president of the University of Miami drummed up support among university personnel, while the vice-president of Burdine's, Miami's leading department store, followed the earlier examples of retailers Sidney Baer and Morton May by lobbying among his company's employees. In Miami as in Cleveland and Saint Louis, the business and academic elite were in the forefront of reform.

Officialdom and the suburban editors assumed their usual places in the forefront of the opposition. The city manager of Miami was a longstanding foe of the metropolitan scheme, and a former mayor of the city maintained that there were one hundred reasons for defeating the plan. The suburban-dominated Dade County League of Municipalities denounced the proposed charter publicly, and the mayor of outlying Homestead expressed fears that the distant metropolitan government would neglect Homestead's interests. In Hialeah and Miami Shores, the city councils appropriated money to fight the scheme; and in Miami Beach the opposition was fierce. A Miami Beach editor lambasted the charter, claiming that it was the product of Coral Gables college professors, central-city newspapers, and washed-up politicians. Miamians were hearing the same charges as those exchanged in Cleveland in 1933, in Saint Louis in 1930, and in Pittsburgh in 1929. And the suburban city councils, mayors, and editors were still the chief sources of this rhetoric.[20]

Not only was the rhetoric familiar in each of the metropolitan contests of the 1950s, but the voting patterns in the charter elections also conformed to the patterns evident in the 1930s. In the Cleveland, Saint Louis, and Miami areas, voters from the elite suburbs were the most ardent backers of the metropolitan proposals. In 1934, 77 percent of the voters of Shaker Heights had favored the election of a commission to draft a metropolitan charter; and in 1958, 84 percent of that suburb's voters backed a similar proposition. Sixty-one percent of Rocky River's electorate had supported the proposal in 1934, while 62 percent of Lakewood's voters had cast their ballots for reform. Twenty-four years later 78 percent of Rocky River's voters favored a charter commission, as did 73 percent of Lakewood's electorate. Forty-two percent of the voters

in the wealthy Clayton, University City, Creve Couer, and Ladue areas
of Saint Louis County backed the 1959 metropolitan scheme, compared
to only 33 percent in the city of Saint Louis and 21 percent in the remainder of the county. And in Dade County, Florida, 66 percent of the
voters in the plush suburb of Coral Gables favored the metropolitan
federation, whereas the proposal received a favorable vote from only 57
percent of those casting ballots in the city of Miami and 51 percent of
those in the county as a whole. Throughout suburban Dade County
those precincts with the most expensive homes led in support of the
reform plan, with 62 percent of the voters in the wealthiest unincorporated areas following the example of Coral Gables in supporting
metropolitan rule. In Miami, Saint Louis, and Cleveland the upper-
middle-class suburbanite was the most dedicated believer in metropolitan federation, remaining steadfast to the reform faith of his counterparts in the 1920s and 1930s. [21]

Though the metropolitan battles of the 1950s closely resembled those
of twenty-five years earlier, a new and disquieting element was gaining
political power and it was using that power to thwart unity. This new
element was the black community that was expanding rapidly, especially
in the northern industrial centers. As their numbers increased so did
their voice in central-city government, and many blacks did not want to
dilute this newly won political power through federation with white
suburbia. During the 1930s black wards in Cleveland voted more heavily
for metropolitan rule than did white wards, with 79 percent supporting
the scheme in 1933 and 63 percent in 1934. By 1958 and 1959, however,
black support for county-wide federation had declined significantly. In
the commission contest of 1958 only 50 percent of the voters in black
wards supported the proposal, and in the charter election of 1959 only
29 percent favored reform. In contrast, 63 percent of the voters in white
wards of the central city endorsed the proposal in 1958, and 46 percent
did so one year later. [22] A new bastion of separatism and particularism
was developing in the black neighborhoods of America's cities, blocking
the efforts of suburban reformers.

The same trend is evident in Saint Louis and Miami. Only 29 percent
of the voters in the four black wards of Saint Louis favored the federative scheme in 1959, as compared to 34 percent of the voters in the
remainder of the city. Only 14 percent of the voters in the overwhelmingly black nineteenth ward expressed approval of metropolitan rule,
and only 15 percent did so in the black sixth ward. In sixteen affluent
precincts of predominantly white suburbia, the federative scheme won
majority approval, but in the core of Saint Louis racial minorities were
not willing to sacrifice their growing clout in local government for the
sake of efficiency, economy, and unity.

Likewise, only 40 percent of the voters in Miami's black precincts supported metropolitan federation, whereas an average of 60 percent of the voters in the city as a whole backed Dade Metro in electoral contests during the late 1950s.[23] Miami blacks, like their brethren to the north, saw little to gain and much to lose if they handed over the reins of power to the whites in Coral Gables.

The rhetoric of Cleveland's metropolitan campaign especially reflected this emerging attitude among blacks. One black councilman in Cleveland told his constituents that the metropolitan charter "is designed to tie a noose around the 'black ghetto,' and we stand to lose all of the strength we have [been] fighting to gain."[24] This official attacked procharter black leaders, charging that "just when we were beginning to come into our own, they deserted us."[25] Another black leader spoke of the diminished power blacks would possess in a metropolitan government and asked, "What good is a city when the citizens have no further voice in its policies, operation, and employment?"[26] And a full-page advertisement in Cleveland's black newspaper admonished readers that "you owe it to your children to prevent this rape of Cleveland" and warned that "Cleveland would become just another suburb in the county and have very little control over its employment, policies and operations."[27]

According to black opponents, the metropolitan charter offered much for the haves and little for the have-nots, much for the affluent suburbanite and little for the Clevelander. A ghetto councilman argued that "people are not going to swallow [a charter] that the downtown boys put forward," especially a charter that "is for the chosen few and not for the little man."[28] Another attacked "those thousands who no longer care to live among the citizens of Cleveland" and who seek to deprive Cleveland "of the essentials that are the very heart of a large municipality" and relegate it to being "nothing more than a suburb in county government."[29] Anticharter forces blasted "smug suburbanites, who rushed to the suburbs to escape carrying the city's tax burden" and claimed that they "would gain every benefit" from metropolitan rule "and offer nothing in return."[30]

Whites were moving to the suburbs, abandoning the central city to blacks, and relinquishing past positions and responsibilities to this minority so long denied political power. In 1959 Cleveland's voters elected eight black councilmen, and the number would continue to increase. Finally the black community was beginning to fall heir to the privilege of local self-government, a privilege traditionally cherished by white Americans. And now that they were acquiring this privilege, they were not going to vote it away for the sake of some untried and untested scheme backed by the white suburban elite. They were not fascinated by efficiency. They cared little about overlapping authorities. They wanted power. For blacks government was not simply a service organization that sold water, paved streets, and laid sewers. Government was a means of gaining power, a means for coercing the majority into granting equality of opportunity. Blacks wanted to hold the reins of city government and to achieve social advancement. They did not want to hand control over to white suburbanites.

Throughout the decade following Cleveland's charter referendum, black demands for local political power mounted. The 1960s was a decade of increasing black militancy, of Malcolm X and the Black Muslims, of riots in the nation's ghettos. Blacks wanted their share of power in the nation; they were tired of waiting for change that they felt was long overdue. And in the 1960s their frustration was as evident in the north as in the south. Blacks had moved north to New York City, Cleveland, Detroit, Chicago, and Saint Louis in droves, and they wanted political power in these cities.

Yet in most major cities blacks constituted only a minority of the voting population, and power continued to rest in the hands of white city administrators who governed the ghetto from downtown office towers. Frustrated by their continuing inability to govern themselves, some black leaders of the late 1960s began to preach neighborhood self-rule. In ghetto areas across the country, blacks demanded self-determination for their neighborhoods and some degree of autonomy from the white bureaucracy. In the 1950s they had blocked efforts at metropolitan reintegration. Now, in the 1960s, they favored further dispersion of political authority and disintegration of the unitary city. The pattern of social segregation that had fragmented suburban America was now threatening the unity of the central city as the chaos of the 1960s disrupted the metropolis.

This desire for dispersed power was most readily apparent in the controversy over the control of New York City's schools. In September 1966 parents in East Harlem demanded that the city school board "either ... bring white children in to integrate [intermediate school] 201 or they let the community run the school—let us pick the principal and the teachers, let us set the educational standards and make sure they are met."[31] The school board proposed the creation of an advisory body of community residents to aid in the government of Harlem's schools, but local leaders rejected the proposal, claiming that the advisory panel would be "nothing more than an elaborate P.T.A."[32] According to advocates of self-determination, the proposal took "its place at the top of a large pile of similar proposals as the season's document of deceit and duplicity from the 'Board of Genocide' of the City of New York."[33] In words reminiscent of earlier separatist rhetoric, Harlem's citizenry accused the board of education of the giant, consolidated city of an "arrogant insensitivity to the legitimate voice of the community."[34] For decades suburban Americans had feared distant, indifferent rule by big-city bosses and bureaucrats, and now the black leaders of Harlem were expressing the same views and demanding the traditional American right of local self-determination.

In 1968 the dispute over community control of school government in the Ocean Hill-Brownsville neighborhood of Brooklyn made the front pages of newspapers across the nation, and mayors and administrators became increasingly alert to cries for self-rule. In that same year a group of black citizens calling themselves the United Front of Roxbury demanded the withdrawal of Roxbury from the city of Boston, and in Watts residents were urging the secession of their neighborhood from the city of Los Angeles. After one hundred years of consolidated rule Roxbury residents were campaigning for a return to separatism, and after fifty years of subordination to Los Angeles some leaders in Watts were also calling for a resumption of autonomy. The forces of fragmentation were on the offensive, and the central city itself seemed on the verge of falling apart.

Numerous writers, officials, and reformers outside the urban neighborhoods responded to these cries for change by urging a decentralization of central-city rule. Milton Kotler of the Institute for Policy Studies denounced the American city of the late 1960s as "a floundering empire, no longer in control of the neighborhoods it has annexed."[35] He repudiated the past emphasis on expansion and consolidation and recommended the creation of neighborhood corporations as a means for furthering local self-rule. In 1968 Mayor Kevin White of Boston initiated a program of neighborhood city halls and observed that "the greatest domestic crisis in America today is the failure of the cities to respond to the human needs of its citizens."[36] The National Advisory Commission on Intergovernmental Relations recommended that "neighborhood initiative and self-respect be fostered by authorizing counties and large cities to establish neighborhood subunits endowed with limited powers of taxation and local self-government."[37] And in 1972 a study sponsored by the Bar Association of New York City urged that the nation's largest city be divided into thirty to forty new governmental units, each with its own mayor and council and each "responsible for carrying out significant service and regulatory functions."[38] There would be an overarching city government that would exercise those functions best handled centrally, but the neighborhoods would be responsible for much of the business of governing.

Others suggested similar dual-level schemes, and reformers turned again to the much-discussed notion of a federative metropolis. In 1970 the Committee for Economic Development, which included among its members Charles P. Taft II, concluded that "to gain the advantage of both centralization and decentralization, we recommend as an ultimate solution a governmental system of two levels. Some functions should be assigned in their entirety to the area-wide government, others to the local level."[39] Two years later Joseph Zimmerman, Thomas Reed's successor as spokesman for the metropolitan cause, likewise wrote of neighborhood government, suggesting "that large city government in the United States be revitalized by converting the existing unitary system into a federation."[40] Moreover, in 1974 the League of Women Voters published a study on the "prospects for two-tier government." As the study noted, experts were concluding that "perhaps urban residents can have the best of all political worlds by moving toward two-tier government: a metropolitan-wide unit—a supercity—combined with local or neighborhood components."[41]

Thus Americans continued to hear the same familiar arguments. In the 1970s, as in the 1920s, the forces of consolidation, fragmentation, and federation were clashing on the metropolitan battlefield. Ghetto spokesmen demanded community power and local self-determination just as vigorously as Oak Park whites had done decades before. Planners spoke of the need for regional cooperation and coordination and an end to waste, inefficiency, and confusion. And reformers such as the ubiquitous Charles Taft continued to back that aging innovation, the federative metropolis. Many battles had been fought over the subject in metropolitan areas across the country, and the conflict had not yet come to a conclusion.

Throughout this long struggle, however, dedication to the ideal of self-rule had remained strong. In dry, old-stock Evanston, in wet, Polish Hamtramck, and in black Harlem, Americans had sought to govern the destinies of their local communities either by retaining local power or obtaining such power. In a nation as diverse as the United States, separatism was inevitable as those of varying social, cultural, and ethnic backgrounds sought to create their little neighborhood havens of particularism. Local self-rule allowed each group, each interest, to pursue its goals with only limited interference. It permitted diversity in government as opposed to central dictation. And, as late as the 1970s, mayors, bar associations, the League of Women Voters, and urban experts were still attempting to structure the law in accord with this ideal.

Dedication to local decision-making, in fact, underlay more than a century of American municipal law. During the late nineteenth and early twentieth centuries lawmakers had adopted permissive incorporation procedures that maximized the possibilities both of local self-rule and of metropolitan fragmentation. These permissive laws had combined with social and economic particularism and with rising material expectations to produce scores of suburban polities in every major metropolitan area. Likewise, a decentralized annexation procedure had enhanced the decision-making power of the local community, but this had not thwarted central-city expansion. Until the early twentieth century the demand for superior central-city services had acted as a countervailing force to the prevalent pattern of localism and particularism. Suburbanites yearned for Cleveland's water, Chicago's fire protection, and Boston's sewerage system, and they elected to unite with the city to gain these advantages. Decision-making authority rested with the locality, but local voters were supporting the cause of consolidation.

With the advent of metropolitan cooperation and improved suburban services, however, the countervailing force diminished. The relative inadequacy of suburban services had been the central city's strong suit in consolidation contests before 1910, but by the 1920s it was playing its last trumps and picking up few tricks. Central cities no longer seemed to provide services markedly superior to those offered by the largest and wealthiest suburbs, and most suburbanites perceived few advantages in abandoning local self-rule and sacrificing themselves to central-city masters. The result was fewer and fewer acquisitions, as the central city conquered those remaining communities that failed to meet the demands of autonomy.

In the hope of uniting the metropolis without yielding local rule, suburbanites in Pittsburgh, Cleveland, and Saint Louis had suggested federative forms of government. Such schemes would allow suburbanites to maintain their superior schools and exclusionary zoning codes while satisfying hopes of central-city growth and metropolitan efficiency. Federation would fulfill the dreams of central-city boosters while placating the local spirit in the suburbs. Thus structural reformers in the universities, business, and the press rallied behind these plans as did voters in the inner ring of white-collar suburbs. Many white-collar suburbanites had opposed earlier annexation attempts, but the federative scheme suited their schizoid devotion to both city and suburb, and they ranked among its most loyal supporters.

Yet again the metropolitan population proved too heterogeneous. Blue-collar suburbanites and semirural exurbanites stymied plans for federation in the 1920s and 1930s, and central-city blacks posed an obstacle to such reforms in the 1950s. Urban America was fragmented socially and culturally, and its political structure reflected these divisions. The political fragmentation of the nation was, in large part, a product of its social and economic fragmentation; and the reform panaceas of gentlemen and club women from Mount Lebanon, Shaker Heights, or

Clayton could not bridge these longstanding rifts. After decades of political impotence in a white man's country, Cleveland blacks were not willing to sacrifice the prospect of power in order to satisfy the scion of the Taft family. Union was not likely in a disunited society.

At the close of the 1860s Thomas Cooley had extolled local self-government as the underlying principle of the American system. More than one hundred years later, the legacy of this principle is all too evident throughout the nation. Hundreds of local units share in the governing of metropolitan New York, the Chicago metropolis, and the sprawling urban mass of Southern California. The movement toward neighborhood rule in the central cities has added still another facet to the complex history of local self-government, for those in the urban core continue to battle for local power just as fiercely as those at the urban fringe had decades ago. Suburb continues to vie with suburb, neighborhood corporations still fight central-city administrators, and everyone seems on the defensive against a relatively new threat, the ever-aggressive hand of the federal bureaucracy and federal judiciary. The conflict persists, and in the 1970s, as in the 1870s, Americans continue to guard jealously the rights and privileges of their local communities.

NOTES

Chapter 1

1. Eli K. Price, *The History of the Consolidation of Philadelphia* (Philadelphia, 1873), p. 53.
2. *Report of the Metropolitan District Commission to the Massachusetts Legislature* (Boston, 1896), p. 12.
3. Paul Studenski, *The Government of Metropolitan Areas in the United States* (New York, 1930), p. 29.
4. Robert Wood, *Suburbia: Its People and Their Politics* (Boston, 1959), p. 10.
5. Norton E. Long, "Citizenship or Consumership in Metropolitan Areas," *Journal of the American Institute of Planners* 31 (Feb. 1965):4-5.
6. Lawrence Lader, "Chaos in the Suburbs," *Better Homes and Gardens* 36 (Oct. 1958):10,12.
7. Francis S. Drake, *The Town of Roxbury: Its Memorable Persons and Places* (Roxbury, Mass., 1878), p. 42.
8. *St. Louis County Leader* (Clayton, Mo.), 29 Oct. 1926, p. 1; *West Allis* (Wis.) *Star*, 14 Feb. 1935, p. 4.
9. Peter Manso, ed., *Running Against the Machine* (Garden City, N. Y., 1969), pp. 11-15.
10. Douglas Yates, *Neighborhood Democracy: The Politics and Impacts of Decentralization* (Lexington, Mass., 1973), p. 11.
11. Howard W. Hallman, *Neighborhood Government in a Metropolitan Setting* (Beverly Hills, Cal., 1974), p. 245.
12. Wood, *Suburbia*, pp. 66-87. For other accounts of the metropolitan problem, see Victor Jones, *Metropolitan Government* (Chicago, 1942) and Kenneth T. Jackson, "Metropolitan Government Versus Political Autonomy: Politics on the Crabgrass Frontier," in *Cities in American History*, ed. Kenneth T. Jackson and Stanley Schultz (New York, 1972), pp. 442-62.
13. Wood, *Suburbia*, p. viii.

Chapter 2

1. Thomas M. Cooley, *A Treatise on the Constitutional Limitations Which Rest Upon the Legislative Power of the States of the American Union*, 3d ed. (Boston, 1874), p. 208.
2. George Edwards and Arthur Peterson, *New York as an Eighteenth-Century Municipality* (New York, 1917), pp. 219-20.
3. *Laws of a Public and General Nature, of the District of Louisiana ...* (Jefferson City, Mo., 1842), pp. 184-87. The Kentucky legislature authorized county courts to establish towns as early as 1796. *Digest of the Statute Laws of Kentucky ...* (Frankfort, Ky., 1834), 2:1505-8.
4. *Laws of the State of Indiana, Passed and Published, at the Second Session of the General Assembly, ... 1817* (Corydon, Ind., 1818), pp. 373-78.

5. Salmon P. Chase, ed., *The Statutes of Ohio and of the Northwestern Territory Adopted or Enacted From 1788 to 1833 Inclusive* ... (Cincinnati, 1834), 2:1014-17.

6. *Laws of the State of Missouri; Revised and Digested* (St. Louis, 1825), 2:764-68; *The Laws of Illinois Passed at Seventh General Assembly* (Vandalia, 1831), pp. 82-87; *The Public and General Statute Laws of the State of Illinois* ... (Chicago, 1839), pp. 381-84; John Purdon, ed., *A Digest of the Laws of Pennsylvania* ... (Philadelphia, 1852), pp. 148-50; *Revised Statutes of the State of Arkansas* ... (Boston, 1838), pp. 750-55; *Laws of the State of New York* ... (Albany, 1847), 2:532-33; *Acts and Resolutions Passed at the First Session of the General Assembly of the State of Iowa* (Iowa City, 1847), pp. 174-79; *The Revised Statutes of the State of Wisconsin, Passed at the Second Session of the Legislature, Commencing January 10, 1849* ... (Southport, Wis., 1849), pp. 290-91; *Acts of the State of Tennessee, Passed at the First Session of the Twenty-Eighth General Assembly for the Years 1849-50* (Nashville, 1850), pp. 37-42; S. Garfielde and F. A. Snyder, comps., *Compiled Laws of the State of California* ... (Benicia, Calif., 1853), pp. 114-15; *Acts of the Legislature of State of Michigan, Passed at the Regular Session of 1857* ... (Detroit, 1857), pp. 420-31. See Richard Bigger and James Kitchen, *How the Cities Grew: A Century of Municipal Independence and Expansionism in Metropolitan Los Angeles* (Los Angeles, 1952) for information on the limited discretionary power of California's county supervisors and the way they used that power. Bigger and Kitchen conclude that in the late nineteenth and early twentieth centuries, the Los Angeles County Board of Supervisors "adopted a laissez faire attitude" toward municipal incorporation (p. 102).

7. *General and Local Acts Passed and Joint Resolutions Adopted by the Seventy-Fifth General Assembly* [of the State of Ohio] (Columbus, 1902), p. 469.

8. A. Hutchinson, comp., *Code of Mississippi: Being an Analytical Compilation of the Public and General Statutes of the Territory and State, With Tabular References to the Local and Private Acts, From 1798 to 1848* ... (Jackson, Miss., 1848), pp. 92-95.

9. Harry Toulmin, comp., *A Digest of the Laws of the State of Alabama* ... (Cahawba, Ala., 1823), pp. 1057-60.

10. Date of incorporation from *Michigan Official Directory and Legislative Manual For the Years 1911-1912* (Lansing, 1911), pp. 214-42.

11. Seymour Sacks and William F. Hellmuth, Jr., *Financing Government in a Metropolitan Area: The Cleveland Experience* (New York, 1959), p. 11.

12. Chicago Bureau of Public Efficiency, *Unification of Local Governments in Chicago* (Chicago, 1917), pp. 20-24; *Local Governments in Chicago and Cook County* (Springfield, Ill., 1919), pp. 905-8.

13. *Thirteenth Census of the United States, 1910: Population by Counties and Minor Civil Divisions 1910, 1900, 1890* (Washington, 1912), pp. 127-33.

14. Harvey Walker, *Village Laws and Government in Minnesota* (Minneapolis, 1927).

15. *California Blue Book or State Roster 1911* (Sacramento, 1913), pp. 140-83.

16. For a further portrait of this integrated city, see Sam Bass Warner, Jr., *The Urban Wilderness: A History of the American City* (New York, 1972), pp. 81-84; Sam Bass Warner, Jr., *The Private City: Philadelphia in Three Periods of Growth* (Philadelphia, 1968), pp. 3-21; Walter Firey, *Land Use in Central Boston* (Cambridge, Mass., 1947), pp. 54-59; Peter G. Goheen, *Victorian Toronto, 1850 to 1900: Pattern and Process of Growth* (Chicago, 1970), pp. 23-38.

17. Warner, *Urban Wilderness*, pp. 85-112; Warner, *Private City*; Goheen, *Victorian Toronto*, pp. 201-18.

18. Harvey B. Hurd et al., eds., *Historical Encyclopedia of Illinois and History of Evanston* (Chicago, 1906), 2:174-75; Viola Crouch Reeling, *Evanston: Its Land and Its People* (Evanston, 1928), p. 347; Everett Chamberlin, *Chicago and Its Suburbs* (Chicago, 1874), p. 381. For more on the controversy over the taxation of Northwestern University, see Arthur Herbert Wilde, *Northwestern University, A History 1855-1905* (New York, 1905), 2:321, 326-29; Northwestern University v. the People, 99 U.S. 309 (1879).

19. William R. Coates, *A History of Cuyahoga County and the City of Cleveland* (Chicago,

1924), 1:76. For similar examples of fragmentation in northern New Jersey and Southern California, see Joseph Fulford Folsom, ed., *The Municipalities of Essex County, New Jersey 1666-1924* (New York, 1925), 2:855; Elizabeth Stow Brown, comp., *The History of Nutley, Essex County, New Jersey* (Nutley, N. J., 1907), pp. 42-43; Walter H. Case, *History of Long Beach and Vicinity* (Chicago, 1927), 1:359-60; Bigger and Kitchen, *How the Cities Grew*, p. 212.

20. Powell A. Moore, *The Calumet Region: Indiana's Last Frontier* (Indianapolis, 1959), pp. 202-8; *Whiting Times*, 4 Aug. 1939, p. 14; Paul H. Giddens, *Standard Oil Company (Indiana), Oil Pioneer of the Middle West* (New York, 1955), p. 10.

21. *Lake County News* (Hammond, Ind.), 26 April 1894, p. 2. For further information on the Hammond-Whiting controversy see: *Lake County News*, 7 June 1894, p. 1, 21 June 1894, p. 1.

22. *Whiting Democrat*, 15 Oct., 12 Nov. 1896, as quoted in Moore, *Calumet Region*, p. 207.

23. Margaret Byington, *Homestead: The Households of a Mill Town* (New York, 1910), p. 18.

24. Byington, *Homestead*, pp. 20-21.

25. Charles Davis Goff, "The Politics of Governmental Integration in Metropolitan Milwaukee" (Ph.D. dissertation, Northwestern University, 1952), p. 31; Bayrd Still, *Milwaukee, A History of a City* (Madison, Wis., 1948), p. 380.

26. Orven Roland Altman, "Problems of Government in the St. Louis Metropolitan Area" (Master's thesis, University of Illinois, 1928), pp. 129-34.

27. Elliot M. Rudwick, *Race Riot at East St. Louis, July 2, 1917* (Carbondale, Ill., 1964), pp. 192-93.

28. J. W. Wood, *Pasadena, California, Historical and Personal* (Pasadena, 1917), pp. 190-94; Bigger and Kitchen, *How the Cities Grew*, pp. 81-82.

29. Bigger and Kitchen, *How the Cities Grew*, p. 82.

30. John L. Wiley, *History of Monrovia* (Pasadena, 1927), pp. 62-65.

31. Bigger and Kitchen, *How the Cities Grew*, p. 83.

32. *Oak Park Reporter*, 19 Apr. 1895, p. 4; Arthur Evans LeGacy, "Improvers and Preservers: A History of Oak Park, Illinois, 1833-1940," (Ph.D. dissertation, University of Chicago, 1967), p. 66.

33. *Oak Park Reporter*, 19 Apr. 1895, p. 4; *Austin Vindicator*, 22 March 1895, p. 4.

34. *Oak Park Reporter*, 24 Oct. 1901, p. 4.

35. G. B. Glasscock, *Lucky Baldwin, The Story of an Unconventional Success* (New York, 1933), p. 262.

36. *Los Angeles Times*, 28 July 1903, Part II, p. 1; Bigger and Kitchen, *How the Cities Grew*, p. 89.

37. *Los Angeles Times*, 28 July 1903, Part II, p. 1; Bigger and Kitchen, *How the Cities Grew*, pp. 89-90.

38. *Los Angeles Times*, 28 July 1903, Part II, p. 1.

39. Ibid.

40. Glasscock, *Baldwin*, p. 295.

41. *Cleveland Plain Dealer*, 24 Apr. 1908, p. 1.

42. *Cleveland Plain Dealer*, 24 Apr. 1908, p. 1; 25 Apr. 1908, p. 6; *Cleveland Leader*, 26 Apr. 1908, Part III, p. 2.

43. Altman, "St. Louis Metropolitan Area," p. 143.

44. See Arthur Evans Woods, *Hamtramck—Then and Now* (New York, 1955).

45. Bigger and Kitchen, *How the Cities Grew*, p. 90.

46. Byington, *Homestead*, pp. 27-28.

47. *Indianapolis Journal*, 28 July 1876, p. 5; 1 Aug. 1876, p. 5; 2 Aug. 1876, p. 3; 7 Aug. 1876, p. 3; 9 Aug. 1876, p. 3; Mary E. Studebaker, *Official Centennial History of Woodruff Place* (Indianapolis, 1972), p. 2.

48. Incorporation proceedings for Woodruff Place are found in "Records of Marion County Commissioners," Book 15, pp. 80-83, City-County Building, Indianapolis, Ind.

49. *Indianapolis News*, 23 Jan. 1895, p. 4.

50. *Indianapolis Journal*, 9 Mar. 1876, p. 7.

51. *Indianapolis Journal,* 28 July 1876, p. 5.
52. Sidney Morse, *The Siege of University City, the Dreyfus Case of America* (University City, Mo., 1912), pp. 215-16.
53. For the early history of Kenilworth and the manner in which village officials persistently refused to annex undesirable tracts, see *Kenilworth, First Fifty Years* (Kenilworth, Ill., 1947).
54. *Oak Park Reporter,* 27 Feb. 1891, p. 1; LeGacy, "Improvers and Preservers," p. 65.
55. *Oak Park Vindicator,* 19 Apr. 1895, p. 4; 26 Apr. 1895, p. 4.
56. *Oak Park Reporter,* 24 Oct. 1901, p. 4.
57. *Oak Park Reporter,* 17 Oct. 1901, p. 1.
58. *Oak Park Argus*, 18 Oct. 1901, p. 1, as quoted in LeGacy, "Improvers and Preservers," p. 103.
59. Iverson B. Summers, "A Negro Town in Illinois," *The Independent,* 65 (27 Aug. 1908):464-70; Altman, St. Louis Metropolitan Area," pp. 134-37; *History of St. Clair County, Illinois* (Philadelphia, 1881), p. 308.
60. *Atlanta Constitution,* 9 Mar. 1887, p. 8.
61. Charles M. Kneier, "Development of Newer County Functions," *American Political Science Review* 24 (Feb. 1930): 134-36.
62. Joseph K. Knight, Edmund Davis, and Henry B. Humphrey, comps., *Memorial Sketch of Hyde Park, Massachusetts* ... (Boston, 1888), pp. 17-20.
63. Harry C. Gilchrist, *History of Wilkinsburg, Pennsylvania* (n.pl., 1940), pp. 116-19; Elizabeth M. Davison and Ellen B. McKee, eds., *Annals of Old Wilkinsburg and Vicinity* (Wilkinsburg, 1940), pp. 538-47.
64. *South Omaha Daily Stockman,* 18 Oct. 1886; James W. Savage, John T. Bell, and Consul W. Butterfield, *History of the City of Omaha, Nebraska and South Omaha* (New York, 1894), pp. 645-49.
65. *Rocky Mountain News* (Denver), 19 July 1890, p. 3; 22 July 1890, p. 3.
66. *Cleveland Leader,* 30 Dec. 1870, p. 1.
67. Ren Mulford, Jr., and Werter G. Betty, *Norwood, Her Homes and Her People* (n.pl., 1894), n.p.
68. *Milwaukee Journal,* 26 Apr. 1942, as quoted in Goff, "Governmental Integration in Milwaukee," p. 49.
69. *Los Angeles Times,* 2 June 1897, p. 9; Bigger and Kitchen, *How the Cities Grew,* p. 84.
70. Walter F. Holzworth, *Men of Grit and Greatness, A Historical Account of Middleburg Township, Berea, Brook Park and Middleburg Heights* (n.p., 1970), pp. 139-40.
71. Folsom, ed., *Municipalities of Essex County,* 2:871.
72. In re Incorporation of Borough of Edgewood, 130 Pa. 348, 350 (1889). For another dispute between a township and a newly created borough in the Pittsburgh metropolitan area, see In re Incorporation of the Borough of West Homestead, 48 Pittsburgh Legal Journal 172 (1900).
73. State, ex rel. Henry Broking et al. v. James M. Van Valen, 56 N. J. 85 (1893).
74. Borough of Glen Ridge v. G. Lee Stout et al., 58 N.J. 598 (1896); G. Lee Stout el al. v. Borough of Glen Ridge, 59 N.J. 201 (1896).
75. Ernest Guebelle et al. v. John J. Epley et al., 1 Colo. App. 199, 200 (1891); *Rocky Mountain News* (Denver), 26 Apr. 1891, p. 7, 10 Nov. 1891, p. 3.
76. W. H. Lawrence v. J. Mitchell et al., 10 Ohio Dec. 265, 8 Ohio N.P. 8 (1900); State ex rel. Osborn v. John Mitchell et al., 22 Cir. Ct. R. 208, 12 O. C. D. 288 (1901); R. Hall v. J. C. Siegrist, 13 Ohio Dec. 46 (1902).
77. For further information on the conflict in the Calumet region, see Moore, *Calumet Region,* especially pp. 249-51.

Chapter 3

1. City of St. Louis v. William Russell, 9 Mo. 507 (1845). Technically the term *annexation* applies only to absorption of unincorporated territory by a city, and *consolidation* applies to the union of two incorporated municipalities. In the text of this work, however, the terms are used interchangeably.
2. Eli K. Price, *The History of the Consolidation of the City of Philadelphia* (Philadelphia, 1873).
3. *Debates and Proceedings in the New York State Convention for the Revision of the Constitution* (Albany, 1846), pp. 738-39. For a similar argument with regard to special legislation, see Atchison v. Bartholow, 4 Kan. 124 (1866).
4. *Report of the Debates and Proceedings of the Convention for the Revision of the Constitution of the State of Indiana,* 2 vols. (Indianapolis, 1850), 2:1766-67.
5. *Report of Debates and Proceedings of the Ohio Convention of 1850-51,* 2 vols. (Columbus, 1851), 1:347.
6. *The Debates of the Constitutional Convention of the State of Iowa,* 2 vols. (Davenport, 1857), 1:531-32.
7. See also *Kansas Constitutional Convention . . . 1859* (Topeka, 1920), pp. 80-81.
8. Ohio, *Constitution,* Art. 13, sec. 6 (1851).
9. Ind., *Constitution,* Art. 11, sec. 13 (1851).
10. Howard Lee McBain, *The Law and the Practice of Municipal Home Rule* (New York, 1916), p. 81.
11. Ibid., pp. 85, 87.
12. Ill. *Constitution,* Art. 4, sec. 22 (1870); Richard Bigger and James Kitchen, *How the Cities Grew: A Century of Municipal Independence and Expansionism in Metropolitan Los Angeles* (Los Angeles, 1952), pp. 42, 240.
13. Joseph R. Swan, comp., *The Revised Statutes of the State of Ohio,* 2 vols. (Cincinnati, 1860), 2:1495-98.
14. Taylor et al. v. The City of Fort Wayne et al., 47 Ind. 274 (1874); The City of South Bend et al. v. Lewis, 138 Ind. 512 (1894).
15. *Chicago Tribune,* 15 Apr. 1872, p. 5.
16. Kelly et al. v. Meeks, 87 Mo. 396 (1885); *Laws of Missouri Passed at the Session of the Thirty Fourth General Assembly* (Jefferson City, 1887), pp. 49-50; Copeland v. City of St. Joseph, 126 Mo. 417, 29 S. W. 281 (1895); *The Annotated Statutes of the State of Missouri 1906,* 5 vols. (St. Paul, Minn., 1906), 3:2832, 2929.
17. *General Law of the State of Kansas; Passed at the Sixth Session of the Legislature* (Lawrence, Kan., 1866), pp. 126-27.
18. *The Compiled Statutes of the State of Nebraska* (Omaha, 1881), pp. 84, 124, 125.
19. *Statutes of Nebraska,* p. 123; City of Westport v. Kansas City, 103 Mo. 141, 15 S. W. 68 (1891); *Laws of Missouri,* pp. 49-50; *Annotated Statutes of Missouri,* 3:3254.
20. William F. Kirby, *A Digest of the Statutes of Arkansas* (Austin, Tex., 1904), pp. 1181-83; Vogel v. Little Rock, 55 Ark. 609, 19 S. W. 13 (1892).
21. *The Code: Containing All the Statutes of the State of Iowa* (Des Moines, 1873), pp. 71-73; *The General Statutes of the State of Colorado, 1883* (Denver, 1883), pp. 962-64.
22. Bigger and Kitchen, *How the Cities Grew,* pp. 128-29.
23. Ohio v. City of Cincinnati, 20 Ohio Rep. 18, 37 (1870). Later annexation scheme upheld in State ex rel. v. Cincinnati, 52 Ohio St. 419 (1895).
24. City of Wyandotte v. Wood, 5 Kan. 603 (1870); City of Topeka and others v. Gillett, 4 Pac. 800 (1884).
25. In re Extension of Boundaries of City of Denver, 18 Colo. 288, 32 Pac. 615 (1893).
26. State ex rel. West v. City of Des Moines, 96 Iowa 521, 65 N. W. 818 (1896). For invalidation of a special act altering village boundaries see Smith v. Sherry, 50 Wis. 210, 6 N. W. 561 (1880).
27. McBain, *Municipal Home Rule,* pp. 457-58; *General Laws of the State of Minnesota Passed During the Twenty-ninth Session of the State Legislature* (St. Paul, 1895), pp. 20-21, 24-25.

28. Paul Studenski, *The Government of Metropolitan Areas in the United States* (New York, 1930), pp. 68–69; McBain, *Municipal Home Rule*, pp. 591–620.
29. McBain, *Municipal Home Rule*, p. 95.
30. State ex rel. Knisely v. Jones, 66 Oh. St. 453 (1902); Town of Longview v. City of Crawfordsville, 164 Ind. 117 (1905).
31. *Cleveland Leader,* 2 Apr. 1872, p. 4; 3 Apr. 1872, p. 2.
32. *Cleveland Leader,* 15 July 1872, p. 4.
33. Ibid.
34. Ibid.
35. Ibid.
36. Ibid.
37. *Cleveland Leader,* 29 July 1872, p. 4.
38. Ibid.
39. Ibid.
40. Ibid.
41. Ibid.
42. *Cleveland Leader,* 3 Sept. 1872, p. 4.
43. Ibid.
44. *Cleveland Leader,* 5 Oct. 1872, p. 2.
45. *Cleveland Leader,* 9 Oct. 1872, p. 2; 22 Oct. 1872, p. 4; 26 Oct. 1872, p. 1; 28 Oct. 1872, pp. 2, 4; 29 Oct. 1872, pp. 2, 4.
46. *Cleveland Leader,* 30 Oct. 1872, pp. 2, 4.
47. *South Brooklyn, A Brief History of the Part of the City of Cleveland Which Lies South of Big Creek and West of the Cuyahoga* (Cleveland, 1946), pp. 50–52.
48. *Cleveland Plain Dealer,* 6 Nov. 1907, p. 3.
49. *Cleveland Plain Dealer,* 14 July 1908, p. 1.
50. Ibid.
51. Ibid.
52. *Cleveland Plain Dealer,* 3 Nov. 1909, p. 10; 9 Nov. 1909, p. 5.
53. *Cleveland Plain Dealer,* 26 Jan. 1910, p. 9.
54. Bessie Louise Pierce, *A History of Chicago,* 3 vols. (New York, 1937, 1940, 1957) 2:306.
55. Harvey B. Hurd, ed., *The Revised Statutes of the State of Illinois, 1887* (Chicago, 1887), pp. 1299–1300.
56. *Chicago Tribune,* 4 Nov. 1887, p. 3.
57. *Chicago Tribune,* 6 Nov. 1887, p. 11.
58. *Chicago Herald,* 3 Nov. 1887, p. 5.
59. Ibid.
60. Ibid.
61. *Chicago Tribune,* 9 Nov. 1887, p. 1.
62. *Chicago Tribune,* 17 Nov. 1887, p. 2; 3 Dec. 1887, p. 5. For actions of Chicago City Council, see *Proceedings of the City Council of Chicago ... 1887–88* (Chicago, 1888), pp. 422–27.
63. Dolese et al. v. Pierce, 124 Ill. 140 (1888); Village of Hyde Park v. City of Chicago, 124 Ill. 156 (1888); *Chicago Tribune* 15 Mar. 1888, p. 1; 16 Mar. 1887, p. 5.
64. *Chicago Tribune,* 15 Mar. 1888, p. 1.
65. *Chicago Tribune,* 16 Mar. 1888, p. 4.
66. *Laws of the State of Illinois Passed by the Thirty-Sixth General Assembly* (Springfield, 1889), pp. 67–77.
67. *Chicago Tribune,* 29 June 1889, p. 1.
68. *Chicago Tribune,* 4 May 1889, p. 2.
69. *Chicago Tribune,* 4 May 1889, p. 2; 28 June 1889, p. 8.
70. *Chicago Daily News,* 21 June 1889, p. 1.
71. *Chicago Daily News,* 21 June 1889, p. 1; *Chicago Herald,* 23 June 1889, p. 17.
72. *Chicago Daily News,* 25 June 1889, p. 1; 21 June 1889, p. 1.
73. *Chicago Herald,* 23 June 1889, p. 17.
74. *Chicago Herald,* 26 June 1889, p. 2.

75. *Chicago Daily News,* 21 June 1889, p. 1.
76. *Chicago Herald,* 22 June 1889, p. 2.
77. *Chicago Tribune,* 4 July 1889, p. 3.
78. *Chicago Tribune,* 30 Oct. 1889; True v. Davis, 133 Ill. 522 (1889).
79. Clyde Lyndon King, *The History of the Government of Denver with Special Reference to Its Relations with Public Service Corporations* (Denver, 1911), p. 176.
80. *Rocky Mountain News* (Denver), 31 Jan. 1893, p. 8.
81. *Rocky Mountain News* (Denver), 31 Jan. 1893, pp. 4, 8; 2 Feb. 1893, p. 8.
82. *Rocky Mountain News* (Denver), 31 Jan. 1893, p. 4.
83. In re Extension of Boundaries of the City of Denver, 18 Colo. 288, 290, 291 (1893).
84. Mayor and Trustees of the Town of Valverde v. Shattuck et al., 19 Colo. 104 (1893).
85. *Rocky Mountain News* (Denver), 29 Jan. 1894, p. 3. For other annexationist activity in South Denver, see *Rocky Mountain News* (Denver), 3 Jan. 1894, p. 5; 4 Jan. 1894, p. 2; 20 Jan. 1894, p. 3.
86. *Rocky Mountain News* (Denver), 9 Jan. 1894, p. 8; 12 Jan. 1894, p. 5; 23 Jan. 1894, p. 3.
87. *Rocky Mountain News* (Denver), 5 Apr. 1893, p. 8; 12 Jan. 1894, p. 5; 30 Jan. 1894, p. 3; 31 Jan. 1894, p. 5; 6 Feb. 1894, p. 3.
88. *Rocky Mountain News* (Denver), 31 Jan. 1894, pp. 4, 5; 7 Feb. 1894, p. 5.
89. Phillips et al. v. Corbin et al., 8 Colo. App. 346, 353 (1896).
90. Phillips et al. v. Corbin et al., 25 Colo. 62 (1898).
91. Martin v. Simpkins, 20 Colo. 438 (1894); for the annexation of Highlands and Barnum, see *Rocky Mountain News* (Denver), 19 Aug. 1896, p. 8; 26 Aug. 1896, p. 8.
92. Perry et al. v. City of Denver et al., 27 Colo. 93, 59 Pac. 747 (1899).
93. John A. Rush, *The City-County Consolidated* (Los Angeles, 1941), p. 322.
94. *Laws of the State of Indiana Passed at the Fifty-Seventh Regular Session of the General Assembly* (Indianapolis, 1891), pp. 155-57; *Laws of the State of Indiana Passed at the Fifty-Ninth Regular Session of the General Assembly* (Indianapolis, 1895), pp. 393-95.
95. *Indianapolis News,* 4 Mar. 1895, p. 2.
96. Ibid.
97. *Laws of Indiana Passed at the Fifty-Ninth Session,* pp. 394-95; *Indianapolis News,* 13 Mar. 1895, p. 8.
98. *Indianapolis News,* 12 Mar. 1897, p. 10.
99. *Indianapolis News,* 11 Mar. 1897, p. 7.
100. *Indianapolis News,* 12 Mar. 1897, p. 10. Indianapolis area residents seem to have accepted these figures as a true index of the comparative tax burdens
101. *Indianapolis News,* 13 Mar. 1897, p. 11.
102. *Indianapolis News,* 11 Mar. 1897, p. 7.
103. *Indianapolis Herald,* 2 Dec. 1949; "Irvington—A History," Scrapbook of newspaper clippings, Indiana State Library, Indianapolis, Ind.
104. *Irvington* (Indiana) *Home Rule Advocate,* 30 Apr. 1898, p. 2.
105. Ibid., pp. 3, 4.
106. *Indianapolis Sentinel,* 4 Mar. 1897, p. 3.
107. *Indianapolis News,* 13 Mar. 1897, p. 11.
108. *Indianapolis Sentinel,* 4 Mar. 1897, p. 3; *Indianapolis News,* 11 March 1897, p. 7.
109. *Indianapolis Sentinel,* 12 Mar. 1897, p. 6; *Indianapolis News,* 11 Mar. 1897, p. 7.
110. *Indianapolis News,* 13 Mar. 1897, p. 11.
111. Jacob P. Dunn, *Greater Indianapolis,* 2 vols. (Chicago, 1910), 1:439-41.
112. *Indianapolis News,* 11 Mar. 1897, p. 7.
113. *Indianapolis Sentinel,* 12 Mar. 1897, p. 6.
114. For annexation of Irvington, see *Indianapolis Sentinel,* 8 Feb. 1902, p. 10; 9 Feb. 1902, p. 12; *Indianapolis Herald,* 2 Dec. 1949; "Irvington—A History," Scrapbook of newspaper clippings, Indiana State Library, Indianapolis, Ind.
115. *Indianapolis News,* 20 Jan. 1906, p. 1.
116. Ibid.
117. *A History of Broad Ripple* (Indianapolis, 1968), p. 40.

118. George H. McCaffrey, *Summary of the Political Disintegration and Reintegration of Metropolitan Boston* (Boston, 1947), pp. 13-14; *Report of the Commissioners and Chief Engineer of the Charlestown Water Works* (Boston, 1865), pp. 3-15.
119. George W. Warren and others v. Mayor and Aldermen of Charlestown, 68 Mass. 84 (1854).
120. McCaffrey, *Political Disintegration,* pp. 14-15. Boston did annex a small section of Dorchester in 1855. James Merino, "A Great City and Its Suburbs: Attempts to Integrate Metropolitan Boston, 1865-1920" (Ph.D. dissertation, University of Texas-Austin, 1968), ch. 1.
121. Ibid., p. 15.
122. *Boston Daily Advertiser,* 7 Sept. 1867, p. 4.
123. Ibid.
124. Ibid.
125. Ibid.
126. Ibid.
127. Ibid.
128. *Boston Daily Advertiser,* 13 Sept. 1867, p. 2.
129. *Boston Daily Advertiser,* 22 June 1869, p. 1.
130. Ibid.
131. *Boston Daily Advertiser,* 23 June 1869, p. 1. For further information on the annexation of Dorchester, see *Report of the Commissioners on the Annexation of Dorchester* (Boston, 1869).
132. *Report of a Committee of the Town of West Roxbury Appointed to Examine the Sources of Water Supply for the Town* (Boston, 1871), p. 5.
133. *Fourth Annual Report of the State Board of Massachusetts* (Boston, 1873), p. 463.
134. John G. Curtis, *History of the Town of Brookline, Massachusetts* (Boston, 1933), pp. 279-90; *Report of the Joint Committee on Water Supply to the Town of Brookline* (Boston, 1873); *Report of the Committee Appointed by the Town of Brookline to Examine the Sources of Water Supply* (Boston, 1873). Winthrop voters defeated annexation by a narrow margin, and Boston voters likewise disapproved union with Winthrop. McCaffrey, *Political Disintegration,* p. 18.
135. *New York Times,* 9 Feb. 1894, p. 5.
136. *New York Times,* 8 Nov. 1894, p. 1; 9 Nov. 1894, p. 1; 10 Nov. 1894, p. 3.
137. Harold C. Syrett, *The City of Brooklyn, 1865-1898* (New York, 1944), pp. 267, 271-72; *New York Times,* 10 Apr. 1897, p. 1.
138. *The Manual of American Water-Works 1889-90* (New York, 1890).
139. Ibid.
140. *Rocky Mountain News* (Denver), 12 Jan. 1894, p. 5.
141. *Rocky Mountain News* (Denver), 4 Jan. 1894, p. 2.
142. *Fourth Report of the State Board of Health of Colorado* (Denver, 1894), pp. 88, 97.
143. *Report on Vital and Social Statistics in the United States at the Eleventh Census: 1890,* 4 vols. (Washington, 1896), 2:161-81.
144. William D. Miller, *Memphis During the Progressive Era 1900-1917* (Memphis, 1957), pp. 64-68.
145. *Birmingham News,* 29 July 1907, as quoted in Jere C. King, Jr., "The Formation of Greater Birmingham" (Master's thesis, University of Alabama, 1935), p. 5.
146. *Birmingham Age-Herald,* 6 August 1907, p. 5.
147. For information on the annexation campaign in Seattle, see State ex rel. West Seattle v. the Superior Court for King County, 36 Wash. 566 (1905); State v. Nicoll, 40 Wash. 517 (1905); Brown's Estate v. West Seattle, 43 Wash. 26 (1906); *Seattle Post-Intelligencer,* 6 Apr. 1907, p. 9; 25 May 1907, p. 5; 26 May 1907, p. 1; 27 May 1907, pp. 6, 10; 28 May 1907, p. 14.
148. *Annexation of the Villages of Avondale, Clifton, Linwood, Riverside, and Westwood* (Cincinnati, 1896).
149. See "Annexation Proceedings" for villages of Evanston, Bond Hill, and Winton Place, Office of Clerk of Council, City Hall, Cincinnati, Ohio.

150. "Report of Delhi Annexation Commissioners," Office of Clerk of Council, City Hall, Cincinnati, Ohio.
151. Ibid.
152. "Annexation Proceedings" for Winton Place and Bond Hill, Office of Clerk of Council, City Hall, Cincinnati, Ohio.
153. "Annexation Proceedings" for Evanston, Office of Clerk of Council, City Hall, Cincinnati, Ohio; *Cincinnati Enquirer*, 4 Apr. 1903, p. 2.
154. "Annexation Proceedings" for Delhi, Winton Place, and Evanston, Office of Clerk of Council, City Hall, Cincinnati, Ohio.

Chapter 4

1. Albert E. Lauder, *The Municipal Manual* (London, 1907), p. 3.
2. A. E. Wood and T. R. Johnson, *Encyclopedia of Local Government Board Requirements and Practice*, 2 vols. (London, 1908), 1:238-39.
3. Lauder, *Municipal Manual*, p. 13.
4. Ibid., pp. 14-15.
5. Josef Redlich and Francis Hirst, *Local Government in England*, 2 vols. (London, 1903), 2:245.
6. Lauder, *Municipal Manual*, p. 18.
7. Redlich and Hirst, *Local Government*, 2:119.
8. *Thirty-Fourth Annual Report of the Local Government Board, 1904-05* (London, 1905), p. xi; Wood and Johnson, *Local Government Board Requirements*, 2:621.
9. *The Municipal Year Book of the United Kingdom for 1922* (London, 1922), p. 239.
10. Figures based on list of boundary alterations in Wood and Johnson, *Local Government Board Requirements*, 1:96-100.
11. Jack Simmons, *Leicester, Past and Present*, 2 vols. (London, 1974), 2:119-21.
12. H. Keeble Hawson, *Sheffield: The Growth of a City 1893-1926* (Sheffield, 1968), pp. 281-283.
13. S. Middlebrook, *Newcastle Upon Tyne, Its Growth and Achievement* (Newcastle Upon Tyne, 1950), p. 299; *Thirty-Eighth Annual Report of the Local Government Board, 1908-1909* (London, 1909), pp. xxvi-xxvii.
14. *Twenty-Third Annual Report of the Local Government Board, 1893-1894* (London, 1894), p. xxxv; Wood and Johnson, *Local Government Board Requirements*, 1:95.
15. *Twenty-Eighth Annual Report of the Local Government Board, 1898-1899* (London, 1899), p. xxvii, Wood and Johnson, *Local Government Board Requirements*, 1:95.
16. *Thirty-Eighth Annual Report*, p. xxviii.
17. *Thirty-Ninth Annual Report of the Local Government Board, 1909-1910* (London, 1910), p. xxxi.
18. *Twenty-Ninth Annual Report of the Local Government Board, 1899-1900* (London, 1900), p. xxxii.
19. *Thirty-First Annual Report of the Local Government Board 1901-1902* (London, 1902), p. xxxii.
20. *Times* (London), 4 Jan. 1888, p. 7.
21. Ibid.
22. Ibid., p. 9.
23. *Twenty-First Annual Report of the Local Government Board 1891-92* (London, 1892), p. xxxvi.
24. *Birmingham Daily Mail*, 7 Nov. 1891, as quoted in Asa Briggs, *History of Birmingham* (London, 1952), p. 143.
25. *Twenty-First Annual Report*, p. xxxvii.
26. *Times* (London), 26 Jan. 1909, p. 13; 14 July 1909, p. 14; Briggs *Birmingham*, 2:145.
27. Briggs, *Birmingham*, 2:149.
28. Ibid.

29. *Birmingham Gazette,* 11 Nov. 1909, as quoted in Briggs, *Birmingham,* 2:152.
30. Briggs, *Birmingham,* 2:149-50.
31. *Birmingham Daily Mail,* 21 Jan. 1910, as quoted in Briggs, *Birmingham*, 2:150.
32. Briggs, *Birmingham,* 2:153.
33. *Times* (London), 28 May 1910, p. 8.; Briggs, *Birmingham,* 2:153.
34. *Times* (London), 14 June 1910, p. 12.
35. *Times* (London), 28 June 1910, p. 3; Briggs, *Birmingham,* 2:153-54.
36. *Times* (London), 21 July 1910, p. 4.
37. *Times* (London), 20 July 1910, p. 4; 15 July 1910, p. 3.
38. *Times* (London), 15 July 1910, p. 3; 23 July 1910, p. 8.
39. *Times* (London), 28 July 1910, p. 4.
40. *Times* (London), 29 July 1910, p. 9.
41. *Times* (London), 27 July 1910, p. 4.
42. *House of Commons Debates* (Fifth Ser.) 18:1714.
43. Ibid., p. 1717.
44. Ibid., pp. 1709-10.
45. Ibid., 21:1351.
46. Ibid., p. 1336.
47. Ibid., p. 1351.
48. Ibid., pp. 1336, 1338.
49. Ibid., p. 1352.
50. Ibid., p. 1344.
51. Norman Chamberlain, "Municipal Government in Birmingham," *Political Quarterly* (Feb. 1914), pp. 90-91.
52. "Now for the Final Passage of Baltimore's Annexation Measure," *Municipal Journal Baltimore* 6 (8 Mar. 1918):1; *The Non-Partisan Greater Baltimore Extension League* (Baltimore, 1917), p. 90.
53. "Judge Harlan Reviews Work of Non-Partisan, Greater Baltimore Committee," *Municipal Journal Baltimore* 6 (8 Feb. 1918):3. See also, *Baltimore Extension League, pp. 76, 77.*
54. *Birmingham Ledger,* 20 (26 July 1907), as quoted in Jere C. King, Jr., "The Formation of Greater Birmingham" (Master's thesis, University of Alabama, 1935), pp. 48, 52.
55. *Birmingham Age-Herald,* 6 Aug. 1907, p. 5; 27 July 1907, p. 1.
56. Pennsylvania's lawmakers authorized similar referenda for the Pittsburgh region, permitting a local vote but denying the suburban veto; see Hunter v. City of Pittsburgh 207 U.S. 161 (1907).

Chapter 5

1. For background material on annexation law in Texas, see Joseph D. McGoldrick, *Law and Practice of Municipal Home Rule 1916-1930* (New York, 1933), pp. 250-53.
2. Data on areas derived from Roderick D. McKenzie, *The Metropolitan Community* (New York, 1933).
3. *Thirteenth Census of the United States ... 1910, Population,* 4 vols. (Washington, 1913), 1:74; *Sixteenth Census of the United States: 1940, Population—Number of Inhabitants* (Washington, 1942), pp. 58-65.
4. Figures based on information from *The Manual of American Water-Works 1889-90* (New York, 1890) and *The McGraw Waterworks Directory 1915* (New York, 1915).
5. Max R. White, *Water Supply Organization in the Chicago Region* (Chicago, 1934), p. 5.
6. *The Manual of American Water-Works 1897* (New York, 1897).
7. *American Water-Works 1889-90*; *McGraw Waterworks Directory 1915.*
8. Langdon Pearse, ed., *Modern Sewage Disposal* (New York, 1938), p. 13.
9. G. P. Brown, *Drainage Channel and Waterway* (Chicago, 1894); C. Arch Williams, *The Sanitary District of Chicago* (Chicago, 1919).

10. City of Chicago v. Town of Cicero, 210 Ill. 290 (1904).
11. *Report of the Massachusetts State Board of Health Upon a Metropolitan Water Supply* (Boston, 1895), pp. 59, 87, 97.
12. *History and First Annual Report of the Metropolitan Water District of Southern California* (Los Angeles, 1939).
13. White, *Water Supply in Chicago Region,* pp. 120-23, 130.
14. Matthew Holden, Jr., *Inter-Governmental Agreements in the Cleveland Metropolitan Area, Staff Report to Study Group on Government Organization* (Cleveland, 1958), pp. 43-46; Matthew Holden, Jr., *County Government in Ohio, Staff Report to Study Group on Government Organization* (Cleveland, 1958); Robert O. Warren, *Government in Metropolitan Regions; A Reappraisal of Fractionated Political Organization* (Davis, Calif., 1966), pp. 92-110.
15. Charles M. Kneier, "Development of Newer County Functions," *American Political Science Review,* 24 (Feb. 1930): 134-40.
16. Paul Studenski, *The Government of Metropolitan Areas in the United States* (New York, 1930), pp. 216-255; Los Angeles County Bureau of Efficiency, *Growth of County Functions, Los Angeles County, California: 1852 to 1934* (Los Angeles, 1936).
17. Victor Jones, *Metropolitan Government* (Chicago, 1942), pp. 140-41.
18. See, Arthur Evans Woods, *Hamtramck—Then and Now* (New York, 1955).
19. *Chicago Record-Herald,* 6 Apr. 1910, p. 6.
20. *Chicago Tribune,* 4 Apr. 1909, Sec. I, p. 5; 8 Apr. 1914, p. 2.
21. W. Hubert Morken, "The Annexation of Morgan Park to Chicago, One Village's Response to Urban Growth (Master's thesis, University of Chicago, 1968), p. 75.
22. Based on data from *Fourteenth Census of the United States . . . 1920,* 11 vols. (Washington, 1921-23).
23. *Fourteenth Census of the United States . . . 1920, Manufactures,* 11 vols. (Washington, 1923), 9:1348.
24. Ibid., p. 1210. Value of products manufactured in 1925: Kenmore, $3,664,250; Barberton, $36,443,790. Both had populations of between 15,000 and 20,000. *Moody's Manual of Investments—Foreign and American Government Securities, 1928* (New York, 1928), pp. 1752, 1792.
25. *Fourteenth Census, Manufactures,* 9:138.
26. *Thirty-Fifth Annual Report of the Department of Labor and Industry, 1920* (Topeka, Kan., 1921), p. 25. In comparing the wealth of municipalities, I have not relied on assessed valuation figures because they are generally unreliable. Valuation practices varied widely during the early twentieth century, and valuations were not accurate indices of wealth. Residential property was commonly valued at a higher percentage of sale value than was industrial property, but there was little consistency. In 1925 in Westmoreland County, Pennsylvania, the ratio of assessed value to sales value in municipalities ranged from 10 percent to 133 percent. In Los Angeles County, California, city and county assessors assessed the same property, but in 1917 in Venice the city official's total assessed valuation was 35 percent higher than the valuation assigned by the county assessor, and in Santa Monica the city figure was 34 percent higher than the county figure. City assessors overvalued property so that these suburban cities could obtain greater revenue without raising the tax rate. Because of overvaluation or undervaluation, one must be wary about comparing tax rates for municipalities. I have attempted in this chapter to compare only those tax rates that are an accurate reflection of the true levels of taxation. See *Final Report of the Pennsylvania Tax Commission to the General Assembly* (Harrisburg, 1927), especially pp. 87-88; *City and County Consolidation for Los Angeles* (Los Angeles, 1917), pp. 55-57.
27. *Chicago Tribune,* 4 Apr. 1909, Sec. I, p. 5.
28. Ibid.
29. Ibid.
30. *Chicago Tribune,* 8 Apr. 1914, p. 2.
31. *Oak Leaves* (Oak Park, Ill.), 26 Feb. 1910, p. 5.

32. *Oak Leaves* (Oak Park, Ill.), 5 Mar. 1910, p. 12.
33. *Oak Leaves* (Oak Park, Ill.), 19 Feb. 1910, p. 8; 5 Mar. 1910, p. 12.
34. *Oak Leaves* (Oak Park, Ill.), 26 Mar. 1910, p. 8.
35. Ibid.
36. Ibid., p. 10.
37. Ibid.
38. Ibid., p. 9.
39. *Oak Leaves* (Oak Park, Ill.), 26 Feb. 1910, p. 4.
40. *Oak Leaves* (Oak Park, Ill.), 26 Mar. 1910, p. 9.
41. *Oak Leaves* (Oak Park, Ill.), 26 Feb. 1910, p. 14; 26 Mar. 1910, p. 10.
42. *Chicago Tribune,* 5 Apr. 1911, p. 3.
43. *Chicago Tribune,* 7 Apr. 1909, p. 3; 6 Apr. 1910, p. 3; 5 Apr. 1911, p. 3; *Chicago Record-Herald,* 6 Apr. 1910, p. 6; 5 Apr. 1911, p. 5.
44. U.S. Bureau of the Census, *Assessed Valuation of Property and Amounts and Rates of Levy 1860-1912* (Washington, 1915), pp. 138-40.
45. U.S. Bureau of the Census, *County and Municipal Indebtedness 1913, 1902, and 1890 and Sinking Fund Assets* (Washington, 1915), pp. 187-89.
46. *Annual Reports of the President and Board of Trustees, Village of Morgan Park, Illinois* (Morgan Park, 1909), p. 8.
47. U.S. Bureau of the Census, *Municipal Revenues, Expenditures and Public Properties 1913* (Washington, 1915), pp. 204-8.
48. Ibid.
49. *Morgan Park* (Ill.) *Post,* 5 Nov. 1910, p. 3.
50. *Morgan Park* (Ill.) *Post,* 22 Oct. 1910, p. 2.
51. *Morgan Park* (Ill.) *Post,* 5 Nov. 1910, pp. 3, 7.
52. *Morgan Park* (Ill.) *Post,* 5 Nov. 1910, p. 3; 18 Apr. 1914, p. 3.
53. *Morgan Park* (Ill.) *Post,* 18 Apr. 1914, p. 3.
54. *Morgan Park* (Ill.) *Post,* 1 Apr. 1911, p. 3. Litigation delayed the annexation of Morgan Park until 1914, see Village of Morgan Park v. City of Chicago, 255 Ill. 190 (1912). For an extensive account of the annexation fight, see Morken, "Annexation of Morgan Park."
55. John D. McCauley, *Pioneers of Progress, the History of Stickney Township* (Stickney Township, Ill., 1969), pp. 17, 19.
56. *Residential Chicago* (Chicago, 1942), pp. 256-57.
57. Ibid., pp. 165, 174, 210-11.
58. Computed from data in the *Real Property Inventory of Allegheny County* (Pittsburgh, 1937).
59. J. Steele Gow, Jr., "Metropolitics in Pittsburgh" (Ph.D. dissertation, University of Pittsburgh, 1952), p. 94.
60. *Homestead* (Pa.) *Messenger,* 15 Feb. 1928, p. 1.
61. *Homestead* (Pa.) *Messenger,* 3 Jan. 1928, pp. 1, 11.
62. *Homestead* (Pa.) *Messenger,* 23 Jan. 1928, p. 1; 24 Jan. 1928, p. 1.
63. Ibid.
64. *Homestead* (Pa.) *Messenger,* 18 Feb. 1928, p. 1; 22 Feb. 1928, p. 1.
65. *Homestead* (Pa.) *Messenger,* 15 Feb. 1928, p. 1.
66. *Homestead* (Pa.) *Messenger,* 20 Feb. 1928, p. 4.
67. *Homestead* (Pa.) *Messenger,* 2 Mar. 1928, p. 8.
68. *Homestead* (Pa.) *Messenger,* 2 Mar. 1928, p. 8; 25 Apr. 1928, p. 1.
69. *Cleveland Plain Dealer,* 2 Nov. 1922, p. 15.
70. Ibid. See also *Cleveland Plain Dealer,* 10 Nov. 1909, p. 1; 5 Jan. 1910, p. 2; 9 Nov. 1910, p. 3; 8 Nov. 1922, p. 4; 9 Nov. 1922, p. 17.
71. *Cleveland Plain Dealer,* 9 Nov. 1910, p. 3. See also *Cleveland Plain Dealer,* 10 Nov. 1909, p. 1; 22 Jan. 1910, p. 7; 26 Jan. 1910, p. 9.
72. *Cleveland Plain Dealer,* 8 Nov. 1912, p. 4.
73. Ibid.
74. Ibid.
75. Ibid.

76. Ibid. See also *Cleveland Plain Dealer*, 6 Nov. 1912, pp. 2, 6.
77. Howard Whipple Green, *An Analysis of Population by Census Tracts ... Cleveland and Vicinity* (Cleveland, 1927), pp. 14-15.
78. *Cleveland Plain Dealer*, 8 Nov. 1922, p. 4. See also *Cleveland Plain Dealer*, 9 Nov. 1922, pp. 10, 17.
79. "Conditions in Miles Heights Village," *Greater Cleveland, A Bulletin on Public Business by the Citizens League* 5 (10 April 1930):140.
80. Ibid., p. 143.
81. Ibid.
82. Howard Whipple Green, *Population by Census Tracts Cleveland, Ohio 1930* (Cleveland, 1931), p. 64; Howard Whipple Green, *Supplement to Population Characteristics by Census Tracts Cleveland, Ohio 1930* (Cleveland, 1933), p. 9.
83. See *City Club News* (Milwaukee) 8 (13 Oct. 1922):18; 8 (18 May 1923):144; 8 (25 May 1923):150; 9 (28 Sept. 1923):6; 9 (9 Nov. 1923):31; 9 (23 May 1924):150; 10 (12 Dec. 1924):42; 10 (29 May 1925):154; 11 (28 May 1926):158; 12 (7 Jan. 1927):75; 12 (27 May 1927):180; 13 (23 Mar. 1928):113; 13 (25 May 1928):149; 14 (9 Nov. 1928):32; 14 (23 Nov. 1928):40; 14 (15 Feb. 1929):92; 14 (5 Apr. 1929):118-19; 14 (31 May 1929):156; 15 (7 Feb. 1930):91; 15 (9 May 1930):139.
84. Arthur Werba and John L. Grunwald, *Making Milwaukee Mightier* (Milwaukee, 1929), pp. 8, 11.
85. *City Club News* (Milwaukee) 8 (18 May 1923):144; 8 (25 May 1923):150.
86. *Wisconsin Senate Journal, 1927* (Madison, 1927), Pt. 1, pp. 977-85.
87. *Milwaukee Journal*, 18 Dec. 1921, as quoted in Charles Davis Goff, "The Politics of Governmental Integration in Milwaukee" (Ph.D. dissertation, Northwestern University, 1952), p. 225.
88. Ibid.
89. Ibid.
90. Ibid., pp. 245-49.
91. *Proceedings of the Board of Supervisors of the County of Milwaukee, 1933-34* (Milwaukee, 1934), pp. 823-26, 856.
92. For wording of referendum proposal, see *Thirteenth Biennial Report of the Board of Election Commissioners of the City of Milwaukee, 1935* (Milwaukee, 1935), p. 188.
93. *Wauwatosa* (Wis.) *News*, 1 Nov. 1934, p. 4.
94. *Wauwatosa* (Wis.) *News*, 18 Oct. 1934, p. 4.
95. *West Allis* (Wis.) *Star*, 25 Oct. 1934, p. 1.
96. *West Allis* (Wis.) *Star*, 21 Mar. 1935, p. 6.
97. *Milwaukee Journal*, 30 Oct. 1934, p. 1 L. For other examples of the suburban response, see *Wauwatosa* (Wis.) *News*, 4 Oct. 1934, p. 4; 11 Oct. 1934, p. 4; 25 Oct. 1934, p. 1; 1 Nov. 1934, p. 3; *West Allis* (Wis.) *Star*, 9 Aug. 1934, p. 1; 18 Oct. 1934, p. 4; 1 Nov. 1934, p. 1; 14 Feb. 1935, p. 4; 7 Mar. 1935, p. 1; 14 Mar. 1935, p. 1.
98. *Thirteenth Report of Election Commissioners*, pp. 188-89. West Allis voters approved consolidation in November 1934 but rejected the merger proposal decisively in a second election in April 1935.
99. *Milwaukee Sentinel*, 6 Dec. 1934, p. 13. For the plan recommended by the joint committee on consolidation, see *Proceedings of Board of Supervisors of the County of Milwaukee, 1934-35* (Milwaukee, 1935), pp. 3-78.
100. *Milwaukee Leader*, 5 Nov. 1934, p. 12.
101. *Los Angeles Times*, 1 Oct. 1925, Pt. II, p. 1; Richard Bigger and James Kitchen, *How the Cities Grew: A Century of Municipal Independence and Expansionism in Metropolitan Los Angeles* (Los Angeles, 1952), pp. 180-83.
102. Ibid.
103. Bigger and Kitchen, *How the Cities Grew*, p. 183.
104. Ibid., pp. 183-84.
105. Walter Wagner, *Beverly Hills: Inside the Golden Ghetto* (New York, 1976), p. 19.
106. Ibid., p. 20.
107. Ibid., p. 21.

108. Ibid., unnumbered photograph page.
109. For information on the Akron annexation contests, see *Akron Beacon Journal,* 2 Nov. 1928, p. 43; 13 Mar. 1929, p. 4; 21 Mar. 1929, p. 9; 8 Apr. 1929, p. 4.
110. For information on the annexation contests in Columbus during the 1920s and 1930s, see *Ohio State Journal* (Columbus), 22 July 1930, p. 2; 23 July 1930, pp. 1, 2; 3 Mar. 1931, p. 2; 2 Nov. 1931, p. 4; 4 Nov. 1931, p. 2; 11 Jan. 1933, p. 2; *Columbus Evening Dispatch,* 4 Nov. 1920, p. 2; 4 Nov. 1925, pp. 6, 21; *City Bulletin, Official Publication of the City of Columbus,* 13 Nov. 1920, p. 257; 6 Aug. 1925, pp. 423, 425; 10 Aug. 1929, p. 401; 28 Sept. 1929, pp. 467, 470; 13 June 1931, p. 167; 11 July 1931, p. 193; 18 July 1931, pp. 200-201; 18 June 1932, pp. 163, 164-65; 26 Nov. 1932, p. 289.
111. For information on the annexation struggle in Spokane, see Russell William Barthell, "Annexation and Consolidation of Local Governments in the State of Washington" (Master's thesis, University of Washington, 1931), pp. 113-16.
112. *Journal of the House of Representatives of the Commonwealth of Massachusetts, 1919* (Boston, 1919), pp. 83, 88, 140, 153, 723, 738, 758, 772, 782, 793, 926, 962, 968; *Journal of the Senate of the Commonwealth of Massachusetts, 1919* (Boston, 1919), pp. 31, 95, 156, 165, 613, 622, 641, 652, 656, 673.
113. *Journal of the House of Representatives of the Commonwealth of Massachusetts 1923* (Boston, 1923), pp. 103, 118, 315, 334; *Journal of the Senate 1923* (Boston, 1923, pp. 122, 142, 261, 277; *Journal of the Senate 1924* (Boston, 1924), pp. 217, 225; *Journal of the House of Representatives of the Commonwealth of Massachusetts 1925* (Boston, 1925), pp. 54, 119-20, 251, 260, 303, 320; *Journal of the Senate 1925* (Boston, 1925), pp. 63, 168, 222, 236, 273, 289; *Journal of the House of Representatives of the Commonwealth of Massachusetts 1926* (Boston, 1926), pp. 30, 81, 112, 129, 141, 235, 243, 247, 253, 383, 411; *Journal of the Senate 1926* (Boston, 1926), pp. 34, 107, 132, 200, 211.
114. *St. Louis County Leader* (Clayton, Mo.), 11 June 1926, p. 1.
115. *St. Louis County Leader* (Clayton, Mo.), 18 June 1926, p. 1.
116. *Maplewood* (Mo.) *News-Champion,* 8 Oct. 1926, p. 4.
117. *Webster News-Times* (Webster Groves, Mo.), 11 June 1926, p. 1.
118. *Clayton* (Mo.) *Watchman Advocate,* 31 Oct. 1924, p. 4.
119. *St. Louis County Leader* (Clayton, Mo.), 12 Feb. 1926, pp. 1, 5. For suburban opinion from the constitutional amendment contest of 1924, see *Clayton* (Mo.) *Watchman Advocate,* 3 Oct. 1924, p. 3; 31 Oct. 1924, pp. 1, 7, 8; *Maplewood* (Mo.) *News-Champion,* 31 Oct. 1924, pp. 4. For further examples of suburban reaction to the merger plan of 1926, see *Maplewood* (Mo.) *News-Champion,* 24 Sept. 1926, p. 1; 8 Oct. 1926, p. 1; 22 Oct. 1926, p. 1; *St. Louis County Leader* (Clayton, Mo.), 26 Mar. 1926, p. 1; 27 August 1926, p. 1; 17 Sept. 1926, p. 1; 29 Oct. 1926, p. 1; *Webster News-Times* (Webster Groves, Mo.), 18 June 1926, p. 4; 2 July 1926, pp. 1, 5.
120. Complete returns published in the *St. Louis County Leader* (Clayton, Mo.), 29 Oct. 1926, p. 1.
121. Charles McKinley, "The Proposed Consolidation of the Governments of Portland and Multnomah County," *Commonwealth Review: A Journal of Applied Social Science* 12 (Nov. 1930):249-56. For information on the history of boundary adjustments in the Portland area, see *Annexation, Incorporation, and Consolidation in the Metropolitan Area* (Portland, 1968).

Chapter 6

1. For background on the reorganization of metropolitan London, see *Times* (London), 8 Apr. 1884, pp. 9-10; 9 Apr. 1884, pp. 6-7; 11 Apr. 1884, p. 7; 25 Sept. 1888, p. 8; Sir Gwilym Gibbon and Reginald W. Bell, *History of the London County Council 1889-1939* (London, 1939).

2. *Report of the Metropolitan District Commission to the Massachusetts Legislature* (Boston, 1896).
3. *Boston Herald,* 6 Jan. 1896, p. 3.
4. *Boston Herald,* 8 Jan. 1896, p. 4.
5. "New York City Charter Revision," *Outlook* 65 (26 May 1900):200.
6. Frederick Shaw, *The History of the New York City Legislature* (New York, 1954), p. 13.
7. Paul Studenski, *The Government of Metropolitan Areas in the United States* (New York, 1930), pp. 357-58.
8. Ibid., p. 342.
9. Richard Bigger and James Kitchen, *How the Cities Grew: A Century of Municipal Independence and Expansionism in Metropolitan Los Angeles* (Los Angeles, 1952), pp. 163, 246.
10. Cal. *Constitution,* Art. 11, sec. 8; Winston Crouch and Beatrice Dinerman, *Southern California Metropolis: A Study in Development of Government for a Metropolitan Area* (Berkeley, 1977), pp. 74-75.
11. Crose v. City Council of City of Los Angeles et al., 175 Cal. 774, 167 P. 386 (1917).
12. Martin J. Schiesl, *The Politics of Efficiency: Municipal Administration and Reform in America, 1880-1920* (Berkeley, 1977), p. 13.
13. Etling B. Morison, ed., *The Letters of Theodore Roosevelt,* 8 vols. (Cambridge, Mass., 1951-54), 1:84.
14. Schiesl, *Politics of Efficiency,* p. 63.
15. In 1925 "Boss" Tom Pendergast backed the city manager plan and most of the poorer neighborhoods of the north side voted strongly in favor of it. But the plan was the handiwork of south side good-government reformers. *Kansas City Times,* 25 February 1925, pp. 1-2; William Reddig, *Tom's Town* (Philadelphia, 1947), pp. 115-18.
16. *Seattle Times,* 11 Mar. 1925, p. 8.
17. *Minneapolis Journal,* 22 June 1926, pp. 1, 16.
18. See, for example, *Cleveland Plain Dealer,* 21 Aug. 1929, p. 5.
19. Chicago Bureau of Public Efficiency, *Unification in Chicago* (Chicago, 1917).
20. Tax Payers' Association of California, *City and County Consolidation for Los Angeles* (Los Angeles, 1917).
21. Thomas H. Reed, "The Government of Metropolitan Areas," *Public Management* 12 (Mar. 1930):77; Thomas H. Reed, "City-County Consolidation," *National Municipal Review* 23 (Oct. 1934):525.
22. Mary C. Schauffler, *The Suburbs of Cleveland: A Field Study of the Metropolitan District Outside of the Administrative Area of the City* (Chicago, 1945), pp. 114, 381-82, 390; Stuart A. Queen and Lewis F. Thomas, *The City, A Study of Urbanism in the United States* (New York, 1939), p. 287.
23. Harlan P. Douglass, *The Suburban Trend* (New York, 1925), pp. 218-19.
24. Frank C. Harper, *Pittsburgh of Today, Its Resources and People,* 4 vols. (New York, 1931), 4:427.
25. Joseph T. Miller, "Pittsburgh Plan of City-County Consolidation," *American Political Science Review* 21 (May 1927):367; Joseph T. Miller, "The Pittsburgh Consolidation Charter," *National Municipal Review* 18 (Oct. 1929):603-9.
26. *Cleveland Plain Dealer,* 2 Nov. 1922, p. 15.
27. William A. Greenlund, "County Reform and Metropolitan Government," *National Municipal Review* 19 (Oct. 1930):696.
28. Based on information from *Cleveland City Directory 1930* (Cleveland, 1930) and *Cleveland City Directory 1932* (Cleveland, 1932).
29. *Who's Who in Ohio* (Cleveland, 1930), p. 48.
30. Mayo Fesler, "City and County Consolidation and County Home Rule in Cleveland," *National Municipal Review* 14 (July 1925):435.
31. *St. Louis Globe-Democrat,* 18 May 1926, p. 4; *St. Louis County Leader* (Clayton, Mo.), 7 Aug. 1925, p. 1.
32. *St. Louis Globe-Democrat,* 18 May 1926, p. 6. For another account of Roessel's antimerger efforts, see *Maplewood* (Mo.) *News-Champion,* 8 Oct. 1926, p. 1.

33. *St. Louis Globe-Democrat,* 18 Oct. 1926, p. 6.
34. *St. Louis County Leader* (Clayton, Mo.), 17 Sept. 1926, p. 1.
35. *Milwaukee Journal,* 29 Mar. 1928, as quoted in Charles Davis Goff, "The Politics of Governmental Integration in Metropolitan Milwaukee" (Ph.D. dissertation, Northwestern University, 1952), pp. 276-77.
36. Arthur Werba and John L. Grunwald, *Making Milwaukee Mightier* (Milwaukee, 1929), p. 43.
37. *San Francisco Chronicle,* 28 July 1923, p. 4.
38. *San Francisco Chronicle,* 27 July 1923, p. 2; 28 July 1923, p. 4.
39. *San Francisco Chronicle,* 28 July 1923, p. 1; 7 Apr. 1926, p. 3; 13 Apr. 1926, p. 5.
40. *San Francisco Chronicle,* 27 July 1923, p. 2.
41. *San Francisco Chronicle,* 28 July 1923, p. 4.
42. For further developments, see *San Francisco Chronicle,* 8 Jan. 1925, p. 6; 12 Mar. 1925, p. 7; 2 Apr. 1926, p. 22; 13 May 1926, p. 13; 14 June 1929, p. 6; 27 Nov. 1930, p. 1; 10 Dec. 1930, p. 4; 19 Mar. 1931, p. 24; 25 Mar. 1931, Sec. 2, p. 15. See also John C. Bollens, *The Problem of Government in the San Francisco Bay Region* (Berkeley, 1948), pp. 70-77; Alfred H. Campion, "San Francisco Approves Plan for Consolidation with San Mateo County," *National Municipal Review* 20 (May 1931):256-59.

Chapter 7

1. J. Steele Gow, Jr., "Metropolitics in Pittsburgh" (Ph.D. dissertation, University of Pittsburgh, 1952), pp. 14-21.
2. Ibid., p. 20.
3. "Many New Activities to be Undertaken by Chamber of Commerce Committees," *Pittsburgh First, Official Bulletin of the Chamber of Commerce of Pittsburgh* 1 (28 June 1919):1.
4. "Opportunity for a Greater Pittsburgh," *Pittsburgh First, Official Bulletin of the Chamber of Commerce of Pittsburgh* 2 (14 Aug. 1920):4. For similar expressions of concern about annexation and metropolitan rule, see *Pittsburgh First,* 26 July 1919; 24 July 1920; 20 Jan. 1923; 27 Jan. 1923; 24 Feb. 1923; 24 Mar. 1923; 21 Apr. 1923; 16 June 1923; 23 June 1923; 7 July 1923; 14 July 1923; 28 July 1923.
5. Gow, "Metropolitics in Pittsburgh," pp. 22-27.
6. Ibid., p. 37.
7. Ibid., p. 56.
8. Ibid., pp. 82-85.
9. Ibid., pp. 75-81.
10. *Journal of the House of Representatives of the . . . State of Ohio . . . 1917* (Columbus, 1917), pp. 477, 727-28.
11. *Journal of the Senate of the . . . State of Ohio . . . 1919* (Columbus, 1919), pp. 121,128.
12. Chester C. Maxey, "The Political Integration of Metropolitan Communities," *National Municipal Review* 11 (Aug. 1922):248.
13. *Journal of the Senate of the Eighty-Fifth General Assembly of the State of Ohio* (Columbus, 1923), pp. 160-62; *Journal of the Senate of the Eighty-Sixth General Assembly of the State of Ohio* (Columbus, 1925), pp. 108-10; *Journal of the Senate of the Eighty-Seventh General Assembly of the State of Ohio* (Columbus, 1928), pp. 36, 44.
14. *Ohio State Journal* (Columbus), 12 Jan. 1927, p. 2; 27 Jan. 1927, p. 3; *Cleveland Plain Dealer,* 12 Jan. 1927, p. 16; 13 Jan. 1927, p. 8.
15. *Cleveland Plain Dealer,* 3 Feb. 1927, pp. 1, 7.
16. *Cleveland Plain Dealer,* 3 Feb. 1927, pp. 1, 7; *Ohio State Journal* (Columbus), 3 Feb. 1927, p. 5.
17. *Journal of Proceedings of the Ohio State Grange, 1928* (n.pl., 1928), p. 27.
18. C. A. Dyer, "News and Views from Columbus," *Ohio State Grange Monthly* 34 (Jan. 1931):12.

19. "City-County Reorganization Proposal," *Greater Cleveland: A Bulletin on Public Business by the Citizens League* 6 (15 Jan. 1931):79, 82.
20. *Cleveland Plain Dealer,* 5 Jan. 1931, p. 11.
21. *Cincinnati Enquirer,* 26 Feb. 1931, pp. 1-2.
22. *Cleveland Plain Dealer,* 5 Jan. 1931, pp. 1, 11.
23. *Cincinnati Enquirer,* 26 Feb. 1931, p. 2; Haskell Penn Short, "Robert Alphonso Taft, His Eight Years in the Ohio General Assembly" (Master's thesis, Ohio State University, 1951), pp. 97-98.
24. Ibid.
25. *Cincinnati Enquirer,* 26 Feb. 1931, p. 2.
26. *Cincinnati Enquirer,* 26 Feb. 1931, pp. 1-2; *Cleveland Plain Dealer,* 26 Feb. 1931, p. 1.
27. *Cleveland Plain Dealer,* 9 Apr. 1931, p. 16.
28. Ibid., p. 1.
29. Ibid., p. 16.
30. Ibid., p. 1.
31. "Records of League of Women Voters of Ohio," Ohio Historical Society, Columbus, Ohio.
32. C. A. Dyer, "News and Views from Columbus," *Ohio State Grange Monthly* 35 (June 1932): 3; "County Charter Amendment," *Ohio State Grange Monthly* 35 (July 1932): 4.
33. Thomas H. Reed, "Dual Government for Metropolitan Regions," *National Municipal Review* 16 (Feb. 1927): 118-26.
34. *Watchman Advocate* (Clayton, Mo.), 2 May 1930, p. 1.
35. *Wellsboro (Pa.) Gazette,* 25 Oct. 1928, p. 8.
36. *Bedford (Pa.) Gazette,* 16 Nov. 1928, p. 6. Other Pennsylvania newspapers examined are *Gettysburg Times, Selinsgrove Time-Tribune, Fulton Democrat* (McConnellsburg), *Forest Press* (Tionesta), *Emporium Press-Independent, Waynesburg Republican.*
37. *Journal of Proceedings of the Ohio State Grange, 1932* (n.pl., 1932), p. 32.
38. *Cadiz (Ohio) Republican,* 2 Nov. 1933, p. 1.
39. *Paulding County (Ohio) Republican,* 2 Nov. 1933, p. 1.
40. *Republican Tribune* (McArthur, Ohio), 1 Nov. 1933, p. 2. See same editorial in *Noble County Leader* (Caldwell, Ohio), 1 Nov. 1933, p. 3.
41. *Preble County News* (Camden, Ohio), 2 Nov. 1933, p. 2. For other small-town commentary on the constitutional amendment, see *Carroll Chronicle* (Carrollton, Ohio), 12 Oct. 1933, p. 2; *Morgan County (Ohio) Democrat,* 2 Nov. 1933, p. 4. For reaction in the central city and suburbs of one of Ohio's smaller metropolitan areas, see *Youngstown (Ohio) Vindicator,* 1 Nov. 1933, p. 3; 2 Nov. 1933, p. 3; *Struthers (Ohio) Journal,* 20 Oct. 1933, p. 1; 27 Oct. 1933, p. 1; 3 Nov. 1933, p. 1; *Mahoning Dispatch* (Canfield, Ohio), 27 Oct. 1933, p. 1.
42. *Troy (Mo.) Free Press,* 24 Oct. 1930, p. 1.
43. *Gasconade County Republican* (Owensville, Mo.), 9 Oct. 1930, p. 1; 16 Oct. 1930, p. 1.
44. *Jefferson County Republican* (DeSoto, Mo.), 30 Oct. 1930, p. 1; *Warrenton (Mo.) Banner,* 31 Oct. 1930, p. 1. Foes of the amendment also placed articles attacking the proposal in rural newspapers throughout the state. See, for example, *Current Wave* (Eminence, Mo.), 30 Oct. 1930, p. 1; *Warrenton (Mo.) Banner,* 24 Oct. 1930, p. 1.
45. *Missouri Farmer,* 22 (1 Nov. 1930):8.
46. *Fiftieth Anniversary Missouri Bar Association, Report of the Proceedings of the 1930 Annual Meeting* (Fulton, Mo., 1931), p. 14.
47. *Homestead (Pa.) Messenger,* 12 Oct. 1928, pp. 1, 9.
48. *Duquesne (Pa.) Times,* 2 Nov. 1928, p. 12.
49. *Duquesne (Pa.) Times,* 28 Sept. 1928, p. 9.
50. *Duquesne (Pa.) Times,* 2 Nov. 1928, p. 12.
51. *Wilkinsburg (Pa.) Progress,* 19 Oct. 1928, p. 3; 26 Oct. 1928, p. 1. See also editorial in *Wilkinsburg (Pa.) Progress,* 10 Aug. 1928, p. 1.
52. *Cleveland Press,* 1 Nov. 1933, p. 6; *Cleveland Plain Dealer,* 19 Oct. 1933, p. 15.
53. *Cleveland Plain Dealer,* 19 Oct. 1933, p. 15.
54. *Lakewood (Ohio) Post and West Shore Post,* 13 Oct. 1933, p. 2.

55. *Berea* (Ohio) *Enterprise*, 6 Oct. 1933, p. 1.
56. *Cleveland Plain Dealer*, 9 Nov. 1933, p. 9.
57. *Lakewood* (Ohio) *Post and West Shore Post*, 20 Oct. 1933, p. 6.
58. *Suburban News and Herald* (Lakewood, Ohio), 3 Nov. 1933, p. 2.
59. *Berea* (Ohio) *Enterprise*, 27 Oct. 1933, p. 1.
60. *St. Louis County Leader* (Clayton, Mo.), 10 Oct. 1930, p. 1.
61. *Maplewood* (Mo.) *News-Champion*, 17 Oct. 1930, p. 1.
62. *St. Louis County Leader* (Clayton, Mo.), 26 Sept. 1930, p. 1.
63. *St. Louis County Leader* (Clayton, Mo.), 3 Oct. 1930, p. 1.
64. *Maplewood* (Mo.) *News-Champion*, 17 Oct. 1930, p. 4.
65. *Clayton* (Mo.) *Watchman Advocate*, 27 June 1930, p. 1.
66. *Maplewood* (Mo.) *News-Champion*, 12 Sept. 1930, p. 4.
67. *Maplewood* (Mo.) *News-Champion*, 24 Oct. 1930, p. 2.
68. *St. Louis County Leader* (Clayton, Mo.), 26 Sept. 1930, p. 1.
69. *St. Louis County Leader* (Clayton, Mo.), 31 Oct. 1930, p. 1; *St. Louis Globe-Democrat*, 28 Oct. 1930, p. 2.
70. *St. Louis County Leader* (Clayton, Mo.), 19 Sept. 1930, p. 1.
71. *Clayton* (Mo.) *Watchman Advocate*, 25 Apr. 1930, p. 1.
72. *St. Louis Countian* (Kirkwood, Mo.), 31 Oct. 1930, p. 1.
73. *Kirkwood* (Mo.) *Monitor*, 17 Oct. 1930, p. 2.
74. *Webster News-Times* (Webster Groves, Mo.), 19 Sept. 1930, p. 4.
75. *St. Louis Globe-Democrat*, 12 Oct. 1930, p. 4b.
76. *St. Louis Globe-Democrat*, 19 Oct. 1930, p. 1.
77. A. L. Humphrey, "Pittsburgh Fifty Years Hence," *Pittsburgh and the Pittsburgh Spirit: Addresses at the Chamber of Commerce of Pittsburgh 1927-1928* (Pittsburgh, 1928), pp. 364-65.
78. Discussion on Metropolitan Area at Board Meeting, 1 Feb. 1927, Civic Club of Allegheny County Records, Archives of Industrial Society, University of Pittsburgh, Pittsburgh, Pennsylvania.
79. Ibid.
80. Ibid.
81. *Cleveland Press*, 4 Nov. 1933, p. 4.
82. *Cleveland News*, 4 Nov. 1933, p. 4.
83. *Cleveland Plain Dealer*, 14 Oct. 1933, p. 8. For other editorials on the reform of county government, see *Cleveland Plain Dealer*, 28 Oct. 1933, p. 8; 3 Nov. 1933, p. 8; 6 Nov. 1933, p. 8.
84. *Cleveland Plain Dealer*, 19 Oct. 1933, p. 15.
85. *St. Louis Globe-Democrat*, 2 Nov. 1930, p. 2.
86. Ibid.
87. Ibid.
88. Ibid.
89. *St. Louis Globe-Democrat*, 15 Oct. 1930, p. 12; *St. Louis County Leader* (Clayton, Mo.), 17 Oct. 1930, p. 1.
90. *St. Louis County Leader* (Clayton, Mo.), 17 Oct. 1930, p. 1.
91. *St. Louis Globe-Democrat*, 29 Oct. 1930, p. 1.
92. *St. Louis Globe-Democrat*, 18 Oct. 1930, p. 2.
93. *St. Louis Globe-Democrat*, 19 Oct. 1930, p. 4.
94. Election data from *The Pennsylvania Manual 1929* (Harrisburg, 1929), p. 506; *Official Manual of the State of Missouri, 1931-1932* (Jefferson City, Mo., 1931), pp. 269-70; *Ohio Election Statistics 1934* (Berea, Ohio, 1935), pp. 257-59.
95. Computed on basis of data from Abstract of Elections 1933, Cuyahoga County Board of Elections, Cleveland, Ohio; Civic Club of Allegheny County Records, Archives of Industrial Society, University of Pittsburgh Library, Pittsburgh, Pennsylvania; Gow, "Metropolitics in Pittsburgh," pp. 304-6. Economic data derived from *Real Property Inventory of Allegheny County* (data collected in February 1934); Green, *Population Characteristics Cleveland 1930;* Green, *Supplement to Population Characteristics Cleveland 1930; Population and Housing, Statistics for Census Tracts—Cleveland, Ohio and Adjacent Area, 1940* (Washington, D.C., 1942), pp. 130-38.

96. Election data by precincts reported in *St. Louis County Leader* (Clayton, Mo.), 7 Nov. 1930, p. 1.

Chapter 8

1. Letter from Joseph Miller to H. Marie Dermitt, 3 Dec. 1928, Civic Club of Allegheny County Records, Archives of Industrial Society, University of Pittsburgh Library, Pittsburgh, Pennsylvania.
2. *Cleveland Plain Dealer*, 9 Nov. 1933, p. 12.
3. J. Steele Gow, Jr., "Metropolitics in Pittsburgh" (Ph.D. dissertation, University of Pittsburgh, 1952), p. 136.
4. Rowland A. Egger, "Pittsburgh—The World's Third Federated City," *American City* 40 (June 1929):120-21; Rowland A. Egger, "The Proposed Charter of the Federated 'City of Pittsburgh,' " *American Political Science Review* 23 (Aug. 1929):718-26.
5. Egger, "Pittsburgh," *American City*, pp. 120-21.
6. Gow, "Metropolitics in Pittsburgh," p. 145.
7. *Pittsburgh Post-Gazette*, 27 Mar. 1929, as cited in Victor Jones, *Metropolitan Government* (Chicago, 1942), p. 284.
8. *Pittsburgh Post-Gazette*, 8 Febr. 1929, as quoted in Jones, *Metropolitan Government*, p. 285.
9. Jones, *Metropolitan Government*, p. 285.
10. Egger, "Pittsburgh," *American City*, pp. 120-21.
11. Martin L. Faust, "Voters Turn Thumbs Down of Pittsburgh's Metropolitan Charter," *National Municipal Review* 18 (Aug. 1929):530, 531.
12. Egger, "Pittsburgh," *American City*, p. 121.
13. Miller, "Consolidation Charter," *National Municipal Review 18* (Oct. 1929):603-9. For Miller's endorsement of the charter, see *Pittsburgh Courier*, 22 June 1929, p. 1.
14. Egger, "Pittsburgh," *American City*, p. 121.
15. *East Cleveland Signal*, 1 Nov. 1934, p. 4.
16. *East Cleveland Signal*, 1 Nov. 1934, p. 4; *Cleveland Press* 20 Oct. 1934, p. 3.
17. *Garfield Heights* (Ohio) *Record*, 4 Oct. 1934, p. 3. Also see *Garfield Heights* (Ohio) *Record*, 27 Sept. 1934, p. 3; 11 Oct. 1934, p. 2; 25 Oct. 1934, p. 2; 1 Nov. 1934, p. 2; 22 Nov. 1934, p. 3.
18. *East Cleveland Signal*, 25 Oct. 1934, p. 4. Also see *East Cleveland Signal*, 1 Nov 1934, p. 1.
19. *Suburban News and Herald* (Lakewood, Ohio), 2 Nov. 1934, p. 2.
20. *Cleveland Press*, 18 Oct. 1934, p. 7.
21. *Cleveland Plain Dealer*, 15 Nov. 1934, p. 1.
22. Ibid.
23. *Cleveland Plain Dealer*, 15 Nov. 1934, p. 6.
24. *Cleveland Plain Dealer*, 17 Oct. 1934, p. 4.
25. *Cleveland Press*, 3 Nov. 1934, p. 4.
26. *Cleveland Plain Dealer*, 26 Sept. 1934, p. 6.
27. Computed on basis of data from Abstract of Elections 1934, Cuyahoga County Board of Elections, Cleveland, Ohio. Economic data derived from Green, *Population Characteristics Cleveland 1930*; Green, *Supplement to Population Characteristics Cleveland 1930*; *Population and Housing—Cleveland and Adjacent Area, 1940*, pp. 130-38. Rental figures averaged from the 1930 and 1940 data.
28. *Cleveland Plain Dealer*, 6 Jan. 1935, p. 20A.
29. *Cleveland Plain Dealer*, 26 Jan. 1935, p. 16.
30. *Cleveland Plain Dealer*, 1 June 1935, p. 9.
31. *Cleveland Plain Dealer*, 9 Mar. 1935, p. 1.
32. Ibid.
33. *Berea* (Ohio) *Enterprise*, 15 Feb. 1935, p. 1. For a short biography of Blythin, see Strongsville Historical Society, comp. *History of Strongsville, Cuyahoga County, Ohio*, 2 vols. (Strongsville, 1967-68), 2:55-56.

34. *Berea* (Ohio) *Enterprise,* 1 Feb. 1935, p. 1.
35. Ibid.
36. Ibid.
37. *History of Strongsville,* 1:6. For a short biography of Bean, see *History of Strongsville,* 2:60.
38. *Berea* (Ohio) *Enterprise,* 8 Mar. 1935, p. 1; 15 Mar. 1935, pp. 1, 2.
39. Ibid.
40. *Cleveland Plain Dealer,* 1 June 1935, p. 9.
41. *Wilkinsburg* (Pa.) *Progress,* 14 June 1929, p. 1.; 21 June 1929, p. 10.
42. *Duquesne* (Pa) *Times,* 14 June 1929, pp. 1, 16. See also *Duquesne* (Pa.) *Times,* 21 June 1929, p. 10.
43. *Homestead* (Pa.) *Messenger,* 12 June 1929, p. 1.
44. *Lakewood* (Ohio) *Post and West Shore Post,* 4 Oct. 1935, pp. 1, 7.
45. *Lakewood* (Ohio) *Post and West Shore Post,* 18 Oct. 1935, p. 6; 25 Oct. 1935, p. 6.
46. *Berea* (Ohio) *Enterprise,* 1 Nov. 1935, p. 4.
47. *Cleveland Plain Dealer,* 25 Oct. 1935, p. 14.
48. *Cleveland Plain Dealer,* 21 Oct. 1935, p. 13.
49. *Cleveland Plain Dealer,* 5 Oct. 1935, p. 10.
50. Faust, "Voters Turn Thumbs Down," *National Municipal Review,* p. 531.
51. *Pittsburgh Post-Gazette,* 24 June 1929, p. 10; 19 June 1929, p. 8.
52. *Wilkinsburg* (Pa.) *Progress,* 14 June 1929, p. 1.
53. State, Ex Rel. Howland v. Krause et al. 130 Ohio State 455 (1936).
54. Election data from Civic Club of Allegheny County Records, Archives of Industrial Society, University of Pittsburgh Library, Pittsburgh, Pennsylvania; *Pittsburgh Post-Gazette,* 27 June 1929, p. 2; Gow, "Metropolitics in Pittsburgh," pp. 304-6. Economic data derived from *Real Property Inventory of Allegheny County* (data collected in February 1934).
55. Election data from Abstract of Elections 1935, Cuyahoga County Board of Elections, Cleveland, Ohio. Economic data derived from Green, *Population Characteristics Cleveland 1930;* Green, *Supplement to Population Characteristics Cleveland 1930; Population and Housing, Statistics for Census Tracts—Cleveland, Ohio and Adjacent Area, 1940,* pp. 130-38. Rental figures averaged from the 1930 and 1940 data.
56. *Homestead* (Pa.) *Messenger,* 26 June 1929, p. 4.

Chapter 9

1. *Government in Metropolitan Areas: Commentaries on a Report by the Advisory Commission on Intergovernmental Relations* (Washington, 1962), pp. 1-5.
2. Computed on the basis of information in John C. Bollens, "Metropolitan Special Districts," *Municipal Year Book* 23 (1956):52-55.
3. For the shortcomings of the metropolitan special district, see John C. Bollens, *Special District Governments in the United States* (Berkeley, 1957).
4. Thomas P. Murphy and John Rehfuss, *Urban Politics in the Suburban Era* (Homewood, Ill., 1976), p. 155.
5. Ibid., p. 151.
6. Stephen B. Sweeney and George S. Blair, eds., *Metropolitan Analysis: Important Elements of Study and Action* (Philadelphia, 1958), pp. 113-16.
7. *Cleveland Plain Dealer,* 4 Nov. 1959, p. 1.
8. Ibid.
9. *Cleveland Call and Post,* 17 Oct. 1959, p. 2A.
10. *Cleveland Plain Dealer,* 4 Nov. 1959, p. 1.
11. *Cleveland Plain Dealer,* 4 Nov. 1959, p. 13.
12. Ibid.
13. Estal E. Sparlin, "Cleveland Seeks New Metro Solution," *National Civic Review* 49 (Mar. 1960):142-43.

14. *St. Louis Post-Dispatch*, 4 Nov. 1959, p. 13A.
15. *St. Louis Post-Dispatch*, 5 Nov. 1959, p. 11A.
16. Scott Greer, *Metropolitics* (New York, 1963), p. 77.
17. Ibid., p. 78.
18. Ibid., p. 85.
19. Ibid., p. 84.
20. For a complete account of the Miami metropolitan struggle, see, Edward Sofen, *The Miami Metropolitan Experiment* (Bloomington, Ind., 1963).
21. *Prologue to Progress* (Cleveland, 1959), p. 16. See correlations of economic status and support for the metropolitan movement in Richard A. Watson and John H. Romani, "Metropolitan Government for Metropolitan Cleveland: An Analysis of the Voting Record," *Midwest Journal of Political Science* 5 (Nov. 1961):365-90.
22. Watson and Romani, "Metropolitan Government," *Midwest Journal of Political Science*, p. 377.
23. Voting returns reported in *St. Louis Post-Dispatch*, 4 Nov. 1959, p. 13A; Sofen, *Miami*, pp. 74-75.
24. *Cleveland Call and Post*, 31 Oct. 1959, p. 4A.
25. Ibid.
26. Ibid., p. 5A.
27. Ibid.
28. Ibid., p. 3A.
29. Ibid., p. 5A.
30. Ibid. For other examples of metropolitan controversy in the black neighborhoods, see *Cleveland Call and Post*, 17 Oct. 1959, pp. 1A, 2A, 1D; 24 Oct. 1959, pp. 2C, 1D; 31 Oct. 1959, p. 7D.
31. *New York Times*, 2 Sept. 1966, p. 3.
32. *New York Times*, 22 Oct. 1966, p. 17.
33. Ibid.
34. Ibid.
35. Milton Kotler, *Neighborhood Government: The Local Foundations of Political Life* (Indianapolis, 1969), p. 26.
36. Douglas Yates, *Neighborhood Democracy: The Politics and Impacts of Decentralization* (Lexington, Mass., 1973), p. 11.
37. Donna E. Shalala, *Neighborhood Governance. Proposals and Issues* (New York, 1971), p. 32.
38. Walter G. Farr, Jr., Lance Liebman, and Jeffrey S. Wood, *Decentralizing City Government: A Practical Study of a Radical Proposal for New York City* (New York, 1972), p. 183.
39. Committee for Economic Development, *Reshaping Government in Metropolitan Areas* (New York, 1970), p. 19.
40. Joseph F. Zimmerman, *The Federated City: Community Control in Large Cities* (New York, 1972), preface, n.p.
41. *Supercity/Hometown, U.S.A., Prospects for Two-Tier Government* (New York, 1974), p. 5.

BIBLIOGRAPHY

Unpublished Sources

Manuscript sources were of limited usefulness in this study of metropolitan fragmentation. County commissioners' journals consulted in Indiana and Ohio included records of the petitions for incorporation and of the county commissioners' orders to incorporate, but these represent only the bare bones of the incorporation process and in many areas county records seem to contain little or no information about the issues surrounding the creation of a new municipality. The records of commissioners and supervisors can, however, offer an outline of the proceedings, and James Kitchen and Richard Bigger in their study of southern California made extensive use of the minutes and files of Los Angeles County. County records also provide generally perfunctory descriptions of the annexation proceedings of county commissioners during the late nineteenth and early twentieth centuries. Municipal records of annexation proceedings survive as well, but these usually offer limited information. In Cincinnati, for example, the records are fairly extensive and conveniently filed, yet primarily they describe the terms of the annexation agreements and report the vote on annexation. For an account of a specific annexation controversy, local newspaper reports can be more useful.

Manuscript sources on the struggle for federative rule survive, but they do not offer considerably greater insights into the problem than do the printed sources. The records of the Civic Club of Allegheny County at the University of Pittsburgh Library provide information on the Pittsburgh experience. The Western Reserve Historical Society holds the papers of the Citizens League and Saul Danaceau, but the Danaceau papers contain virtually nothing about the metropolitan struggle. The Ohio Historical Society in Columbus is the repository for the papers of the League of Women Voters of Ohio, and these papers offer some additional information on the subject. The most useful unpublished sources, however, are a series of dissertations and theses relating to the metropolitan issue.

Unpublished Dissertations and Theses

Altman, Orven Roland. "Problems of Government in the St. Louis Metropolitan Area." Master's thesis, University of Illinois, 1928.

Barthell, Russell William. "Annexation and Consolidation of Local Governments in the State of Washington." Master's thesis, University of Washington, 1931.

Cassella, William N., Jr. "Governing the St. Louis Metropolitan Area." Ph.D. dissertation, Harvard University, 1952.

Goff, Charles Davis. "The Politics of Governmental Integration in Metropolitan Milwaukee." Ph.D. dissertation, Northwestern University, 1952.

Gow, J. Steele, Jr. "Metropolitics in Pittsburgh." Ph.D. dissertation, University of Pittsburgh, 1952.

King, Jere C., Jr. "The Formation of Greater Birmingham." Master's thesis, University of Alabama, 1935.

LeGacy, Arthur Evans. "Improvers and Preservers: A History of Oak Park, Illinois, 1833-1940." Ph.D. dissertation, University of Chicago, 1967.

Merino, James. "A Great City and Its Suburbs: Attempts to Integrate Metropolitan Boston, 1865-1920." Ph.D. dissertation, University of Texas, 1968.

Morken, W. Hubert. "The Annexation of Morgan Park to Chicago, One Village's Response to Urban Growth." Master's thesis, University of Chicago, 1968.

Short, Haskell Penn. "Robert Alphonso Taft, His Eight Years in the Ohio General Assembly. Master's thesis, Ohio State University, 1951.

Printed Sources

Newspapers

Alabama
  Birmingham Age-Herald

California
  Los Angeles Times
  San Francisco Chronicle

Colorado
  Rocky Mountain News (Denver)

Georgia
  Atlanta Constitution

Illinois
  Austin Vindicator
  Chicago Daily News

Chicago Herald
Chicago Record-Herald
Chicago Tribune
Morgan Park Post
Oak Leaves (Oak Park)
Oak Park Reporter
Oak Park Vindicator

Indiana
Indianapolis Herald
Indianapolis Journal
Indianapolis News
Indianapolis Sentinel
Irvington Home Rule Advocate
Lake County News (Hammond)
Whiting Times

Massachusetts
Boston Daily Advertiser
Boston Herald

Minnesota
Minneapolis Journal

Missouri
Clayton Watchman Advocate
Current Wave (Eminence)
Gasconade County Republican (Owensville)
Jefferson County Republican (DeSoto)
Kansas City Times
Kirkwood Monitor
Maplewood News-Champion
St. Louis Countian (Kirkwood)
St. Louis County Leader (Clayton)
St. Louis Globe-Democrat
St. Louis Post-Dispatch
Troy Free Press
Warrenton Banner
Webster News-Times (Webster Groves)

New York
New York Times

Ohio
Akron Beacon Journal
Berea Enterprise

Cadiz Republican
Carroll Chronicle (Carrollton)
Cincinnati Enquirer
Cleveland Call and Post
Cleveland Leader
Cleveland News
Cleveland Plain Dealer
Cleveland Press
Columbus Evening Dispatch
East Cleveland Signal
Garfield Heights Record
Lakewood Post and West Shore Post
Mahoning Dispatch (Canfield)
Morgan County Democrat (McConnellsville)
Noble County Leader (Caldwell)
Ohio State Journal (Columbus)
Paulding County Republican (Paulding)
Preble County News (Camden)
Republican Tribune (McArthur)
Struthers Journal
Suburban News and Herald (Lakewood)
Youngstown Vindicator

Pennsylvania
Bedford Gazette
Duquesne Times
Homestead Messenger
Pittsburgh Courier
Pittsburgh Post-Gazette
Wellsboro Gazette
Wilkinsburg Progress

Washington
Seattle Post-Intelligencer
Seattle Times

Wisconsin
Milwaukee Journal
Milwaukee Leader
Milwaukee Sentinel
Wauwatosa News
West Allis Star

United Kingdom
Times (London)

Municipal and Civic Newsletters and Bulletins

City Bulletin, Official Publication of the City of Columbus
City Club News (Milwaukee)
Greater Cleveland, A Bulletin on Public Business by the Citizens League
Municipal Journal Baltimore
Pittsburgh First, Official Bulletin of the Chamber of Commerce of Pittsburgh

Statutes

Alabama

Toulmin, Harry, comp. *A Digest of the Laws of the State of Alabama.* ...
Cahawba, Ala., 1823.

Arkansas

Kirby, William F. *A Digest of the Statutes of Arkansas.* Austin, Texas,
1904.
Revised Statutes of the State of Arkansas. ... Boston, 1838.

California

Garfielde, S. and Snyder, F. A., comps. *Compiled Laws of the State of
California.* ... Bernicia, California, 1853.

Colorado

The General Statutes of the State of Colorado, 1883. Denver, 1883.

Illinois

Hurd, Harvey B., ed, *The Revised Statutes of the State of Illinois, 1887.*
Chicago, 1887.
The Laws of Illinois Passed at Seventh General Assembly. Vandalia, Illinois,
1831.
Laws of the State of Illinois Passed by the Thirty-Sixth General Assembly.
Springfield, 1889.
The Public and General Statute Laws of the State of Illinois. ... Chicago,
1839.

Indiana

*Laws of the State of Indiana, Passed and Published, at the Second Session
of the General Assembly.* ... *1817.* Corydon, Ind., 1818.
*Laws of the State of Indiana Passed at the Fifty-Ninth Regular Session of
the General Assembly.* Indianapolis, 1895.
*Laws of the State of Indiana Passed at the Fifty-Seventh Regular Session of
the General Assembly.* Indianapolis, 1891.

Iowa

Acts and Resolutions Passed at the First Session of the General Assembly of the State of Iowa. Iowa City, 1847.

The Code: Containing All the Statutes of the State of Iowa. Des Moines, 1873.

Kansas

General Law of the State of Kansas; Passed at the Sixth Session of the Legislature. Lawrence, Kan., 1866.

Kentucky

Digest of the Statute Laws of Kentucky. . . . 2 vols. Frankfort, Ky., 1834.

Louisiana Territory

Laws of a Public and General Nature, of the District of Louisiana. . . . Jefferson City, Mo., 1842.

Michigan

Acts of the Legislature of State of Michigan, Passed at the Regular Session of 1857. . . . Detroit, 1857.

Minnesota

General Laws of the State of Minnesota Passed During the Twenty-Ninth Session of the State Legislature. St. Paul, 1895.

Mississippi

Hutchinson, A., comp. *Code of Mississippi Being an Analytical Compilation of the Public and General Statutes of the Territory and State, With Tabular References to the Local and Private Acts, From 1798 to 1848.* . . . Jackson, Miss., 1848.

Missouri

The Annotated Statutes of the State of Missouri 1906. 5 vols. Saint Paul, Minn., 1906.

Laws of Missouri Passed at the Session of the Thirty-Fourth General Assembly. Jefferson City, 1887.

Laws of the State of Missouri; Revised and Digested. 2 vols. Saint Louis, 1825.

Nebraska

The Compiled Statutes of the State of Nebraska. Omaha, 1881.

New York

Laws of the State of New York. . . . 3 vols. Albany, 1846–48.

Ohio

Chase, Salmon P., ed. *The Statutes of Ohio and of the Northwestern Territory Adopted or Enacted from 1788 to 1833 Inclusive.* ... 3 vols. Cincinnati, 1833-35.

General and Local Acts Passed and Joint Resolutions Adopted by the Seventy-Fifth General Assembly. Columbus, 1902.

Swan, Joseph R., comp. *The Revised Statutes of the State of Ohio.* 2 vols. Cincinnati, 1860.

Pennsylvania

Purdon, John, ed. *A Digest of the Laws of Pennsylvania.* ... Philadelphia, 1852.

Tennessee

Acts of the State of Tennessee, Passed at the First Session of the Twenty-Eighth General Assembly for the Years 1849-50. Nashville, 1850.

Wisconsin

The Revised Statutes of the State of Wisconsin Passed at the Second Session of the Legislature Commencing January 10, 1849. ... Southport, Wis., 1849.

Constitutional Convention Proceedings and Debates

Indiana, Report of the Debates and Proceedings of the Convention for the Revision of the Constitution of the State of. 2 vols. Indianapolis, 1850.

Iowa, The Debates of the Constitutional Convention of the State of. 2 vols. Davenport, 1857.

Kansas Constitutional Convention. ... *1859.* Topeka, 1920.

New York State Convention for the Revision of the Constitution, Debates and Proceedings of the. Albany, 1846.

Ohio Convention of 1850-51, Report of Debates and Proceedings of the. 2 vols. Columbus, 1851.

Cases Cited

Atchinson v. Bartholow, 4 Kan. 124 (1866)
Borough of Glen Ridge v. G. Lee Stout et al., 58 N.J. 598 (1896)
Brown's Estate v. West Seattle, 43 Wash. 26 (1906)
City of Chicago v. Town of Cicero, 210 Ill. 290 (1904)
City of St. Louis v. William Russell, 9 Mo. 507 (1845)
City of South Bend et al. v. Lewis, 138 Ind. 512 (1894)
City of Topeka and others v. Gillett, 4 Pac. 800 (1884)

City of Westport v. Kansas City, 103 Mo. 141, 15 S.W. 68 (1891)

City of Wyandotte v. Wood, 5 Kan. 603 (1870)

Copeland v. City of St. Joseph, 126 Mo. 417, 29 S.W. 281 (1895)

Crose v. City Council of City of Los Angeles et al., 175 Cal. 774, 167 Pac. 386 (1917)

Dolese et al. v. Pierce, 124 Ill. 140 (1888)

Ernest Guebelle et al. v. John J. Epley et al., 1 Colo. App. 199 (1891)

G. Lee Stout et al. v. Borough of Glen Ridge, 59 N.J. 201 (1896)

George W. Warren and others v. Mayor and Aldermen of Charlestown, 68 Mass. 84 (1854)

Hunter v. City of Pittsburgh, 207 U.S. 161 (1907)

In re Extension of Boundaries of the City of Denver, 18 Colo. 288, 32 Pac. 615 (1893)

In re Incorporation of Borough of Edgewood, 130 Pa. 348 (1889)

In re Incorporation of the Borough of West Homestead, 48 Pittsburgh Legal Journal 172 (1900)

Kelly et al. v. Meeks, 87 Mo. 396 (1885)

Martin v. Simpkins, 20 Colo. 438 (1894)

Mayor and Trustees of the Town of Valverde v. Shattuck et al., 19 Colo. 104 (1893)

Northwestern University v. the People, 99 U.S. 309 (1879)

Ohio v. City of Cincinnati, 20 Ohio Rep. 18 (1870)

Perry et al. v. City of Denver et al., 27 Colo. 93, 59 Pac. 747 (1899)

Phillips et al. v. Corbin et al., 8 Colo. App. 346 (1896)

Phillips et al. v. Corbin et al., 25 Colo. 62 (1898)

R. Hall v. J. C. Siegrist, 13 Ohio Dec. 46 (1902)

Smith v. Sherry, 50 Wis. 210, 6 N. W. 561 (1880)

State, ex rel. Henry Broking et al. v. James M. Van Valen, 56 N.J. 85 (1893)

State, ex rel. Howland v. Krause et al., 130 Ohio St. 455 (1936)

State, ex rel. Knisely v. Jones, 66 Ohio St. 453 (1902)

State, ex rel. Osborn v. John Mitchell et al., 22 Cir. Ct. R. 208, 12 Ohio C. D. 288 (1901)

State, ex rel. v. Cincinnati, 52 Ohio St. 419 (1895)

State, ex rel. West Seattle v. the Superior Court for King County, 36 Wash. 566 (1905)

State, ex rel. West v. City of Des Moines, 96 Iowa 521, 65 N.W. 818 (1896)

State v. Nicoll, 40 Wash. 517 (1905)

Taylor et al. v. City of Fort Wayne et al., 47 Ind. 274 (1874)

Town of Longview v. City of Crawfordsville, 164 Ind. 117 (1905)

True v. Davis, 133 Ill. 522 (1889)

Village of Hyde Park v. City of Chicago, 124 Ill. 156 (1888)

Village of Morgan Park v. City of Chicago, 255 Ill. 190 (1912)

Vogel v. Little Rock, 55 Ark. 609, 19 S.W. 13 (1892)

W. H. Lawrence v. J. Mitchell et al., 10 Ohio Dec. 265, 8 Ohio N.P. 8 (1900)

Legislative Proceedings

Illinois
Proceedings of the City Council of Chicago. . . . 1887–88. Chicago, 1888.

Massachusetts
Journal of the House of Representatives of the Commonwealth of Massachusetts, 1919. Boston, 1919.
Journal of the House of Representatives of the Commonwealth of Massachusetts, 1923. Boston, 1923.
Journal of the House of Representatives of the Commonwealth of Massachusetts, 1925. Boston, 1925.
Journal of the House of Representatives of the Commonwealth of Massachusetts, 1926. Boston, 1926.
Journal of the Senate of the Commonwealth of Massachusetts, 1919. Boston, 1919.
Journal of the Senate 1923. Boston, 1923.
Journal of the Senate 1924. Boston, 1924.
Journal of the Senate 1925. Boston, 1925.
Journal of the Senate 1926. Boston, 1926.

Ohio
Journal of the House of Representatives of the . . . State of Ohio . . . 1917. Columbus, 1917.
Journal of the Senate of the . . . State of Ohio . . . 1919. Columbus, 1919.
Journal of the Senate of the Eighty-Fifth General Assembly of the State of Ohio. Columbus, 1923.
Journal of the Senate of the Eighty-Sixth General Assembly of the State of Ohio. Columbus, 1925.
Journal of the Senate of the Eighty-Seventh General Assembly of the State of Ohio. Columbus, 1928.

Wisconsin
Proceedings of the Board of Supervisors of the County of Milwaukee, 1933–34. Milwaukee, 1934.
Proceedings of the Board of Supervisors of the County of Milwaukee, 1934–35. Milwaukee, 1935.
Wisconsin Senate Journal, 1927. 2 vols. Madison, 1927.

United Kingdom
House of Commons Debates (Fifth Ser.), vol. 18. London, 1910.
House of Commons Debates (Fifth Ser.), vol. 21. London, 1911.

Local Studies and Sources

Allegheny County, Real Property Inventory of. Pittsburgh, 1937.

Annexation, Incorporation, and Consolidation in the Metropolitan Area. Portland, Ore., 1968.

Avondale, Clifton, Linwood, Riverside, and Westwood, Annexation of the Villages of. Cincinnati, 1896.

Baltimore Extension League, The Non-Partisan Greater. Baltimore, 1917.

Bell, John T.; Butterfield, Consul W.; and Savage, John W. *History of the City of Omaha, Nebraska and South Omaha.* New York, 1894.

Bell, Reginald W. and Gibbon, Sir Gwilym. *History of the London County Council 1889-1939.* London, 1939.

Betty, Werter G. and Mulford, Ren, Jr. *Norwood, Her Homes and Her People.* n.p., 1894.

Bigger, Richard and Kitchen, James D. *How the Cities Grew: A Century of Municipal Independence and Expansionism in Metropolitan Los Angeles.* Los Angeles, 1952.

Bollens, John C. *The Problem of Government in the San Francisco Bay Region.* Berkeley, 1948.

Briggs, Asa. *History of Birmingham.* London, 1952.

Broad Ripple, A History of. Indianapolis, 1968.

Brookline to Examine the Sources of Water Supply, Report of the Committee Appointed by the Town of. Boston, 1873.

Brookline, Report of the Joint Committee on Water Supply to the Town of. Boston, 1873.

Brown, Elizabeth Stow, comp. *The History of Nutley, Essex County, New Jersey.* Nutley, N.J., 1907.

Brown, G. P. *Drainage Channel and Waterway.* Chicago, 1894.

Byington, Margaret. *Homestead: The Households of a Mill Town.* New York, 1910.

Campion, Alfred H. "San Francisco Approves Plans for Consolidation with San Mateo County." *National Municipal Review* 20 (May 1931):256-59.

Case, Walter H. *History of Long Beach and Vicinity.* 2 vols. Chicago, 1927.

Chamberlain, Norman. "Municipal Government in Birmingham." *Political Quarterly* (Feb. 1914): 89-119.

Chamberlin, Everett. *Chicago and Its Suburbs.* Chicago, 1874.

Chicago and Cook County, Local Governments in. Springfield, Ill., 1919.

Chicago Bureau of Public Efficiency. *Unification of Local Governments in Chicago.* Chicago, 1917.

Chicago, Residential. Chicago, 1942.

Cleveland City Directory 1930. Cleveland, 1930.

Cleveland City Directory 1932. Cleveland, 1932.

Coates, William R. *A History of Cuyahoga County and the City of Cleveland.* 3 vols. Chicago, 1924.

Crouch, Winston and Dinerman, Beatrice. *Southern California Metropolis: A Study in Development of Government for a Metropolitan Area.* Berkeley, 1963.

Curtis, John G. *History of the Town of Brookline, Massachusetts.* Boston, 1933.

Davis, Edmund; Knight, Joseph K.; and Humphrey, Henry B., comps. *Memorial Sketch of Hyde Park, Massachusetts.* ... Boston, 1888.

Davison, Elizabeth M. and McKee, Ellen B., eds. *Annals of Old Wilkinsburg and Vicinity.* Wilkinsburg, Pa., 1940.

Dorchester, Report of the Commissioners on the Annexation of. Boston, 1869.

Drake, Francis S. *The Town of Roxbury: Its Memorable Persons and Places.* Roxbury, Mass., 1878.

Dunn, Jacob P. *Greater Indianapolis.* 2 vols. Chicago, 1910.

Edwards, George and Peterson, Arthur. *New York as an Eighteenth-Century Municipality.* New York, 1917.

Egger, Rowland A. "Pittsburgh—The World's Third Federated City." *American City* 40 (June 1929):120-121.

Egger, Rowland A. "The Proposed Charter of the Federated 'City of Pittsburgh.'" *American Political Science Review* 23 (Aug. 1929):718-26.

Farr, Walter G., Jr.; Liebman, Lance; and Wood, Jeffrey S. *Decentralizing City Government: A Practical Study of a Radical Proposal for New York City.* New York, 1972.

Faust, Martin L. "Voters Turn Thumbs Down of Pittsburgh's Metropolitan Charter." *National Muncipal Review* 18 (Aug. 1929): 529-32.

Fesler, Mayo. "City and County Consolidation and County Home Rule in Cleveland." *National Municipal Review* 14 (July 1925):435.

Firey, Walter. *Land Use in Central Boston.* Cambridge, Mass., 1947.

Folsom, Joseph Fulford, ed. *The Municipalities of Essex County, New Jersey, 1666-1924.* 4 vols. New York, 1925.

Gilchrist, Harry C. *History of Wilkinsburg, Pennsylvania.* n.pl., 1940.

Goheen, Peter G. *Victorian Toronto, 1850 to 1900: Pattern and Process of Growth.* Chicago, 1970.

Green, Howard Whipple. *An Analysis of Population by Census Tracts ... Cleveland and Vicinity.* Cleveland, 1927.

Green, Howard Whipple. *Population by Census Tracts Cleveland, Ohio 1930.* Cleveland, 1931.

Green, Howard Whipple. *Supplement to Population Characteristics by Census Tracts Cleveland, Ohio 1930.* Cleveland, 1933.

Greenlund, William A. "County Reform and Metropolitan Government." *National Municipal Review* 19 (Oct. 1930):694-96.

Greer, Scott. *Metropolitics.* New York, 1963.

Grunwald, John L. and Werba, Arthur. *Making Milwaukee Mightier.* Milwaukee, 1929.

Harper, Frank C. *Pittsburgh of Today, Its Resources and People.* 4 vols. New York, 1931.

Hawson, H. Keeble. *Sheffield: The Growth of a City 1893-1926.* Sheffield, 1926.

Hellmuth, William F., Jr. and Sacks, Seymour. *Financing Government in a Metropolitan Area: The Cleveland Experience.* New York, 1959.

Holden, Matthew, Jr. *Inter-Governmental Agreements in the Cleveland Metropolitan Area, Staff Report to Study Group on Government Organization.* Cleveland, 1958.

Holzworth, Walter F. *Men of Grit and Greatness, A Historical Account of Middleburg Township, Berea, Brook Park and Middleburg Heights*. n.pl., 1970.

Humphrey, A. L. "Pittsburgh Fifty Years Hence." *Pittsburgh and the Pittsburgh Spirit: Addresses at the Chamber of Commerce of Pittsburgh 1927–1928*. Pittsburgh, 1928.

Hurd, Harvey B., et al., eds. *Historical Encyclopedia of Illinois and History of Evanston*. Chicago, 1906.

Kenilworth, First Fifty Years. Kenilworth, Ill., 1947.

King, Clyde Lyndon. *The History of the Government of Denver with Special Reference to Its Relations with Public Service Corporations*. Denver, 1911.

Los Angeles County Bureau of Efficiency. *Growth of County Functions, Los Angeles County, California: 1852 to 1934*. Los Angeles, 1936.

McCaffrey, George H. *Summary of the Political Disintegration and Reintegration of Metropolitan Boston*. Boston, 1947.

McCauley, John D. *Pioneers of Progress, the History of Stickney Township* (Stickney Township, Ill., 1969).

McKinley, Charles. "The Proposed Consolidation of the Governments of Portland and Multnomah County." *The Commonwealth Review: A Journal of Applied Social Science*. 12 (Nov. 1930):249–56.

Manso, Peter, ed. *Running Against the Machine*. Garden City, N.Y., 1969.

Middlebrook, S. *Newcastle Upon Tyne, Its Growth and Achievement*. Newcastle Upon Tyne, 1950.

Miller, Joseph T. "The Pittsburgh Consolidation Charter." *National Municipal Review* 18 (Oct. 1929):603–9.

Miller, Joseph T. "Pittsburgh Plan of City-County Consolidation." *American Political Science Review* 21 (May 1927):367

Miller, William D. *Memphis During the Progressive Era 1900–1917*. Memphis, 1957.

Milwaukee, 1935, Thirteenth Biennial Report of the Board of Election Commissioners of the City of. Milwaukee, 1935.

Moore, Powell A. *The Calumet Region: Indiana's Last Frontier*. Indianapolis, 1959.

Morgan Park, Illinois, Annual Reports of the President and Board of Trustees, Village of. Morgan Park, 1909.

Morse, Sidney. *The Siege of University City, The Dreyfus Case of America*. University City, Mo., 1912.

"New York City Charter Revision." *Outlook* 65 (26 May 1900):198–201.

Pierce, Bessie Louise. *A History of Chicago*. 3 vols. New York, 1937, 1940, 1957.

Price, Eli K. *The History of the Consolidation of the City of Philadelphia*. Philadelphia, 1873.

Prologue to Progress. Cleveland, 1959.

Reading, Richard, comp. *Municipal Manual of the City of Detroit*. Detroit, 1928.

Reddig, William. *Tom's Town*. Philadelphia, 1947.

Reeling, Viola Crouch. *Evanston: Its Land and Its People*. Evanston, 1928.

Report of the Massachusetts State Board of Health Upon a Metropolitan Water Supply. Boston, 1895.

Report of the Metropolitan District Commission to the Massachusetts Legislature. Boston, 1896.

Romani, John H. and Watson, Richard A. "Metropolitan Government for Metropolitan Cleveland: An Analysis of the Voting Record." *Midwest Journal of Political Science* 5 (Nov. 1961):365-90.

Rudwick, Elliot M. *Race Riot at East St. Louis, July 2, 1917.* Carbondale, Ill., 1964.

St. Clair County, Illinois, History of. Philadelphia, 1881.

Schauffler, Mary C. *The Suburbs of Cleveland: A Field Study of the Metropolitan District Outside of the Administrative Area of the City.* Chicago, 1945.

Schmid, Calvin F. *Social Saga of Two Cities: An Ecological and Statistical Study of Social Trends in Minneapolis and St. Paul.* Minneapolis, 1937.

Shaw, Frederick. *The History of the New York City Legislature.* New York, 1954.

Simmons, Jack. *Leicester, Past and Present.* London, 1974.

Sofen, Edward. *The Miami Metropolitan Experiment.* Bloomington, Ind., 1963.

South Brooklyn, A Brief History of the Part of the City of Cleveland Which Lies South of Big Creek and West of the Cuyahoga. Cleveland, 1946.

Southern California, History and First Annual Report of the Metropolitan Water District of. Los Angeles, 1939.

Sparlin, Estal E. "Cleveland Seeks New Metro Solution." *National Civic Review* 49 (Mar. 1960):142-44.

Still, Bayrd. *Milwaukee, A History of a City.* Madison, Wis., 1948.

Strongsville Historical Society, comp. *History of Strongsville, Cuyahoga County, Ohio.* 2 vols. Strongsville, 1967-68.

Studebaker, Mary E. *Official Centennial History of Woodruff Place.* Indianapolis, 1972.

Summers, Iverson B. "A Negro Town in Illinois." *Independent.* 65 (27 Aug. 1908):464-470.

Syrett, Harold C. *The City of Brooklyn, 1865-1898.* New York, 1944.

Tax Payers' Association of California. *City and County Consolidation for Los Angeles.* Los Angeles, 1917.

Wagner, Walter. *Beverly Hills: Inside the Golden Ghetto.* New York, 1976.

Warner, Sam Bass, Jr. *The Private City: Philadelphia in Three Periods of Growth.* Philadelphia, 1968.

West Roxbury Appointed to Examine the Sources of Water Supply for the Town, Report of a Committee of the Town of. Boston, 1871.

White, Max R. *Water Supply Organization in the Chicago Region.* Chicago, 1934.

Wiley, John L. *History of Monrovia.* Pasadena, 1927.

Williams, Arch. *The Sanitary District of Chicago.* Chicago, 1919.

Wood, J. W. *Pasadena, California, Historical and Personal.* Pasadena, 1917.

Woods, Arthur Evans. *Hamtramck—Then and Now.* New York, 1955.

Other Sources

Blair, George S. and Sweeney, Stephen B., eds. *Metropolitan Analysis: Important Elements of Study and Action*. Philadelphia, 1958.

Bollens, John C. "Metropolitan Special Districts." *Municipal Year Book* 23 (1956):52–55.

Bollens, John C. *Special District Governments in the United States*. Berkeley, 1957.

California Blue Book or State Roster 1911. Sacramento, 1913.

Committee for Economic Development. *Reshaping Government in Metropolitan Areas*. New York, 1970.

Cooley, Thomas M. *A Treatise on the Constitutional Limitations Which Rest Upon the Legislative Power of the States of the American Union*. 3d ed., Boston, 1874.

"County Charter Amendment." *Ohio State Grange Monthly*. 35 (July 1932):4.

Douglass, Harlan P. *The Suburban Trend*. New York, 1925.

Dyer, C. A. "News and Views from Columbus." *Ohio State Grange Monthly* 34 (Jan. 1931):12.

Dyer, C. A. "News and Views from Columbus." *Ohio State Grange Monthly* 35 (June 1932):3.

Fiftieth Anniversary Missouri Bar Association, Report of the Proceedings of the 1930 Annual Meeting. Fulton, Mo., 1931.

Final Report of the Pennsylvania Tax Commission to the General Assembly. Harrisburg, 1927.

Fourteenth Census of the United States ... 1920. 11 vols. Washington, 1921–23.

Fourth Annual Report of the State Board of Massachusetts. Boston, 1873.

Fourth Report of the State Board of Health of Colorado. Denver, 1894.

Giddens, Paul H. *Standard Oil Company (Indiana), Oil Pioneer of the Middle West*. New York, 1955.

Government in Metropolitan Areas: Commentaries on a Report by the Advisory Commission on Intergovernmental Relations. Washington, 1962.

Hallman, Howard W. *Neighborhood Government in a Metropolitan Setting*. Beverly Hills, Cal., 1974.

Hirst, Francis, and Redlich, Josef. *Local Government in England*. 2 vols. London, 1903.

Holden, Matthew, Jr. *County Government in Ohio, Staff Report to Study Group on Government Organization*. Cleveland, 1958.

Jackson, Kenneth T. "Metropolitan Government Versus Political Autonomy: Politics on the Crabgrass Frontier." *Cities in American History* ed. Kenneth T. Jackson and Stanley K. Schultz. New York, 1972.

Johnson, T. R. and Wood, A. E. *Encyclopedia of Local Government Board Requirements and Practice*. 2 vols. London, 1908.

Jones, Victor. *Metropolitan Government*. Chicago, 1942.

Journal of Proceedings of the Ohio State Grange, 1928. n.pl., 1928.

Journal of Proceedings of the Ohio State Grange, 1932. n.pl., 1932.

Kneier, Charles M. "Development of Newer County Functions." *American Political Science Review* 24 (Feb. 1930):134–40.

Kotler, Milton. *Neighborhood Government*: *The Local Foundations of Political Life*. Indianapolis, 1969.

Lader, Lawrence. "Chaos in the Suburbs." *Better Homes and Gardens* 36 (Oct. 1958):10, 12, 14, 17, 121, 129, 166.

Lauder, Albert E. *The Municipal Manual*. London, 1907.

Long, Norton E. "Citizenship or Consumership in Metropolitan Areas." *Journal of the American Institute of Planners* 31 (Feb. 1965):2-6.

McBain, Howard Lee. *The Law and the Practice of Municipal Home Rule*. New York, 1916.

McGoldrick, Joseph D. *Law and Practice of Municipal Home Rule 1916-1930*. New York, 1933.

McGraw Waterworks Directory 1915. New York, 1915.

McKenzie, Roderick D. *The Metropolitan Community*. New York, 1933.

Manual of American Water-Works 1889-90. New York, 1890.

Manual of American Water-Works 1897. New York, 1897.

Maxey, Chester G. "The Political Integration of Metropolitan Communities." *National Municipal Review*. 11 (Aug. 1922):229-53.

Michigan Official Directory and Legislative Manual For the Years 1911-1912. Lansing, 1911.

Missouri Farmer. 22 (1 Nov. 1930):8.

Moody's Manual of Investments—Foreign and American Government Securities. 1928. New York, 1928.

Morison, Etling E., ed. *The Letters of Theodore Roosevelt*. 8 vols. Cambridge, Mass., 1951-54.

The Municipal Year Book of the United Kingdom for 1922. London, 1922.

Murphy, Thomas P. and Rehfuss, John. *Urban Politics in the Suburban Era*. Homewood, Ill., 1976.

Official Manual of the State of Missouri, 1931-1932. Jefferson City, Mo., 1931.

Ohio Election Statistics 1934. Berea, Ohio, 1935.

Pearse, Langdon, ed. *Modern Sewage Disposal*. New York, 1938.

The Pennsylvania Manual 1929. Harrisburg, 1929.

Queen, Stuart A. and Thomas, Lewis F. *The City, A Study of Urbanism in the United States*. New York, 1939.

Reed, Thomas H. "City-County Consolidation." *National Municipal Review* 23 (Oct. 1934):523-25.

Reed, Thomas H. "Dual Government for Metropolitan Regions." *National Municipal Review* 16 (Feb. 1927):118-26.

Reed, Thomas H. "The Government of Metropolitan Areas." *Public Management* 12 (Mar. 1930):75-78.

Report on Vital and Social Statistics in the United States at the Eleventh Census: 1890. 4 vols. Washington, 1896.

Rush, John A. *The City-County Consolidated*. Los Angeles, 1941.

Schiesl, Martin J. *The Politics of Efficiency: Municipal Administration Reform in America 1880-1920*. Berkeley, 1977.

Shalala, Donna E. *Neighborhood Governance, Proposals and Issues*. New York, 1971.

Sixteenth Census of the United States: 1940, Population—Number of Inhabitants. Washington, 1942.

Studenski, Paul. *The Government of Metropolitan Areas in the United States.* New York, 1930.

Supercity/Hometown, U.S.A., Prospects for Two-Tier Government. New York, 1974.

Thirteenth Census of the United States ... 1910, Population. 4 vols. Washington, 1913.

Thirty-Eighth Annual Report of the Local Government Board, 1908-1909. London, 1909.

Thirty-Fifth Annual Report of the Department of Labor and Industry, 1920. Topeka, Kan., 1921.

Thirty-First Annual Report of the Local Government Board 1901-1902. London, 1902.

Thirty-Fourth Annual Report of the Local Government Board, 1904-05. London, 1905.

Thirty-Ninth Annual Report of the Local Government Board, 1909-1910. London, 1910.

Twenty-Eighth Annual Report of the Local Government Board, 1898-99. London, 1899.

Twenty-First Annual Report of the Local Government Board, 1891-92. London, 1892.

Twenty-Ninth Annual Report of the Local Government Board, 1899-1900. London, 1900.

Twenty-Third Annual Report of the Local Government Board, 1893-1894. London, 1894.

U.S. Bureau of the Census. *Assessed Valuation of Property and Amounts and Rates of Levy 1860-1912.* Washington, 1915.

U.S. Bureau of the Census. *County and Municipal Indebtedness 1913, 1902, and 1890 and Sinking Fund Assets.* Washington, 1915.

U.S. Bureau of the Census. *Municipal Revenues, Expenditures and Public Properties 1913.* Washington, 1915.

Walker, Harvey. *Village Laws and Government in Minnesota.* Minneapolis, 1927.

Warner, Sam Bass, Jr. *The Urban Wilderness: A History of the American City.* New York, 1972.

Warren, Robert O. *Government in Metropolitan Regions: A Reappraisal of Fractionated Political Organization.* Davis, Calif., 1966.

Who's Who in Ohio. Cleveland, 1930.

Wood, Robert. *Suburbia, Its People and Their Politics.* Boston, 1959.

Yates, Douglas. *Neighborhood Democracy: The Politics and Impacts of Decentralization.* Lexington, Mass., 1973.

Zimmerman, Joseph F. *The Federated City: Community Control in Large Cities.* New York, 1972.

INDEX

THE JOHNS HOPKINS UNIVERSITY PRESS

This book was set in Times Roman Compu-
graphic by Action Comp. Co., Inc. It was
printed on 50-lb. Publishers Eggshell Wove
and bound by Universal Lithographers.

Library of Congress Cataloging in Publication Data

Teaford, Jon C.
  City and suburb.

  (Johns Hopkins studies in urban affairs)
  Bibliography: pp. 209–24
  Includes index.
  1. Municipal government—United States.
2. Metropolitan government—United States.
3. Cities and towns—United States—Growth.
I. Title. II. Series.
JS323.T4   352'.008'0973   78-20519
ISBN 0-8018-2202-5